P9-DWJ-660

No Laughing Matter

OTHER BOOKS BY JOSEPH HELLER

Catch-22

Something Happened

Good as Gold

God Knows

JOSEPH HELLER
&
SPEED VOGEL

No Laughing Matter

G. P. PUTNAM'S SONS NEW YORK

Published by G. P. Putnam's Sons
200 Madison Avenue, New York, NY 10016.
Published simultaneously in Canada by
General Publishing Co. Limited, Toronto

The text of this book is set in Caslon

Designed by MaryJane DiMassi

Library of Congress Cataloging-in-Publication Data

Heller, Joseph.
No laughing matter.

1. Heller, Joseph—Biography—Health.
2. Polyradiculitis—Biography. 3. Novelists, American—
20th century—Biography. I. Vogel, Speed, date.
II. Title.
PS3558.E476Z466 1986 813'.54 85-19421
ISBN 0-399-13086-1

Printed in the United States of America
1 2 3 4 5 6 7 8 9 10

What follows is essentially a true account that is accurate in every detail but those in which it is not: some names have been omitted or changed, and here and there an imperfection in technical terminology may have been left standing to help make our work easier.

THE AUTHORS

In August of 1982 a twenty-six-year-old man in New Jersey wrote to tell me he had been on a respirator in the intensive care unit of a hospital for fifty-eight days and had not been able to talk all that time. He was admitted to the hospital on February 1, 1982, and released five months later on June 30. His wife informed me in a separate letter that he was able by August to do just about everything but play softball and run. His rate of recovery from the effects of the ailment from which he had suffered was exceptional. But what struck me more profoundly was the information that he had been deprived of the ability to speak for the fifty-eight days he required the mechanical assistance of a respirator in order to breathe. I was stunned by the knowledge. Although more than eight months had elapsed since the date of my own hospitalization with the identical ailment, and over three since my discharge, the thought had not once occurred to me that I would have been unable to talk if I too had required a tracheostomy.

My attending doctors were twin brothers who maintained their medical practice together. In my instance they had adopted the sensible approach of not giving me any distressing information about my illness unless they had to; and I had adopted the sensible defense of not seeking any. I do not remember their telling me that I would not be able to speak once the tracheostomy they mentioned as all but inevitable had been performed and I had been connected through an incision at the throat to the ventilating machine which I believe, perhaps incorrectly, was already there, built into the wall at the head of my bed. I cannot recall even associating the procedure with the need for an apparatus to breathe for me.

I believe now that I would have lost my mind had I not been able to talk. I talked incessantly, from the moment I was moved as an emergency admission into the Medical Intensive Care Unit of Mount Sinai Hospital in New York. Conversation was all that prevented me from going mad. I wisecracked boisterously, commented, criticized, interrupted, counseled. I gave lengthy replies to all questions that were asked me by anyone and garrulous responses to thousands that were not. I was curious initially about every person there with whom verbal communication was possible—the man who came daily with the mobile apparatus for taking chest X rays stood a distance away and was outside the range of conversation. I sought as much knowledge from the bedside psychiatrist prescribed for me in my second week as he did of me. I was gregarious, affable, agreeable. The nurses embraced my volubility. To them I was a rarity: for all of my twenty-two days in the intensive care unit I was usually their only patient who was not completely unconscious from one pathological cause or another. I could hear, I could answer, I could joke, I could laugh; and compulsive and insatiable was my appetite for distraction.

Activity upon which to focus my attention was never a problem with the morning shift of nurses and orderlies. From 7:00 a.m., when they reported and took over, they raced against time to complete multitudes of duties, and friends and relatives who came to visit, my daughter among them, were incredulous to observe so many people working so assiduously at high speed for so many hours, one day after the next. There was too much to be done, and they were always in a rush. And all were unfailingly good-humored. At no time, on any of the shifts, did I observe even one moment of friction among them, any hint of irritation. The second shift was all right for me, too. There were doctors who came to check in the latter part of the afternoon, and often in the evening, and a considerable number of other medical activities were conducted as well. There was my feeding at dinnertime. Visitors came from work or after their own evening meal. Friends made social arrangements to meet at my bedside.

It was only toward the end of the second shift that things began to taper off. Then, from ten to midnight, the gloom and boredom began to settle in, the silence and weariness. I was very seldom asleep at ten, when the shifts changed again and the nurses coming on duty for the night were taken around by those making ready to depart, to be briefed on each patient. Rather, I was wide awake and suspiciously alert, anxious to discern immediately which one had already been assigned to me. There were always favorites I wanted desperately. My vital signs—my temperature, pulse, and blood pressure—would be taken by my new nurse, and my respiratory capabilities, "parameters," would be measured by three individual tests and recorded. The numbers for my respiratory capacities soon began going down drastically, but I felt no change. I was afraid to sleep, but I didn't know that then. Except for a late admission or the death of another patient, the period after midnight was eerie, endless, and routine. On this shift, only two nurses were assigned to the four beds in my section of the unit. And for two successive hours there would be but one available, as each spent an hour away for a meal break. For long stretches the stillness was unbearable. I welcomed the urge to urinate, for I was given a legitimate need for summoning aid. By the end of my first week I could no longer reach down into my groin to place or remove a urinal. Extending and retracting a hand that far requires the use of the shoulder and trunk muscles in addition to those of the arm, and all of these muscles of mine were by then already very much gone. I could not turn over. To minimize the danger of skin breakdown and resultant bedsores,

I was encouraged to lie on my sides alternately, rather than on my back continually. At night the nurse would prop me onto my side, with the call button near and the suction tube in both hands, where I would lie for approximately two hours, or less if, as usually happened, the position in which I had been placed grew uncomfortable. I could when I chose, by turning my head and shifting my center of weight just a bit, make use of gravity and momentum and allow myself to roll over down onto my back. I already knew that I could not free my feet if they were crossed, and that they quickly became almost painful when locked at the ankles. Using the small velocity generated in this changing of position from my side to my back, I could make an effort to elevate my upper leg while in motion in order to come to rest with my ankles separated, and I often would succeed. But at night I often wouldn't try. I wanted a reason to ring for the nurse.

I KNOW IT'S RIDICULOUS and bordering on the superstitious to suggest it but I have a queasy feeling nonetheless. I simply cannot get *The Picture of Dorian Gray* out of my head. . . . I'm sure it's mere coincidence, but my life started to get terrific at the same exact time that Joseph Heller's got terrible. As he got worse, I got better. As he started to look his age, I started to look more youthful. As he got sicker, I got healthier. As he got poorer, I got to live like a rich man.

Before Joe contracted Guillain-Barré syndrome, I was living in a cold-water walk-up. After he was stricken, I left my tiny cluttered flat for his newly furnished apartment in midtown. From there to a friend's ninety-four-foot yacht in Cannes, to a stay at the Gritti Palace in Venice, to a spectacular apartment on the Left Bank of Paris, where I was treated like a VIP at the sold-out Simon and Garfunkel concert, back to a beautifully landscaped house with swimming pool in East Hampton, then south to occupy a villa on Saint Croix, Virgin Islands, for much of the winter, then north to East Hampton again to welcome spring and summer. All at practically no cost.

Heller and I have known each other for twenty-five years.

When we met I was sitting on the beach reading *Catch-22*, which had recently been published, and I told him I loved it. We became friends. I am not implying that Heller will become an intimate of anyone who likes his work, but it is fair to say that he isn't exactly offended when something he has written is praised. During those twenty-five years I have had ups and downs, both financial and emotional. I have also had several interesting careers. We've managed to stay friends, although Heller has been nothing but a writer.

When Joe was in the hospital, I saw that he needed help. Since I had the time, I gave him some assistance. Simultaneously, conditions for me started to improve and are still getting better. I did not bargain for this, but I won't complain about it either. Because I never bore Joe any malice and had not been hoping for an improved life for myself prior to his illness, I did not feel the least twinge of guilt about the strange juxtaposition of our circumstances and the benefits that accrued to me as things were getting rotten for him. I did become uncomfortable and terribly embarrassed when other people praised me for my selflessness and kindness. My protestations only served to make me seem more modest. There was no way out.

Joe and I are really very different fellows. I have never met anyone so totally inept in the kitchen or laundry as he. Joe had been married at twenty-two, and he and his wife had separated about a year before. Before his marriage he was in the army. Before the army he had lived at home with his mother and an older brother and sister. Here was a fifty-eight-year-old man who had never had to keep house for himself. He had never baked a potato or scrambled an egg, never used a washing machine or dryer, nor ever even gone to a laundromat. (I think he understood what a dry cleaner did but had little idea about what should be taken there.) Heller was like someone from another planet. I believe he was always apprehensive about having to take care of himself.

But now, separated from his wife, he was, for the first time in his life, faced with learning how. And he was terrified. In the past he had no difficulty in getting others to work for him, and he isn't stupid, so why should he ever have to learn to do these things for himself? He is, on the contrary, very smart and very spoiled. I'm spoiled too—maybe more than he is—but I am very much at home in the kitchen and I actually love to do laundry and other household chores. I prefer ironing my shirts to sending them out. I even look forward to fixing appliances when they need repairs. Joe just throws them away.

Heller grew up in Coney Island. I grew up in Manhattan. I was a rich kid and was driven to school in our chauffeured limousine. Joe was poor and walked. Later on, when he rode a bicycle, it was for Western Union. I ride one for sport. Joe is tall; I am short (but getting taller). I was a lousy student; Joe was Phi Beta Kappa and a Fulbright Scholar (which he didn't tell me—I had to find out for myself). He was in the army. I was so laid-back I had a stomach ulcer at age twenty-two and was deferred from military service. In response to any invitation, my immediate answer is "Yes." His is an automatic "No!" He is an insomniac. I can sleep anytime and anywhere.

Before Heller's big affliction, his close and dear friends used to commiserate with each other about his exceptional impatience, rudeness, insensitivity, selfishness, arrogance, duplicity, obstinacy, malevolence, insincerity, negativity, and general unpleasantness. We liked him . . . but we were extremely hard put to explain why. All of us, in our own ways, tried to apologize to others who happened to meet Heller and whose misfortune it was to be exposed to his charming manifestations. We'd explain that underneath it all he was a good guy. We were less than convincing. People thought we were crazy.

After experiencing Guillain-Barré, Joe's manifest behavior was so much nicer in every way that we, his friends, pondered how we could manage to give him another foreign ailment after he recovered from this one and was back to normal. I am still working on it, for my sake as well as humanity's.

* * *

It all began on Saturday, December 12, 1981. Heller had commissioned me to decorate his apartment. His nephew, Paul, had urged us to look at some furniture a friend of his was willing to part with for practically nothing. The stuff we saw was less than wonderful, and we passed. We walked back to his apartment house, where my friend Joe seemed unable to pull open the entrance door. I opened it with ease. He then said that he couldn't remove his own sweater; I indulged him by pulling it deftly over his head. He said he was hungry so I baked a couple of sweet potatoes for us. I was taking very little notice of his minor complaints about weakness because he is not very strong and he is inclined to complain. And when, that evening at dinner at Simon's, a small restaurant on the West Side of mid-Manhattan, he said that the food tasted metallic, the meal seemed only more delicious to me. But when he then mentioned that he was experiencing trouble swallowing, I was alarmed. At that point I knew something was seriously wrong. My friend Joe is lots of things to lots of people, but to those of us who know him best, he remains the most prodigious eater in the world. The very last thing to expect from him is trouble swallowing. However, though he may have had trouble swallowing, Joe nevertheless managed to skip not a beat in the race to bring spoon and fork to mouth, which also helped make me forget my earlier anxiety about his health.

I called him the next morning and he told me once more about an unusual weakness in his limbs. This time I truly began to feel concerned and agreed that he should call his internist, even though it was Sunday. I asked him to call me back as soon as he had some information because I was leaving early to visit my sister in New Jersey. I waited about an hour before I tried him and got his answering machine. I thought perhaps he was out shopping for food and had forgotten to phone me before leaving the house. I called once more after a few minutes, with the same result. I was slightly annoyed but not yet terribly concerned. When I arrived at my sister's house, I called and got the machine again. I was now worried. At about one-thirty I decided to phone a close mutual friend, Julie Green, to tell him what was going on with Joe and to ask him to continue trying to reach him while I was away. When I returned to the city, about eight in the evening, I called Joe and still got no answer. Then I called Julie, who told me Joe had telephoned him from the emergency room of Mount Sinai Hospital. Julie added that when Joe was then sent to the intensive care unit, he collapsed completely.

THAT'S NOT EXACTLY the way I remember it, although I recall the sweet potato.

The sweet potatoes I enjoyed as a child are no longer obtainable in New York. They tended to be smaller than the yams that substitute for them now. The color of the inside usually was a pale yellow and the taste was starchy rather than sweet. Martha Hume, a Kentucky-bred journalist in New York who writes mainly about rock and country music, responded compassionately to the longings she had heard me express for the true sweet potatoes of my past, and she thoughtfully brought back a few of a local variety when she returned from a visit to the family homestead. They were not the same, but they were good enough. These were white inside.

We cooked a big one, Speed and I, before going out to dinner that night. By "we" I mean that Speed did: Speed prepared the potato for both of us in the course of showing me how a potato is baked and demonstrating for me the uses of the small toaster-baker unit he had purchased while furnishing my apartment. The potato was delicious. However, I was not able after a few mouthfuls to swallow any more of it easily. That premonitory touch of dysphagia, actually my second of the day, made me begin to suspect that something might be wrong.

That word "dysphagia" was one I had never heard until my son, Ted, came to visit me in the intensive care unit on my second day there. In attempting to minimize his alarm when I phoned, I had urged him to make certain the medical reference book I knew he would consult about my ailment was a recent one. He later thanked me for this clear-headed precaution, having looked into different medical dictionaries published several decades apart and observed the favorable change in fatality rates that had taken place over the years.

The decrease in mortality from Guillain-Barré has been dramatic, as diagnostic recognition has improved and mechanical respirators have become standard equipment in almost all hospitals. Most deaths are caused by respiratory failure stemming from paralysis of those muscles we normally and unconsciously employ to expand and contract the chest in order to breathe. One of my physicians regularly quoted statistics that were obsolete: fifteen percent die, thirty-five percent are left with significant residual paralytic damage. At the outset, I assumed that I myself, merely by being in the hands of doctors, had already escaped the dangers imperiling others, until the fifth or sixth day arrived and I could no longer deny to myself that I had not. These melancholy figures were in contrast to the sunny predictions of my neurologist, Dr. Walter Sencer, who did not waver in assurances that my case probably would not be a severe one (he was right, for what I had) and that I might even be jogging again by August (here he was off: it was not until the third August that I was able to take my first running steps). The conflicting reports I was receiving ceased when, with deliberate malice and some irritation, I referred each of these specialists to the comments of the other. From that point on we unanimously chose optimism.

Speed and I had dinner that Saturday evening with Cheryl McCall, a journalist then with *People* magazine. My drink tasted queer, metallic. The others had no complaint. I enjoyed the fish I ordered as my main course. But midway through the meal I began to have trouble swallowing just the vegetables. I could not seem to chew them finely enough. I felt them resting immovably on the right side of my tongue toward the rear of my mouth. I think I may have said so.

I felt well enough after dinner to walk from the restaurant back to my apartment, nearly a mile away, and Speed accompanied me, to retrieve his bicycle. Speed Vogel had been on this earth some six decades and three years at that time, and he had parked his bicycle in my apartment. When he was gone, I found myself having trouble with the Sunday *Times*. The sections felt heavier than ever as I lay in bed trying to read. I gave up halfway through and fell into a deep sleep. The pages of the newspaper were all about me when I was awakened by the harsh ring of the telephone many hours later. Tedda Fenichel was calling.

Tedda is a busy, perky, very intelligent woman somewhere in her thirties, I'd estimate, who is able to type with an efficiency that is fairly embarrassing even to her. She had assisted me in the past with my manuscripts. She was phoning now on Sunday morning to inform me that she had completed the section of the King David novel I had given her and to fix a time to deliver it. She remembers how disoriented I was at first, and she knew instantly, and regretfully, that she had wrested me from a sound sleep. For a full minute I was convinced it was still night. When she told me it was Sunday, I inquired if it was Sunday night, wondering in a daze if I could possibly have slumbered through an entire day after sleeping all the night before. I told Tedda I would call her later as soon as I could figure out my schedule.

Without unusual effort, I dressed as customary upon getting out of bed, large-size trousers over my underpants and then a loose sweatshirt—I have never gotten used to pajamas or a bathrobe—and prepared my normal breakfast. The grapefruit tasted wrong; there was definitely that metallic taint again. The rest of my breakfast was fine, a cold cereal with a banana sliced in and raisins added, although I found myself chewing more slowly than usual. My coffee was perfect. But I was reflecting soberly as I moved into the living room with my second cup that something neurologically unpleasant was taking place inside me, something I could not control and could not fathom. All of my limbs felt tired. With reluctance, I rose from the couch to call my doctors. I left my name and number with the answering service.

Speed telephoned as I waited, to find out how I was, and I told him I was going to try to talk to one of the Baders, the two brothers who were my doctors. He told me he was spending the day in New Jersey with his sister and promised to call when he returned. I received another call shortly after, regarding an invitation I had forgotten. Friends from California, Norman and Gloria Barasch, were in New York for the week and had asked me to join them for brunch that day at the Russian Tea Room. I told Norman I wasn't feeling so hot and begged off. He remembers my telling him I was probably going to talk to a doctor. I remember my advocating that the scrambled eggs with imported ham at the Russian Tea Room was exceptionally apt on a late Sunday morning, especially when accompanied by a bottle of ale.

While continuing to wait, I found myself rehearsing guiltily the catalogue of symptoms I would recite to whichever physician returned my call, and I understood instantly that the sequence of bizarre effects I'd been experiencing was longer than I had supposed and had commenced earlier. Friday evening I'd had dinner with Norman and Gloria in a restaurant on East Forty-fourth Street. Some time had passed since we'd seen each other, and they were pleased to find me in good spirits and looking radiant with health. I was lean, bright-eyed, and suntanned. I had spent the summer in a rented apartment in Aspen, Colorado, exercising daily and writing outdoors when the sky was clear, and twice for short periods that autumn I had been to Santa Fe, writing and sunbathing there too. Through a light snowfall we walked back uptown into the high Fifties, to their hotel and my partly furnished apartment. Although it was winter, I wore only a trench coat, which had a lining of wool. Toward the end of our walk I complained of a chill.

The following day, Saturday, I was scheduled to go with

Speed to look at the furniture of a man who was leaving the city and giving up his apartment. This meeting had been arranged by my nephew, who was a talent agent for International Creative Management and is my godson, qualities that combine to make him nearly irresistibly attractive to pretty young girls who find his noted uncle now a bit forbiddingly too mature. With time to kill in the morning, I had a hearty second breakfast alone in a neighborhood coffee shop, the Red Flame. Midway through the meal, which I was devouring robustly, all at once, without a solitary hint of any diminution of motor ability, I was unable to swallow the forkful of hash brown potatoes I had put into my mouth. I thought that most odd. The rest of the meal, eggs, bacon, buttered toast, and coffee, went down smoothly. Outside the coffee shop, I met briefly with Norman and Gloria Barasch, who again were impressed by my appearance. And indeed, I did look good! I had returned but ten days before from my second trip to Santa Fe, where I had taken a small apartment for a year, doing so at the suggestion of a woman who had popped fortuitously back into my life at just that time when I wanted to move somewhere and had no idea where to go. Her name was Maia Wojciechowska and she formerly had been married to Selden Rodman, the art critic. She was living in Santa Fe and wanted my assistance in bringing a manuscript she had written to the attention of the editors of the publishing house she preferred. I did what I could. She in turn found me the bedroom-kitchen-and-bathroom apartment right in town, which I leased for one year for two hundred dollars a month.

Though you would not know it from the level terrain surrounding the city, Santa Fe is a city of an altitude almost as high as Aspen's. The air in November is cold and dry. Nevertheless, I was able to jog just about every day on the four-mile route I had marked out. During the day, the sun shone almost continually. Before and after my run, I would sit outside, dressed in thermal underwear and socks, a heavy shirt, goose-down jacket, and woolen watch cap, and I would sunbathe as I wrote in longhand the third chapter of my novel about King David, which eventually was published as *God Knows*. I had never in my life been in better physical condition than when I returned to New York. In my twenties, I could not run one mile, not even downhill. But now I was in the best of health—right up to the moment some small biological process in my body, for reasons still unknown to anyone, began manufacturing monocellular antibodies with a pathological affinity for infiltrating and degenerating the tissues surrounding the fibers in my peripheral nervous system, and I began to have trouble swallowing my hash brown potatoes and after that could not remove my sweater.

The incident with the sweater took place about two hours later, when Speed and I had returned to my apartment after looking at the furniture and finding nothing I wanted. Because the day was a cold one, I had worn a thick sweater over a velour shirt, and I could not take it off when I tried. My illogical belief was that perspiration or static electricity was in some way causing these two garments to adhere. I said so to Speed when I asked him to help me. I did not know then that this inability to execute so commonplace a function was resulting from the failure of my shoulder muscles to respond as usual to my intention, or that the failure was being caused by something impairing the transmission of nerve signals from the spinal cord to the muscles the nerves normally activated. Or that this same thing was taking place with the nerves governing the actions of my tongue and my throat. At no time ever did I experience numbness or pain.

I felt well enough to go with Speed to the gym to jog later that afternoon. We used the Business Men's Club of the West Side YMCA, on Sixty-third Street, just off Central Park West, along with several close friends and with a number of acquaintances made there who included Israel Horovitz, Paddy Chayevsky, when he was alive, and Paul Simon, when he still had time.

The West Side "Y" has an indoor track. Years before, I had been given a few stretching exercises by an orthopedist to help alleviate a lower-back problem, and I had incorporated these into my warm-up routine. The first of the exercises went well, alternately raising each leg from the hip as high as I could while lying supine on a mat. The second was a startling surprise. Bending each leg in succession, I was supposed to wrap my arms about the shin and lift my head to touch my chin to my knee. I could not come close, on either side. Executing this simple action had not been impossible for me from the day I first tried. It struck me then that something was wrong. And I recalled with a flash of recognition the weird moment I had experienced in that same exercise room the day previous. I do—or used to do—fifteen push-ups rapidly as one of my preliminaries. I had reached seven or nine, and then came to a halt abruptly in astonishment, without feeling any signal of tiring, with no sense of fatigue, without any sense of strain. It was as though I had suffered a loss of communication between my wish and my capability to achieve it. I could not even *begin* to try to accomplish even one more. Prudently, I limited myself on the track to three miles instead of my regular four. I optimistically concluded then that I was getting a virus. Now, a day later, I was unable to bring my head up far enough to touch my chin to my knee.

I am not the first middle-aged athlete to discover that jogging will overcome and dispel at least temporarily just about every sensory physical symptom of just about every incubating disease. Feeling both stoic and martyred, I walked upstairs one floor to the track and grimly and sluggishly did a mile and a half. I felt wholesomely purified when I came back down. But at my locker, I could not readily take off my T-shirt. I was sweating, of course; and again I assumed the difficulty had something to do with the dampness of the garment. By pulling and twisting at the neck and shoulders, I succeeded at last in wrestling it free.

And so, by the following morning, I found myself brooding over the accumulation of disturbing signs as I waited for a return call from my doctor. I had, I felt with somewhat clearer conscience, an impressive aggregation of symptoms with which to extenuate my seeking judgment from a physician. I was, in fact, growing so concerned by then that I decided to telephone one of my doctors at his home. To do that, though, I first had to speak to friends of mine, Joseph and Elisa Stein, to obtain the home numbers I needed and to explain why.

Richard and Mortimer Bader are internists my own age who are identical twins, and they have shared a medical practice from the beginning. So alike are they that, as Speed Vogel observed once, it would have been necessary for only one of them to go through medical school for both to practice. For over a dozen years they had been attending my wife's parents, and they had not once imposed a charge greater than that paid by Medicare.

Richie lived with his family. Morty, at that time, dwelt alone, and he was the one I chose. To me he seemed grouchy when he answered, and I was contrite. He brushed my apologies aside. I told him my story and responded to his questions: I was afebrile (had no fever); the disorder was bilateral (occurring on both sides); it was even symmetrical (affecting the same limbs on both sides with the weakness I described). While talking to him I noted with a kind of nervous vindication still another manifestation. I could not cross my right leg over my left. Only with an effort could I raise my left. I felt as though much of what I was accustomed to possessing in the way of physical abilities was mysteriously draining from me. The feeling was almost "quaint."

When I'd finished my short recitation, Morty muttered something I could not grasp.

"Guillain-Barré syndrome," he informed me more distinctly when I asked him to repeat what he'd said.

Those were words I had never heard before. "Okay. Now what does it mean?"

"Can you get over here? To my apartment?" He was speaking softly, calmly.

"Sure."

I have heard much about Guillain-Barré since, and his rapid, accurate diagnosis by telephone borders on the miraculous when contrasted with the experiences of so many other people who've been struck with this illness. Typical of this rare and special form of polyneuritis is that so few cases *are* typical, and mine was not.

I knew intuitively that I was going into the hospital—an experience for me that was entirely new—and I tried to pack accordingly. I thought first of a dictionary, a thesaurus, some pads, pens, and pencils, a book or two, and my pocket diary of telephone numbers. The ingenuous picture I conjured up for myself had me ensconced comfortably on a pile of pillows for hours at a time, reading, writing, dozing, and talking on the telephone—in short, continuing my life in a fashion not much different from what I do in my prime. I caught myself planning to pack a variety of toilet articles and home remedies appropriate to an extended travel adventure, and I perceived that I was indulging in a disconcerted fantasy. In an embarrassment of vanity, I regretted owning neither pajamas nor a bathrobe. How was I going to look? In the end I took only my toothbrush, my electric shaver, my address book, several blank checks, and, a last moment addition, a pair of floppy sweatsocks. In dressing, I had experienced so much difficulty putting on stretch socks that I doubted I would be able to replace them if required to remove them. Even so simple an action as holding open and pulling on socks required more strength in the fingers, forearms, triceps, biceps, and shoulder muscles than I now could summarily command, not to mention the coordinated articulation of leg, hips, and trunk muscles needed to bring the foot in reach of the hand.

As I was going out the door the telephone rang. On my answering machine I heard the voice of the doctor filling in for my Baders that weekend. I did not turn back. In the hall I met Bruce Addison, an acquaintance who'd been instrumental in my finding this apartment when I needed one quickly. I mentioned I was on my way to check something out with my doctor and promised to call him for a drink or cup of coffee when I got back. Three and a half months went by before I did call him, on my first overnight trip out of the rehabilitation hospital.

Downstairs, I hailed a taxi and thought mistakenly that the driver had neglected to unlock the door. I needed both arms to pull it open. I needed both to push the door open when it was time to get out.

Dr. Bader was awaiting me in his apartment upstairs. He directed me to undress as we exchanged greetings. When I expressed doubts about getting my socks back on, he said he would help. He asked me to walk, bend, touch things—I forget the rest. His examination did not take long. He put my socks on for me when I dressed. He revealed that he had already talked about me with Richie, his brother, and with a neurologist, Wally Sencer, and the three were in accord: Guillain-Barré. We had an appointment at three with Dr. Sencer, who would come from his home to his office to examine me. Much more rare than a day in June are two top-flight medical specialists available in New York on a Sunday in December.

In the time we had to wait, Morty had lunch for both of us sent up from a delicatessen on Madison Avenue. I asked for a tuna fish salad on rye bread and coffee. I consumed only the coffee. I gave up on the sandwich after a minute. I could not widen my jaws enough to take a full-sized bite, could barely chew what I did manage to get into my mouth, could not manipulate my tongue and throat into swallowing what I did chew. Morty said nothing about what he observed. He said nothing more about Guillain-Barré. And I didn't ask. We talked instead about almost everything else, a lot about his children and mine. He said nothing about any other patients of his with the same complaint. Knowing how small is the incidence of affliction, I understand now that he may never have had any. It is equally plausible that he was shying away from telling me anything that could exacerbate the anxiety and latent terror I unconsciously was striving so successfully to repress. Dr. Sencer, the neurologist, eventually told me that, in twenty-five years of practice, I was his first victim of Guillain-Barré who had not required a tracheostomy. This too becomes less remarkable statistically when I reflect that he could have been talking about no more than four or five others.

I can think of only a very few of my friends who had ever heard of Guillain-Barré syndrome before. It will not come as a surprise to anyone who knows him that the humorist and gifted thespian and film producer Mel Brooks was one. Standard reference works like the *Merck Manual*, *Harrison's Principles of Internal Medicine*, and *Dorland's Medical Dictionary* are Mother Goose to him. He is the only person I'm acquainted with who subscribes to *Lancet*, the English medical periodical. As a Boy Scout, his sole merit badge was in first aid.

Another was the literary critic and Joseph Conrad biographer Frederick Karl, now at New York University and a good friend for more than thirty years. Fred walks around with more factual knowledge in his head than any other human being I know of, and he remembered the malady as the adverse concomitant of the swine flu national immunization program back in 1976. Mercifully, he withheld from me something else he knew, until June, when I was out of the hospital and beginning to walk unaided. He also knew that people really do die from it and others remain severely disabled.

The ailment in discussion appears earliest in modern medical writing as "Landry's ascending paralysis." The disorder affects the peripheral nervous system, which consists of those nerve structures growing outside the spinal column. These include all of the cranial and spinal nerves.

In 1916 three Parisian physicians, Georges Guillain, Jean Alexander Barré, and André Strohl added to this description the characteristic anomaly they discovered of an elevation in protein in the spinal fluid of victims in the *absence* of any corresponding increase in cellular activity that could be an indication of infection.

The *Merck Manual* cautions that the condition always represents a medical emergency requiring constant monitoring to protect against respiratory failure and cardiovascular complications, which are the most frequent causes of death.

No one knows where it comes from, or, indeed, at the beginning, if it's even really there. It does not seem to discriminate as to age, sex, season, or geographical location. As with all things in life, both good and bad, it comes alike to the wicked and the just, to those who sacrifice and those who do not.

Technically, it is called a syndrome rather than a disease because no ways exist to verify its presence other than the course taken by the aggregate of symptoms.

In many cases, paralysis commences at the bottom of the lower extremities, the feet, and progresses upward for as far as it goes, but in many more cases it does not. Mine began in the middle, moving upward and downward simultaneously.

It is not caused by a virus but frequently comes after an upper respiratory infection, surgery, or vaccination, factors suggesting an etiology that is autoimmunological; that is, the body manufactures cells to destroy its own tissues.

Spontaneous remission and recovery may be the traits distinguishing this illness from all others with which it may be initially confused.

Recovery can be as quick as six weeks, I'm told, or take longer than two years. And there is nothing known to man that can moderate the severity or influence the pace or extent of recovery.

Because my case was atypical, both hospitals in which I was confined accepted a diagnosis of Guillain-Barré only because there was no other ailment they knew of that better fit the picture.

Wally Sencer takes a more pragmatic approach: "If it looks like Guillain-Barré, and acts like Guillain-Barré, it's Guillain-Barré."

Only with the elevation in protein shown by the last of my three lumbar punctures would the medical hospital, Mount Sinai, accede to his opinion. Till then, I was on the books as someone with an "acute nonspecific polyneuritis."

The rate of occurrence is small, but not so small that you won't shortly after reading this run into at least one person who knows of at least one person who has had it. Somewhere between 1.6 and 1.9 Americans per one hundred thousand are afflicted each year, or between sixteen and nineteen out of a million. In a population exceeding two hundred million, this implies a figure of more than four thousand new cases annually.

Among people receiving swine flu vaccinations in 1976, the risk was multiplied about eight times, still insignificant in likelihood, except for the nine hundred or so who contracted it after having been inoculated. Epidemiologists urged a halt in the national swine flu immunization program when reports of Guillain-Barré among people recently given the vaccine started flowing in from Minnesota, Alabama, and New Jersey. Then came seven confirmed cases in Pittsburgh alone, and the program was suspended.

Adding to the enigma of the Guillain-Barré syndrome is that in no other country administering the same vaccine was there observed any increase in the rate of incidence.

I doubt very much that my physician that day, Dr. Mortimer Bader, was as familiar with the anecdota of the pathology as I am now. But he knew enough to appreciate the dangers and had the good sense to omit telling me about them. People praising me for my gallant fortitude with the perils ahead overlooked that I was not aware I faced any until the most serious had been left behind.

Morty helped me on with my jacket when it was time to leave. By then I could not lift my left arm high enough against resistance to slide it through the sleeve. This Dr. Bader has a walking impairment of his own. We were ruefully aware of the sight we made together as we hobbled to the corner and assisted each other into the taxicab. The building we drove to had a circular courtyard with a sidewalk and a driveway for automobiles as well. Stepping up to the curb from the driveway, my right knee gave a funny, unexpected jerk, as though it might buckle. I revealed this with a laugh. Morty Bader made no comment as he guided me into the building to the door of an office inside, where the neurologist he was taking me to see was already waiting.

Dr. Walter Sencer is tall and heavyset, bluff, with glinting bright eyes and a way of looking at a patient directly in a gruff, no-nonsense manner that does not quite disguise the kindly and almost fearfully sentimental nature underneath. He is both a neurologist and a psychiatrist, having taken up a second specialty when the first seemed undernourishing to his active and experimental imagination. I imagine it was the psychiatry that came after, for neurology seems limited to diagnosis and grim prediction, affording limited possibility for healing. He told me he enjoyed my novels, relishing particularly my outspoken disapproval of Henry Kissinger in *Good as Gold.*

He too did not take long. There were things he watched me do involving motions and coordination, tests for movement, even of the mouth, eyeballs, and tongue, checks for strength in arms and legs against the pressure of his hand. He lay his hands on my shoulders and asked me to shrug. He saw what he needed to in a matter of minutes. "Better call the hospital and make sure there's a bed for him," he said almost casually to Dr. Bader, without diverting his attention from me. Had I been sick from a virus in the past few weeks? Been vaccinated recently? I had not.

"You're going to have a mild case, probably," he told me. "And you're going to get everything back."

I forgot to ask him what I was going to lose.

He drove us to Mount Sinai Hospital in his blue car, remarking sardonically that with passengers like Morty and me, he felt he was piloting an ambulance. He left his car outside the emergency room. This time my right knee did buckle when I stepped up to the sidewalk, and I came close to falling. They held me between them the rest of the way inside, till I came to the tall and tactful resident on duty in the emergency room, with whom I went through the formalities of admission.

Again, I believe the medical examination given me was brief and simple, but my ability to reconstruct events is far from absolute. There were questions to be answered. I gave my Blue Cross number. I gave my wife as the person to be notified in case of "emergency," doing this with evil humor, for by then we had been separated nearly a year. Why put the burden on either of my children? A supervisor of nurses appeared and gently inquired if there were any people I wanted called. She urged me to reconsider when I shook my head, if only, she suggested, to take possession of my clothing and valuables. Were there no closets upstairs in my room? I was seated on a mobile stretcher now, swinging my legs with the nonchalance of habit. I would need a telephone upstairs, I remember letting her know. She assured me I'd have the use of one. The first number I gave her to call for me now was that of my friends Julie and Edie Green, who lived just across town. Luckily, they were home. Julie would not, however, believe she was speaking the truth when she told him who and where she was and that I wished them to come to the hospital as soon as they conveniently could.

"All right, what's the joke?" he wanted to know.

I took the phone. "I'm really here," I told him, laughing. Had there been a joke, I would not have thought it so funny.

I next had her place a call to my nephew, who, coincidentally, was already on the phone to Mount Sinai on one of his two telephone lines when this second call from Mount Sinai came on the other. He was talking to a friend of his and a lawyer of mine, Alan Altman, who had gone in as a patient that same day for gallbladder surgery scheduled to follow shortly. Paul too had trouble believing his ears, for I'd been the picture of health when he'd seen me the afternoon before. Somewhere along the line I telephoned Tedda Fenichel with a request that she deliver my manuscript to me at the hospital, for she arrived with it that first night. Tedda knew more about intensive care units than I did and recalls being struck with puzzlement by my jovial demeanor and obtuse absence of concern.

I remember nothing at all about tests, examinations, or procedures right after I was brought, now lying down on the mobile stretcher, into the Medical Intensive Care Unit upstairs, but there must have been plenty: vital signs, respiratory parameters, blood and urine samples, weight measurement, attention to the oral directives of both my internist and my neurologist. At a certain point a nurse, no older than twenty-five, came near. She told me her name was Kim Kudzin and she would be the one primarily in charge of me. In less than a week, I believe we had a crush on each other.

I was free to make as much use of the telephone on the desk at the nurses' station as I wanted to, and for the two more days I was able to walk the few steps there, I placed and received my calls. There were looks of general puzzlement when I asked where the toilet was. I did not know yet that I was going to be bedridden. The nurses did not understand that I had not been told. I avoided looking closely at the other three beds in the unit.

Julie and Edie Green hardly knew what to say when they finally were permitted inside to see me. There I was, sitting up and still fully dressed in my usual weekend attire, brimming with friendliness, humor, and good cheer, in a small area containing three other beds with three other patients, two of whom would shortly die. The third, a Canadian man with myasthenia gravis, would leave to go home and be replaced by an elderly woman who also would die.

I had trouble getting my clothes off, Julie Green remembers, and he assisted. I told the Greens where the insurance policies had been left in the apartment from which I had moved at the beginning of the year. Among them was my only life insurance policy, of which my wife was still the sole beneficiary. I wanted Julie to sift out my two major medical policies and discover for me what steps had to be taken to initiate a claim. Compliance with my request would necessitate their informing my wife where I was and why, although I did not ask specifically that they do so. She and I had seen each other but once since January and that was in Family Court of the State of New York about two months before, to which I had been summoned by subpoena for some reason that remains to this day a mystery both to me and to my attorney. It must have been over money, though, because that's what most of the talk in the courtroom was about before the matter was adjourned. I found her lawyer, Mr. Norman Sheresky, an amusing fellow. Excerpts from the transcript of that hearing appear later at a more appropriate place, along with unsuccessful arguments of his for the record made that following June in opposition to my plans to move to my summer house when I was out of the hospital.

It was after the Greens were gone that I telephoned my son to tell him where I was and the name of the disease I had and that it was not much to worry about. I could not reach my daughter until the following morning, at her office.

"Guess where I am," I began my conversation with her.

I gave the bare details, minimizing a possible seriousness of which I was not cognizant yet myself, and repeating to her Dr. Sencer's prediction that I probably was going to get everything back.

"I should hope so!" she declared, which was an exclamation I could have plausibly made myself. It did not occur to me for three more months that I might not.

Joseph and Elisa Stein showed up later, having phoned Morty Bader about me and learning I'd been hospitalized. Because of the close relationship of the three, he had told them confidentially what I and none of my other friends then knew: that the disease could be serious, that there was no way to know the extent of the damage I would suffer or the degree of return that would ensue, and that there was nothing he could do but keep me alive until the production of antibodies destructive to the myelin sheath insulating the medullary nerve fibers had ceased.

I had a visit also that first night from my nephew, who, overcoming his disbelief, met the occasion with a jollity equaling my own. "What are you doing in here?" Paul demanded with feigned indignation when he entered. "You look like a million dollars."

I would need, I informed him, two dozen number-two pencils, finely sharpened and replaced in their original boxes, to make changes in my manuscript in the several days I would be in the hospital, and perhaps some photocopying too if my emendations were completed while I was still confined. The resident on duty knew no more about the course my Guillain-Barré would take than anyone else and answered, when Paul questioned her upon leaving, that I would get weaker for about two weeks until my decline leveled off at what was called a plateau. These definitions had no more meaning to him than to me, for he brought the pencils a day or so later. It was my nephew who recalled for all at my bedside in the visits afterward, when my speech had been grossly affected, that I had always had trouble with my *r*'s, *w*'s, *s*'s, and *l*'s, and surmised that the whole illness was no more than a ruse I had concocted to camouflage these defects.

The nurses and supervisors on the night shift also could not get over how good I looked when they laid eyes on me for the first time. One came to my bed soon after reporting for work and began drawing the curtains closed around me, shutting off my view on all sides. Repentantly, as though bemoaning an offense against me that was not possible to avoid, she told me that the man in the bed beside mine was going to die. "I'm sorry," she said. "That happens in here." The event seemed a bit less of an atrocity when I found out from her the following night that he'd been in his seventies. His wife was there, weeping: I could hear her on the other side of the curtain, laying curses on his doctor, for no greater provocation I could perceive than his having advised the patient to go home and drink a beer and enjoy himself, he would be all right.

"It should happen to him, that bastard," she wailed repeatedly.

I do not remember if I slept that night. I do know I soon was in terror of sleeping, although I tried continually. It was not until seven weeks later, on February 3, when I was already out of Mount Sinai and at the "Rusk" Institute of Rehabilitation Medicine,* that a notation on a nurse's report states that the patient "slept well until morning." The observation was made by Herman Bryan, one of the private-duty nurses I still needed there for the first two weeks. He came on at midnight, and I was awake when he arrived.

---

* In September 1984 the name of the Institute of Rehabilitation Medicine of New York University Medical Center, established by Dr. Howard A. Rusk in 1947, was changed officially to the Howard A. Rusk Institute of Rehabilitation Medicine.

WHEN I ASKED my comical friend Julie Green for the straight story on Heller, he confessed that Joe hadn't actually collapsed—that was an exaggeration. But he really was in the intensive care unit of Mount Sinai. Julie's diagnosis was hypochondriasis. He said Joe looked great, was ordering people around (as usual), and wanted me to get there as soon as possible so that he could give me some special assignments. Joe told Julie that he did not expect to be there very long, but he wanted me to take care of a few things in the meantime.

I went to see Joe in the hospital for the first time on Monday, December 14. A nurse stopped me at the entrance of the ICU and asked for credentials. I told her that I was looking for Joe Heller and that my name was Speed. She smiled, as I figured she would. A camp counselor gave me the name "Speed" when I was four years old—long before amphetamines became a popular drug—for the same reason they call bald men "curly." It stuck. My pace never got faster. In 1969 Joe and I went to Washington for the big moratorium protest against the war in Vietnam. There was a huge crowd, and we became separated during the march. Heller stood where he was and started yelling "Speed!" Three kids hurried up to him and asked, "How much?"

Joe was sitting up in bed making notes on a legal pad when he saw me. He looked fine. At least as good as he had two days before when we'd had dinner together. He asked for his phone messages and mail. He'd called me earlier that morning to be sure I would not forget to stop and pick them up at his apartment on my way uptown, as Julie had already asked me to do. I remembered. He then began to tell me what else he wanted me to do for him. He made me repeat everything back to him, which I felt was rather insulting, even though I am inclined to forget words sometimes. I am the person who once heard myself saying, "My mind is as sharp as a . . . watchamacallit," a line that popped up later as dialogue in one of Joe's . . . er . . . whatcha . . . er . . . books.

Anyway, Joe asked that I return several calls, emphasizing that if returning all those calls was too much for me, I should at least be sure to cancel an appointment for dinner he had that week with his friend Sydney Gruson and his wife, Marit, and ignore the rest. That remark, so typical, left me feeling still that there wasn't much wrong with him.

When I asked, Joe told me he had something called Guillain-Barré, which neither of us had ever heard of before. It sounded fancy but not serious. I made him pronounce it a couple more times so I could tell others who might ask what he had. He said he expected to be out before very long. I told him not to worry. I would continue to pick up his mail and phone messages until he was back home.

At the time, I was living in a small studio on Twenty-eighth Street between Broadway and Sixth Avenue, in the heart of Manhattan's wholesale flower district, which was also one of the city's lesser known centers for working artists. Before the flower people took over, the area had been occupied by publishers of sheet music, songwriters, and song pluggers and in the twenties had been known as "Tin Pan Alley." The florists used only the storefronts and basements, and the upper floors were largely vacant. In the forties, painters, sculptors, and writers were attracted to this neighborhood because of the high ceilings and low rents. I'd first started coming there to visit Herbert Kallem, the sculptor, to whom I'd been introduced by my longtime friend, actor Stanley Prager, who in turn had met Herby through his friend Zero Mostel. Although he was best known as a brilliant comic and actor, Zero had begun as a painter, and at that time he was sharing a studio with Herby. While Herby taught sculpting on the premises, his brother, Henry, lived and taught a painting class on the floor above; I enrolled in both. I was meeting many fascinating characters in that neighborhood and soon found it more pleasant in the flower district than at my home on the Upper West Side.

One of the people Zero introduced me to there was Ngoot Lee, a fine painter who soon became a good friend. When he was about ten, Ngoot left Canton to visit an uncle, a wealthy Chinatown merchant. Ngoot liked New York and decided to stay, attending school, then working in restaurants and at odd jobs until he moved to Twenty-eighth Street some ten years later. It was one day around 1960 that Ngoot told me his next-door neighbor had found more affordable space in Hoboken and was moving. I was introduced to his landlord, who said he could let me have the space if I would agree to an increase in rent. With a sly smirk, he asked, "Would a total of forty-five dollars a month be okay?" Ngoot thought the price was an outrage, but I was anxious to have my own studio, so I grabbed it.

True, it was unheated and the toilet was in the hall, but the previous tenant had left a good stove, and we discovered a blocked-up but usable fireplace, which improved the general ambiance and prevented frostbite as well. The studio became a hangout for me and my friends. After a meal in Chinatown, Joe, Julie, George Mandel, Ngoot, Mel Brooks, and I would stop off at Harry's all-night fruit stand (later, to our dismay, torn down to make way for the World Trade Center), and then on our way back to Twenty-eighth Street we would forage for crates that we could break up to feed my fire.

Mel's job was to toss the bits of wood on the fire, while Julie, George, and I engaged in a frantic effort to break up the crates fast enough to keep Brooks supplied. Mel loved a big blaze. Heller, however, reposing on the daybed, did nothing but drink my booze and coffee, while waiting for a slice of ripe pineapple or melon, carved up by Mr. Lee, to be served him. When they left, the place was a mess but I didn't care.

As long as I used it as a studio away from home, with my extensive wardrobe and various belongings contained in a spacious ten-room apartment on Riverside Drive, the place was fine. It was charming, though somewhat crowded with the cast-off furniture I always accepted when friends redecorated their apartments. Heller thought it was a dump. I thought it was wonderful.

In short, it served very well as a place to sculpt, paint, or just be with my friends on weekends, odd evenings, or anytime I could manage to get away from my office—which was considerably more often than my partners would overlook without complaint. The business I was ostensibly engaged in was textiles. Our beautiful offices, conveniently located just a few blocks from my studio, had been designed by my friend Charles Gwathmey, the famous architect. My partners, however, did not appreciate Gwathmey's work. And, as it turned out, they didn't appreciate mine any better. So, with some motivation from them, I found myself out of the textile business in 1972, and soon thereafter, out of my family home. When life's circumstances left me with the tiny studio as my only residence in New York, I will confess I began to find it less than ideal. It was now overflowing with too many things. It was cozy, but one was more likely to notice its special appeal in the spring.

Who could have guessed when more of life's relentless circumstances showed up with Guillain-Barré for my friend Joe that they would have the effect of providing better living arrangements for Joe's poor friend Speed?

On the day of his admission to intensive care, Joe had told Julie Green that after he had made his initial call to me, he should also notify George Mandel, an old friend. Julie told George that Guillain-Barré wasn't serious, but George, always something of a skeptic when it came to illness, wanted to see for himself.

One day during Joe's first week in ICU, Mandel came as I was leaving. Joe had been taken downstairs for what is known as an EMG, a test to determine nerve response. George decided that since he was already there, he would hang around outside the test room until Joe was finished. When he was approached by an orderly who asked what he was doing there, he identified himself and asked some questions of his own. The orderly told George he should be prepared for some unpleasantness because the EMG is a very painful procedure. When Heller was wheeled out of the room, Mandel asked, with considerable trepidation, "Was it terrible?" Joe said, "No, it was nothing." George thought at first that Heller was just being brave. But then he began to dread that Joe had felt nothing because his nerves were completely dead.

I asked George later on what Joe had requested of him during those days in the hospital. "He just asked me to do some dirty work for him and then did nothing but insult me," George replied.

I was mildly surprised that George, an old friend, would even bother to mention this latest example of Heller's famed rudeness. Where lives the friend who hasn't heard his bark and felt his bite? Insults are simply his way of saying hello. Joe's nephew, who adores him, said that whenever he called his uncle in the past just to find out how he was, Joe would growl after a minute, "What did you call me for?" But Paul's a kid. George is a grown man and knows Joe well enough to have told me, "When you phone that guy, he wants you to come right to the point. When he phones you, however, he can blather away for hours about matters of absolutely no consequence."

I recently phoned my friend Israel Horovitz, the playwright, who got to know Joe when they both taught at CCNY. He asked how Heller was feeling—two years after the onset of Guillain-Barré. Before I could respond, he started complaining about Joe. "What is wrong with that man? I saw him at Paul Simon's wedding and merely asked about his children. Joe's response was, 'What do you care? Do you think I'm going to ask about yours?' " I had to suppress a giggle as I explained to Israel that Joe's ungracious reply was just his way of announcing that he was practically his old self again.

Every time George Mandel went to visit Joe in the hospital, Heller asked belligerently, "What're you doing here again?" (With whom but a close friend would Joe practice his old persona in preparation for his recovery? If he'd tried it with some of us who are not as sweet and understanding as Mandel, we might have dumped his urinal on him.)

In the first few days Joe was in ICU I received many phone calls from people who wanted to find out what had happened to him. After much repetition, I developed a short, concise story that satisfied most inquiries and kept people away, yet permitted me to make a good impression: "Joe's got something they don't know very much about. It can sometimes take a while, but most people recover completely. It's like a short circuit in the nerves. They call it Guillain-Barré." By then I was able to pronounce "Guillain-Barré" as smoothly as Charles Boyer.

Among the friends who called were Barbara Howar, Wyndom Robertson, then an editor of *Fortune*, Bruce Addison, publisher and aficionado of fast horses and fast boats, and Helen Bransford, a lovely friend of Joe's who had given me a wonderful ten-speed bicycle. I, of course, knew most of his friends and informed those who called of his whereabouts. Everyone, without exception, was stunned to learn that Joe was ill, and immediately volunteered assistance and wished to visit at such time that it became possible. I discouraged most people from going to the hospital to see him. I did notify Joe in case I was inadvertently excluding someone he would like to see, but he preferred that everyone be discouraged from visiting in the ICU.

One of the messages I brought Joe off his answering machine

was short and to the point: a woman's voice said, "Joe, why haven't I heard from you? You dead or something?" I realize a woman's intuition is infallible, but this one was inclined to overshoot the mark. Heller was not quite dead. . . .

She was a friend who was expecting him to come to Santa Fe before Christmas. I phoned her and introduced myself. She was very pleasant to talk to, and I felt like a creep having to break her good mood by telling her why Heller was unable to go to Santa Fe as planned. She happens to be one of those perennial "up" types. She took the news so well it was almost insulting.

When I explained to her why Joe had not been able to contact her and that the "dead or something" she mentioned in her phone message was actually Guillain-Barré, she seemed rather unperturbed. She didn't even ask, as most others did, "What's that?" I found out she had once worked at Duke University Medical Center in the department of epidemiology, so if she was not familiar with the syndrome, she knew enough physicians who could supply her with the information. I told her that Joe was getting great medical attention and his friends were giving him all kinds of support. It was not at all necessary for her to come east, I said. In fact, I told her it would actually be counterproductive because I thought it might upset Joe. I did a good convincing job and she agreed to stay put provided I call her regularly to keep her informed. She added that she thoroughly enjoyed speaking to me in any case. (I didn't mention that part of the conversation to Heller for fear that he might get it into his head that I was beating his time.) I told her that it had indeed been a pleasure to speak with her, that it would be an even greater pleasure to meet her in person at an appropriate time in the future. I promised to call her frequently. I urged her not to hesitate to call me collect at Heller's apartment anytime at all. She called me just about every day.

I was now virtually in residence at Joe's. It was the most practical place to be. I would have had to pick up his mail, packages, and telephone messages there anyway, so this saved me time. Moreover, the decor happened to be exactly to my taste, since I was the one who had been commissioned to design it, with explicit instructions and admonitions from my client: "Do it any way you like and spend whatever you have to. Just don't ask me questions or talk to me about it." I had taken him at his word—and, except for the time he looked at his nephew's friend's furniture, he didn't involve himself at all—and I must confess, it turned out perfectly . . . for me.

Actually, that was my second commission from Heller. My first had been for a painting when he was living in a large apartment in a landmark building on West End Avenue. He wanted a specific size for a particular wall. I told him it was no problem; I would even do it in colors compatible with the rest of the decor. I knew that my artist friends would have been appalled, but I wanted that commission despite the fact I was aware that Joe's principal motive was to annoy other painters who had much better credentials than mine. The results were gratifying. The painting was successfully executed, the professionals were irritated, and Joe and I, for different reasons, were delighted. I later hung the painting in Joe's new apartment so that it faced me while I dined at his table.

There were a few other advantages to living in Joe's place. For example, the building management provided hot as well as cold running water, and each and every room contained a steam radiator. The management also provided three passenger elevators and a service elevator suitable for transporting my bicycle to Joe's apartment. The service elevator also went to the basement laundry, which contained several rows of coin-operated washers and dryers. When I ran out of the stacks of quarters Joe had left, I had to provide my own, but I managed. I even had a first-class cleaning woman Joe had hired to come once a week. Doormen, who thought I was Mr. Heller, greeted me accordingly as they opened the front door when I appeared with my bicycle, and a security guard helped ward off panhandlers, burglars, and would-be muggers. It was perfectly reasonable for the personnel to think that I was the real tenant, since I had been on the scene from the time Joe signed the lease. They saw much more of me than they did of him, even before he went to the hospital. One of the early duties I performed for Joe was to distribute his Christmas envelopes stuffed with cash, which he had already prepared. It didn't hurt my standing any. A concierge accepted messages, packages, and other deliveries. Often when returning to his home I would be given a box, envelope, or special package that had arrived for us, always with ingratiating smiles from the staff. I loved opening his packages and inspecting the contents, most of which were books or clothes from L. L. Bean and Eddie Bauer.

The apartment was cheerful and sunny. I thought the living room turned out well, but the bedroom with its beautiful built-in red oak furniture and mirrored closets was simply outstanding. What I enjoyed most, though, was the queen-sized bed with its goose-down comforter and eiderdown pillows. Joe already owned superb hi-fi components, and I had picked up a little beauty of a tape deck for him and designed a wall-hung cabinet that contained the whole system elegantly and at eye level. By intuition rather than plan, I knew we would never wish to stoop again. It was quite pleasant to sit and sip Joe's booze while listening to his stereo. It's really a shame that he can't tolerate my music while I have no difficulty at all with his: Bach, Beethoven, Brahms, Mahler, and even Villa-Lobos are duck soup for me. Whereas he does not even recognize the Doobie Brothers when he hears them, he thinks Fleetwood Mac is a truck and Alice Cooper a girl.

Another good feature of Heller's apartment was its location: close to the West Side YMCA and closer than my studio to the hospital.

By his fourth day in intensive care, Joe's hands were trembling and he was no longer able to tear open the envelopes of letters that came to him. Thereafter, they had to be opened for him, if they were opened at all. He also preferred to have someone read them to him. Sifting through his mail was great fun—for me. I never met anyone else who had such little interest in his own personal mail. Most of us like to get letters. Not our pal Joey. At times I would begin to read a letter and, before I could finish the first sentence, Heller would croak, "Throw it out!" He hardly permitted me to tell him who sent his get-well cards before he canned them. That's another difference between us. I save everything. He, nothing. He did permit me to keep the checks and hold them for deposit, and I ended up keeping better records for him than I ever did for myself. From time to time I would forward information to his accountants and lawyers.

I really did not mind running errands for Joe. In ICU he needed little besides a comb, brush, and disposable razors. Once in a while there was a special document that had to be dropped off somewhere, or something to be picked up and brought to the hospital. I accomplished these tasks on my faithful ten-speed Peugeot. It was a joy to ride a bike through the city. Bicycling is clearly the fastest and least expensive way to travel, and I was getting exercise and fresh air, as well as solace for my soul.

Visiting Heller in ICU was not a chore either. The new Joe had wasted no time getting friendly with the nurses and residents. The entire staff was utterly charmed by him and therefore treated his friends accordingly. Plus, most times there was at least one other visitor around to have fun with. None of us could believe he was seriously ill. And compared with the average intensive care patient, he wasn't. Our attitude was never contradicted by his doctors, who gave us no reason to believe he was in real trouble. We, his good friends, began to refer to him as the "cripple." Heller, himself a famous black humorist, could scarcely take offense. In fact, he referred to himself similarly. Later, after he was discharged from Mount Sinai and was a patient at Rusk Institute, his wheelchair was being pushed down a corridor by an attendant when I heard him shout, "Make way for the handicapped!" And this, at a place where almost everyone except the staff and some visitors was in worse shape than Joe.

I had started out by bringing Joe his checks so that his bills could be paid promptly. They had already been made out and the mailing envelopes prepared. All that was required was his signature. By the fourth day in intensive care, though, he could no longer hold a pen firmly enough to sign his name. Then came the days when I saw he couldn't raise his arms. Even with help he couldn't write. Since he does have a distinctive signature, it was a cinch for an accomplished artist like me to copy it. And that was much less complicated than having him execute a legal power-of-attorney. So from then on, after making out the checks and entering them in the ledger, I simply signed them as well, a practice that was to have amusing consequences at Joe's divorce proceedings.

Joe had been in ICU only three days when my friend Paula Batson, then director of publicity for CBS Records, called me with disturbing news. She had just gotten a fact-checking call from James Brady, a columnist for the New York *Post*, who wanted to confirm that Joe was seriously ill. Paula played dumb, but an item appeared on "Page Six" of the *Post*, December 17, 1981. It sounded pretty ominous: Joseph Heller was in the intensive care unit of Mount Sinai Hospital with a form of polyneuritis, was partially paralyzed, and his condition was serious but stable.

The word "paralyzed" was indeed shocking. Mario Puzo, Heller's friend for over thirty years, since well before *The Godfather* and *Catch-22*, had used it first. Mario had gotten it from Heller's agent, who'd heard it from Heller's editor, who'd heard it from a friend, who'd got it from Cheryl McCall, our friend who was then a senior writer for *People* magazine. Mario had called George Mandel to say he'd heard that Joe was paralyzed. "No, Mario, you heard it wrong. I've already been to see him and he's not that bad," George assured him. "He's got something called Guillain-Barré."

"My God," Mario blurted out. "That's terrible!"

A surprised George murmured, "Hey, Mario, you know about Guillain-Barré?"

"No, I never heard nothing about it," Mario replied. "But when they name any disease after two guys, it's got to be terrible!"

I was at Joe's bedside when he first saw the *Post*. His face was ashen as he muttered, "Jesus Christ! How am I going to make a deal with a publisher when this gets out?"

A Mount Sinai public relations woman arrived and frantically began explaining to Joe that the hospital had nothing to do with planting the story. We both reassured her that we knew the source. Joe requested that the hospital tell callers his condition was good and improving and that he preferred not having visitors.

I was getting ready to leave that afternoon when I realized I had forgotten an envelope I wanted to take with me. The letter was on Joe's night table, on the wrong side for me but within easy reach for him, so I simply asked him to hand it to me. He saw the envelope, tried to reach out to pick it up . . . and couldn't quite make it. We looked at each other and began to laugh.

"Hey, Joe, wanna know something? You *are* paralyzed, you dope. What the hell were we so angry about?"

"Jesus Christ," he said, "I am."

KEEPING MY SISTER and my brother away from New York became a matter of pressing concern once the notice appeared in the newspaper that Thursday.

Ask any novelist, dramatist, poet: let the smallest unwelcome mention be made in the most obscure publication anywhere in the English-speaking world and you can be positive that some well-meaning person will bring it to the attention of the people you want least to know about it—especially yourself. And this was on "Page Six" of the New York *Post*, a prominent and flamboyant feature with a large, avid readership. A paragraph crackling with such terms as "sudden attack," "intensive care section," "polyneuritis," and "partial paralysis" was not likely to be received with apathy by friends and relatives reading it. There could be no doubt that Sylvia and Lee, my sister and brother, would soon be getting long-distance telephone calls from people in New York wishing to learn more about a crisis of which they themselves had not been given a word.

Both live in West Palm Beach, Florida, near one another in modest condominiums to which they retired after long working lives. My sister was an employee of the same firm for more than forty years, R. H. Macy's. My brother was manager of the mail room in the New York office of MCA–Universal Pictures for more than twenty, until he was sixty-five. I am the spoiled youngest of three children. Both are considerably older than I, and both have catered to me unselfishly from the day I was born. Our father died when I was five, and a good deal of the burden of my rearing and support fell upon both while they were still in their teens. There was nothing they would not have done for me at any time in my life. There is nothing they would not do for me now. All I've ever been asked by either one in return was to give a signed book to someone they knew who valued having it. The most I was allowed to do for my brother when he moved from Brooklyn to Florida was give him a small amount of money—I think it was fifteen hundred or two thousand dollars—to help with the purchase of a used car. The most my sister would permit was to allow me to pay the annual premiums on a major medical noncancelable insurance policy I had recommended that she and George, her husband, obtain for themselves. The notice of premium would go to them. My sister would forward it to me with a note attesting again that they were able to pay it themselves if it was a strain for me to do so. In Florida, after several months of tenacious searching, she had found work a few days a week in a department store, George had found work in a liquor store: both had spent too much of their lives in steady, full-time employment to adjust to idleness as readily as I can.

Since 1982, the year mainly about which I am writing, she has not forwarded the premium notices to me. Instead, in the summer of 1982, shortly after I was out of the hospital, there came from her in an envelope sent registered mail a thick pack of shiny, cardboard U.S. government securities of a kind known to us since the time of World War II as defense bonds. Each bond was in both our names, but I had never seen them before. Almost all were in denominations of twenty-five and fifty dollars. In face value they totaled twelve hundred dollars. They went back in date of purchase at least as far as 1952, when she was still an employee of Macy's, and she had paid for the bonds through a system of voluntary payroll deductions. She had read in *People* magazine that I had borrowed sixty thousand dollars already to cover my medical costs, and she wished to help me to the extent she could in paying it back and with the expenses of the physical therapy and nursing attendance I still required. I returned them to her, of course, explaining on the telephone good-naturedly that only a person who is very well off can borrow sixty thousand dollars.

My sister had not herself been in the best of health that year; Lee, my brother, the oldest of us, had lost his wife to cancer several months earlier. Both had problems of their own to which I did not wish to add. I succeeded in keeping them away with the cooperation of my nephew, and with some adventitious help from my varlet, chef, and decorator, Poor Speed.

Paul is my brother's son. "Pop called me at the office a few times today," he related to me at the hospital in the evening of the day the item about me appeared in the *Post*. "He wants to know what's going on."

"I hope you told him I'm fine and there's nothing to worry about."

"Of course," Paul answered.

"Tell them all I'm okay and in no danger of anything, and that I'm only here for observation, as a matter of routine."

"I already did," said Paul. "But Aunt Syl wants to come up anyway, and I don't know how to stop her. She says she'll stay at your apartment or mine, until you're out of the hospital and all better and don't need anyone to help you."

I weighed that one a moment. "She can't stay at your place," I let him know. He nodded at once. "And tell her she can't stay at mine. Tell her my friend Speed has moved in to take care of my mail and my bills and everything else. I'll be out in a few days, explain to her, and I promise to let them know when I do need anything from them."

When Speed arrived dutifully the next afternoon in the course of his normal rounds, I greeted him somewhat hesitantly with a request I feared was perhaps unreasonable.

"Do me a favor if you can," I asked, "and move into my apartment for a day or two. I don't like to lie to my sister."

"I already have," he answered, smiling. "I thought I might have to go downtown to my studio this afternoon for some winter shirts, but a package from L. L. Bean came to you today with some beauties."

"Is that one of them?" I asked. I had been admiring the cornflower-blue turtleneck of luxurious texture he had on.

"Do you mind?"

"Of course not," I answered sadly. "But if it looks that good on you, it means I ordered the wrong size for all of them. Where'd you get that trench coat? Is that mine too?"

He looked keenly dashing in the wool-lined trench coat I had purchased at Brooks Brothers just about two weeks earlier and had worn but once. It looked better on him than it had on me. In the coat department also I had ordered the wrong size.

I knew I didn't want my brother or sister to see me in the intensive care unit. I did not like to have even my daughter and son observe me there, bereft of privacy and almost helpless physically, with a nasogastric tube hanging out of a nostril, through which I was fed, and a suction tube always close at hand to clear from my mouth the phlegm, saliva, and other mucous secretions I now could not swallow or expectorate. I could move my arms laterally and stretch my hand out to the side table if the back of my bed had been raised. But otherwise, I was in a losing match against gravity.

Before that first Thursday, I had an intravenous tube in the back of my hand, mainly, I have since found out, to keep a vein open for any medication to be administered that way, and I was connected to a cardiac monitor that displayed the heart action of a healthy jogger. Consistent with the nature of the disease, my ability to move had diminished substantially. William Boepple, a thirty-eight-year-old sculptor in New York, came down with Guillain-Barré a year after I did, to the very day. In the morning he experienced a cough and then a burning sensation in his feet. By the afternoon of the following day, he was completely paralyzed in University Hospital of the New York University Medical Center, hooked up by an endotracheal tube to a respirator, on which he was to remain for the next six months. The deterioration I suffered was not as rapid or severe, but it was steady and pronounced.

By Thursday, daily entries made in the hospital record state that I needed assistance in placing the urinal to void.

Marked weakness characterized the movements of all my extremities, and I could not lift either of my arms or legs.

I was on a blenderized diet, pumped by hand syringe and plunger into my stomach through the nasogastric tube, because my dysphagia had grown worse. Involvement of the cranial nerves controlling mouth and face had affected movements of the cheeks, tongue, and lips. Try to count for yourself the number of muscular activities required just to spit.

I was slurring my speech and showing signs of dyspnea (shortness of breath), although I was not conscious of either.

My respiratory parameters, normal upon admission, began declining after the second or third day: these are breathing measurements that were conducted every three hours to ascertain the maximum volume of air I could inhale and expel, the amount of air I was taking when breathing normally, and the maximum strength of my breathing muscles to inhale against resistance, or, put more simply, against the opposition of the thumb of a nurse placed over the opening of a tube to close it.

I could no longer turn myself over in bed. This depletion in motor ability I was undergoing was painless and so insidiously gradual that I was able to be cheerfully oblivious to the significant deterioration which was dramatically apparent to everyone else. It was only, for example, when my son walked in one day toward the end of my second week and exclaimed with delight, "Hey, you're moving your hands again!" that I realized I had not for several days had the power to. When I crowed jubilantly to Dr. Alvin Teirstein, the senior physician in charge of the Medical Intensive Care Unit, that I had been able during the night to bend my right knee while lying on my side, I had erased from my memory that the day before I had been able to bend it while on my back and to elevate my whole leg from the hip. I was losing function while believing I was recovering. Charitable people might call this positive thinking.

On December 16, three days after my admission, I needed the help of two nurses to be transferred out of bed to a wheelchair, in which it was good for me to sit for an hour or so at a time two or three periods a day. By Friday, my fifth day, I was described as without ability to move my right leg, and I was able to assist only slightly in my transfer to a chair.

I could not sit up.

I could support my head when seated and turn it from side to side, but I could not raise it. Blame the sternocleidomastoid muscles, which connect the lobes at the back of the skull to the rear of the center of the shoulders.

By Saturday, December 19, after one week in the hospital, it was recorded that I could not bend either knee and that I was able to move each leg at the ankle only. I was complaining daily to my doctors about the amount of noise in the unit at night—the lights were lowered, but the voices were not—and I was in fearful and increasing misery over my failure to sleep.

And the summary of the resident on duty that day states I was "inordinately depressed"!

I am aware that a stroke or heart attack can fell a human more abruptly with more serious irreversible consequences. But it was precisely the gradual, silent nature of my impairment that produced so haunting and morbid an effect on many of my visitors. Marian Berkman, a friend since childhood, was enraged that it should happen to someone as healthy and vigorous as I. Others could not wholly conceal their ghastly apprehensions that it could just as easily be happening to them. In the second and third week, when my weight began to melt away voluminously, just about everybody seeing me for the first time had no doubt I was dying.

* * *

The nasogastric tube through which I was to be given almost all nourishment for the next three and a half months was inserted some time on my first full day in the hospital. On Monday, my first morning there, I could not get down plain yogurt. I did no better at lunchtime. I would have bet a million it would prove impossible, without the administration of anesthesia, to work a flexible plastic tube up my nose to the roof of whatever cavity lay at the top, then down my throat behind my tongue and into my stomach without my howling and thrashing defensively and gagging and vomiting and choking to death. I would have lost: it was possible. It wasn't pleasant, but there was no pain, and after a short time I could grow oblivious to the presence of the tube. I was most aware it was there only those few times it had to be removed and replaced by a fresh one, a daunting prospect that put me in very low spirits each time the need arose.

I ate, so to speak, from the regular daily menus. Ordering these meals became a ritual of amusement, for everything on the tray was blenderized together in the nurses' section and fed to me through the tube, a process consuming about half an hour. I ordered a lot. I tasted nothing, as I explained to people who asked and heard my answer with looks of incredulity. "Want some?" I would offer generously to anyone present at feeding time. I could go right on talking. I could feel changes in temperature in my throat when anything hot or cold was given me, but nothing else. Institutional food being all it's cracked up to be, I'm not sure I missed much.

Once the atrophy started and the precipitous weight loss I was to suffer began, the nurses and I leaned heavily toward carbohydrates when ordering my meals, in a resolute but futile effort to arrest the decline. Between meals were double orders of ice cream, cookies, and chocolate milk, all blenderized and given through my tube. We should have known better. The loss was in muscle tissue, and nothing would have helped.

Without exception, every nurse's report states that I tolerated my blenderized meals well—which would come as no surprise to any soul who has ever eaten with me—and that I was "alert and oriented × 3," oriented to time, to place, and to person. I knew who I was and where I was, and I knew there were personal matters to be taken care of and what most of them were.

On Wednesday or Thursday of that week, I was scheduled for a reappearance in Family Court in connection with that aspect of my marital dispute that had been adjourned a month or two earlier. Jeffrey Cohen, the gallivanting, swashbuckling young lawyer representing me in what I found to be a most peculiar legal forum in which to air my matrimonial altercation, was in California. I discovered this when I telephoned his office from the nurses' station Monday morning. I left word with an associate that I was in the Medical Intensive Care Unit of Mount Sinai Hospital and that the condition for which I had been hospitalized was not anything serious. I failed to appreciate how incongruous these pieces of information could sound to someone more worldly than I in matters of illness.

On Monday, that full first day, I was tested with a substance called Tensilon, with results definitely excluding myasthenia gravis as the malady from which I was suffering.

Then came the first of my spinal taps. I had three of these lumbar punctures in a period of two weeks, and each was without pain or any kind of discomfort, a fact some people who have undergone the same procedure are startled to hear. I was not even susceptible to the headache I was warned might ensue. The findings from this first examination of my cerebrospinal fluid, I was told when I asked, were normal.

I was proud when I heard this. I ought to have been distraught. At the end of the month, on December 29, when I was given my third lumbar puncture and had a much broader conception of the game and the odds, I rooted like hell for the abnormal elevation in protein that would provide some laboratory corroboration of Guillain-Barré. By then I *wanted* Guillain-Barré! By then I knew that Guillain-Barré syndrome is a very good illness to have—if you've already been afflicted with an acute and diffuse idiopathic polyneuropathy with indications of demyelinating inflammation. It may, in fact, be the only one that affords the consolation of a favorable prognosis.

On Tuesday, according to the hospital records, I could still stand and walk, but I was having difficulty sitting up. My gag reflex was becoming weak. A hoarseness of which I had not been aware had been noted by my physicians, and this was growing worse. I was astounded by the amount of information obtained by both doctors that first Sunday in examinations I thought of as cursory. I doubt that the one in Wally Sencer's office took as long as ten minutes. But it was enough for him to observe and write that there was masseter weakness, weakness of the tongue as seen in alternating movements, weakness of both sternocleidomastoid muscles and weakness in head extension, that there was a paraparesis of the hips, bilateral weakness of both upper extremities, along with a proximal weakness at each joint, including the fingers, that I had a diffuse radiculoneuropathy, and that, by virtue of the involvement of the upper cervical roots as well as the cranial roots, I should be admitted as an emergency for close monitoring for spreading paralysis and impairment of my breathing functions and be given the tests I've mentioned. Dr. Sencer came back to check on me at 11:15 p.m. that same Sunday evening and saw me three times the following day.

The electromyographic examination for which I was scheduled on Tuesday was a study of the conduction velocity of stimuli along my nerve fibers that would establish neurological damage as the cause of my condition rather than some primary muscle disease producing symptoms that were similar. Put plainly, I think, this EMG test measures the speed with which sensations of pain induced by needles and electric shocks travel along specific nerves far enough to be recognized as pain.

I was wheeled away on a stretcher, leaving Speed behind to assemble the paperwork I'd left for him and then embark for the completion of his duties on his bicycle, which he had locked to a parking stanchion downstairs in the street. The EMG test I was given that day, though sufficient to the purpose, was superficial compared with the one I was to undergo at Rusk in February. That one lasted two hours, and every accessible nerve in my four limbs was subjected repeatedly to electric shock or the traumatic stab of a needle until a legible pattern of response was recorded by the machine, as well as at least one nerve in the right side of my face.

I don't believe this one at Mount Sinai lasted longer than fifteen minutes, including the few needed to effect the necessary electrical connections. The doctor administering it (I assume he was a doctor and not merely an electrician) was articulate, pleasant, understanding. He alerted me each time to the location of the needle puncture or electric shock I was about to receive. His sparse, sympathetic conversation made a difference. I don't think there were more than a dozen applications all told, and none to me was singularly acute. The worst both times, at Mount Sinai and at Rusk, was the needle plunged into the palm of the hand near the base of the thumb. That one inspects, I think, the ulnar nerve. In the test at Rusk, during which I endeavored to divert myself by counting, I one time got up as high as thirty-eight painful electrical impulses administered to one nerve in my leg before a significant reading was recorded by the monitoring equipment. It was hard for me to believe what was going on. I was more sensitive to pain than the machine was.

As my EMG examination at Mount Sinai was ending, the man administering it inquired almost in digression if I suffered from a stomach ulcer, his curiosity aroused, he told me, by an odor from my mouth he knew to be associated with that condition. As far as I knew I did not, I informed him, but vowed I would mention it when I was back upstairs. (I did not have one.)

Wheeled out on my stretcher, I was surprised to see my old friend George Mandel in the waiting room, leaning on the counter in his unbuttoned brown sheepskin coat and conversing gravely with the clerk there. I was stunned by his wan and dejected expression. My humanitarian impulse was to spring up off my stretcher and to beseech him to please, please lie down, at once, and let me get or do something for him.

George Mandel and I have been friends since I was about fourteen, for close to fifty years. We met while I still lived in Coney Island. I have known George through thick and thicker, in sickness and in health—I had seen him after World War II, from which he had returned with a head wound from a German sniper's bullet, I had seen him with a heart attack, and I had seen him with a stone in his salivary gland—and I had never seen him looking worse, more glum, than he did just then. He looked just awful, and what was making him look so bad was the way I looked to him, lying on a stretcher, limp and exhausted, with a tube in my nose. He had just been told by the clerk that the test to which I had been subjected was experienced by many as excruciating, intolerable. This would have been news to me had he come right out and said so.

But instead he asked solemnly, "How're you feeling?"

"Okay, I guess," I answered promptly. I knew I felt tired. "How'd you find me down here?"

"Speed. Did it hurt a lot?"

"What? No, not really. What's the matter?"

His look was a startled one. "No? Are you really okay? Are you sure it didn't hurt?"

"Of course I'm sure. What are you talking about?"

George stared at me piercingly. "Do you know who I am?" he demanded. "Do you know where you are? Do you know why you're down here?"

"Sure I do. Why are you asking me that?"

"I was checking your memory. Are you sure it didn't hurt? Maybe you forgot already."

George, who by instinct is both heroically diplomatic and infinitely tolerant, assumed control of the area of human relations in the division of labor that began to evolve about me among a rather sizable and growing number of people who would visit frequently and upon whom I knew I could depend.

It was he who received phone calls and letters from old friends who did not know how to reach me and did know how to reach him. There was the shocked phone call from Marian Berkman, who'd been friends with me since the seventh grade in elementary school in Coney Island, and who'd been widowed earlier that year when her husband, Lou, who'd been a friend of mine since the fifth grade, had died of cancer. George took calls from others who inquired about my condition and wished to visit, and he tactfully put them off to allow me to adjust more stably to my plight and my surroundings. To George came that phone call from Mario Puzo, who was the first to use that paralyzing word "paralyzed" and then was curious to learn if I was going to "croak." I had met Mario through George, back about 1950 or so, before any of the three of us had published a novel. George was in communication with my friend Marvin Winkler in California, with whom I had shared a playpen as an infant, if both our mothers were to be believed, and who maintains to this day, calumniously, that I used to empty both our milk bottles. With finesse, George undertook the ticklish assignment of telling the woman who had been my literary agent for thirty years that, because of the expenses I envisioned, I wished to spare myself her commission in connection with my newest novel.

"Candida, I've got some bad news for you about Joe," was the inspired way George Mandel began.

And after that, of course, whatever he had to say could only come as a relief.

George showed most devotion and nobleness of all, though, in submitting at my bedside with unflagging grace, politeness, and self-control to the company of several other people I knew he could not stand—including, at times, me.

Jeffrey Cohen was another soon serving in my kitchen cabinet, an evolvement all the more remarkable because I did not know him all that well and because Jeffrey Cohen is a person without spare time. I had met and retained him only three months before. He came in a rush directly from the airport upon returning from California and probably was my most frequent night-caller in those twenty-two days I was in the intensive care unit, embarking with aggressive zeal each evening on the execution of menial favors wholly unrelated to any of the legal difficulties for which I had retained him to represent me. The appearance in Family Court was postponed. For a while, he was carrying papers back and forth between me and my other lawyer in the hospital, the one with gallstones. I believe I stopped just short of burdening Jeffrey then with responsibilities having to do with razors, laundry, and underwear. For that I had Julius Green. But along with Green, Speed, George, and such others as Joe Stein, A. Robert Towbin, the genial jogger and investment banker, and Barbara Gelb, I include Jeffrey in the corps of diligent factotums I had at my disposal in that grotesque period. My power over people increased as my strength waned. Among my self-discoveries was an unsuspected genius I possessed for delegating responsibility. I should have been in the White House instead of the hospital.

Although Jeffrey generally has a poker-faced control of himself that stands him in good stead in the confrontational arena of matrimonial law, I could tell he was appalled. To him I did not look so good. Jeffrey is dark, strong, and handsome and he is twenty-five years my junior, but I looked better and younger than he did the last time he'd seen me. He works harder. And because he takes his work more seriously than I take mine, including the work he was doing for me, he suffers more. He works incessantly, passionately—when he does have spare time he begins to train for the New York marathon, which he has not yet ever found time to enter—and it was all the more extraordinary, therefore, to find him spending so much of his time with me.

He generally would come to the hospital very late, when his business and social activities were over, arriving at my bedside in punctual devotion and servitude to the dead and the dying: months later he confessed that he was all but certain in that first week that I was already among the dying and destined very shortly to take my place with the dead. He thought I was mad when, with one tube in my nose and another suctioning my mouth, I ebulliently repeated the information from my neurologist that I was suffering only a mild case of something that was not going to affect me seriously or permanently. To Jeffrey even now, I am a walking miracle, a breathing refutation of all of the laws of experience and probability.

Believe it or not, despite his field of specialization, he has an impartial sense of outrage. And this illness of mine in the midst of other difficulties with which he knew I was struggling infuriated his sense of cosmic fairness.

It was good to have Jeffrey visit regularly. What brought him so loyally was a mixture of decency, affection, and esteem. He was habitually shamefaced to show to me, an author for whom he had so much admiration, the letters and papers he was preparing in my behalf. It pleased me enormously to correct his punctuation. To him I was a living—now a dying—legend.

He came as well in gaping fascination with the kind of people he was apt to find around me, the author of *The Godfather;* the author of *Fiddler on the Roof,* Joseph Stein; the star of *Kramer vs. Kramer* (a film with a subject, I imagine, that is very close to his heart); Mel Brooks; the clever and inventive George Mandel, whose newest novel is *Crocodile Blood;* the idiosyncratic Julius Green; and others of mordant misanthropic wit in what to him was an all-star cast. And every one of them was described by me to Jeffrey, on my deathbed, as an opulent prospect for a young matrimonial lawyer eager to make his fortune.

"Mel Brooks?" he questioned with amazement.

"An annuity."

"Joe Stein?"

"On the verge."

"Dustin Hoffman?"

"She finds him meek."

Jeffrey Cohen was not *that* gullible, of course, but the temptation to believe was strong and his delight in being kidded was part of the entertainment. It was in perverse humor that I enjoyed hushing him one night before he could begin addressing me in that ringing voice of his, adjuring him in almost a whisper to speak softly this time because the man in the bed on my left had died but a few minutes before. Jeffrey paled. This was no joke: the man was younger than I and had perished from something occurring in the brain stem caused by a rampaging leukemia. He had been transferred in beside me from a different part of the hospital about four hours before, and there had not been much hope for him from the start.

Earlier that night Mel Brooks had materialized out of nowhere to pay me the first of his visits. Nothing could have been more unexpected to me than the sight of Mel in my intensive care unit at about nine o'clock on a frigid, black winter evening in late December. I had not even known he was in New York. For reasons no more arcane than a very solid and self-centered intelligence, Mel does not take any more warmly to the idea of dying than I do. His face was pinched and gloomy, he regarded me sorrowfully. I could see he had not come to make me laugh. He had bigger fish to fry.

"Tell me honestly," he said right off, "did it begin with a numbness or tingling in your feet and work its way up along the peripheral nerves of the spine and into your cranial nerves to affect your pharynx and face?"

I shook my head and studied him with amazement and respect. "You know about Guillain-Barré?" I exclaimed.

"Of course I do," he answered matter-of-factly. "Who doesn't? Landry's ascending paralysis. Eighteen-sixty-nine, right? I know all about the polyneuritises."

"How come?" I questioned him. "I never even heard the word 'polyneuritis' before, and I've been a hypochondriac longer than you. I'm older."

"How come?" He seemed surprised by my question. "I've got my medical dictionaries, of course. Why are you looking at me like that? Lots of people have medical dictionaries."

"But not everybody memorizes them," I said as a joke.

He took me seriously. "I do. Was there any paresthesia anywhere beforehand? Did you have a respiratory infection of any kind? Any other viral infections? No bronchitis? No rabies shot? Get any other vaccinations? How about childhood viral diseases? Smallpox, measles, hepatitis—"

"Mel, Mel," I broke in benevolently when it began to dawn upon me what lay most heavily on his mind. "I know why you're here. I think I can give you what you've come for, the protection you want. I know how to immunize you." I paused to clear my mouth with the suction tube. "I'll have them shave my head and let you rub my baldy for good luck."

The laugh he gave was perfunctory. "It isn't funny, you know," he admonished me somberly. "Guillain-Barré is no joke. As many as one-point-six to one-point-nine per hundred thousand get it every year. That's between sixteen and nineteen people per million."

Who could help being impressed? "Let me try to build up the odds for you," I said, going all out to comfort him. "Not many people have *two* close friends who get it, right? Can we begin with that?"

"Practically no one," he gave in, after considering.

"Well, you and I have some of the same friends, Julie and Speed and George, and they've already got me. Now all three are not going to have *two* friends with Guillain-Barré, are they? Statistically, you're practically guaranteed."

Reassured a little by that line of reasoning, he talked of other things for a while. He whirled and tongue-lashed the resident on duty severely when he learned I was unable to sleep. Valium relaxes the muscles and sleeping potions depress the respiratory system, and Mel was not disposed to prescribe either. "Give him tryptophan," he then commanded in that same brusque tone which I imagine resonates for years in the recollection of film editors with whom he has worked. "It's mother's milk to him. You can get it in any health food store. I'll send up a bottle of tablets tomorrow." Reminded that I couldn't swallow tablets, he exploded, "Pulverize them in the blender and pour them down his Levin tube. Do I have to tell you people everything? And give him a clean Yankaur tube. That one's filthy. I don't like the color of those secretions."

It was not long after Mel left that the man in the bed beside me passed away. And not long after that, Jeffrey came, and I shushed him and told him what had happened. And when Jeffrey was going, I was able to entrust him with another new commission that must have seemed to him of somewhat ghoulish tenor. I asked him to get word to Mel that very same night through Speed or Julius Green, both close friends of Mel's, that the Malach ha-Mavet, the Jewish angel of death, had missed him just by minutes and had taken the man on my left in sullen consolation upon arriving at my bedside and finding Mel already gone. I could easily picture Mel's moody snicker when that piece of information was given to him.

Julie Green and his wife, Edie, are the friends in New York to whom Mel is closest, and not even they were aware he was in town and had slipped in to see me.

Upon Julie and Edie there fell the largest burden in those first three weeks of executing most of the pedestrian matters that had to be taken care of for me, and they came through, with both good and bad. Julie is a singular eccentric among all my closest friends: he is the only one who regularly goes to, as it is with some dignity called, a place of business, a trait of behavior he often is embarrassed to account for when he is with the rest of us. Our meetings, therefore, except for weekends, took place in the very late afternoon or early evening, when his working day was through.

Among the good things that came from Mr. and Mrs. Green was a tiny transistor radio that allowed me for a time to tune into the news and to the classical music on WQXR. Bad was that after several days I could no longer reach out for the radio or manipulate the small controls. Not so good either was the report that a major medical umbrella insurance policy had been allowed to lapse early that year because of my failure to pay the annual premium of just one hundred and thirty-two dollars. Lost somewhere in the confusion attending the dissolution of my marital household were the notices of premiums due and of policy cancellation. This was a policy with a ten-thousand-dollar deductible provision that would pay eighty percent of all costs above that. I was not all that concerned upon finding this out from Julie: in the short run it would not matter, I knew, for Blue Cross was paying for everything in intensive care and I did have in effect a ten-thousand-dollar major medical policy to cover the rest. But unfortunately, there was no short run; and in the long run the failure to pay that small premium resulted in a loss of benefits of more than forty thousand dollars. I stopped calculating after the figure passed that amount because I began to feel sick again.

Edie Green brought me books, Jane Austen's *Emma*, which I had asked for, and, on her own initiative, for the emotional boost it might give me, Norman Cousins's *Anatomy of an Illness*. As it turned out, I had not much pleasure from either of them, for in a day or two, I could not hold a book steady with both hands, or hold it at all with one when I removed the other to try to turn a page. One evening after I had lost almost all use of my fingers, Julius Green arrived and, with a smile, drew from his pocket a Chinese puzzle, two interlocked metal rings which one would be hard put to separate even when in the pink of condition. "Let's see you do it," he challenged. "Very funny," I answered him dryly. When I gave up after a second or two he said, "Try this one." And he gave me another. He had about twenty in his pocket. Other people toyed with them the rest of that week.

I came close to getting my revenge in the episode of the sheet-burn and the underwear. Sheet-burn: by the end of my first week my scrotum was painfully inflamed from the continual friction of the bare skin against the bedsheet. One of the nurses recommended Jockey shorts. Julius brought me six pairs—none of my friends would let me reimburse them for any of the money they spent buying things I requested. Before the end of the second week some of the shorts were visibly in need of laundering. I was restricted to a bedpan now and could not assist in cleaning myself. Julius recoiled with a look of repugnance when I told him what I wanted done.

"Get out of here!" he objected vehemently. "I'm not going to take those. I won't even touch them."

"They have to be washed," I pointed out blandly. "I can't wear them like that."

"Throw them away, there in the basket. I'd rather buy you new ones."

"You shouldn't have bought white," I muttered reproachfully.

More good news came in the person of the woman from the public relations department of the hospital, who'd been so abashed by the incident of the New York *Post* and so earnest in assuring me that the hospital had not had anything to do with initiating the item. Now *The New York Times* wanted to know the true story. I welcomed the chance to set the record straight, to restore my credit and my credibility simply by presenting the specifics in conjunction with my physicians and the hospital. All I wanted was to have the ailment named and identified as one that was trivial and transitory, and an unequivocal statement from doctors and hospital that I was already on my way to a full recovery and would be back on my feet as good as new in a week or two. When neither my Baders nor the hospital would go quite that far, I began to suspect I might be in trouble.

EVEN WHEN JOE could no longer stand, could no longer lift his arms, had no strength in his hands, and required help to turn in bed, I still didn't think his condition was serious or was going to last very long.

Except for that ridiculous tube hanging out of his nose, he looked like a man in perfect health and was an incongruity in a place with seriously ill and terminal patients. When I asked him, "Why the tube?" he explained that he could not swallow and was afraid that he would choke if he tried eating in normal fashion. I thought it was another unnecessary precaution. I was proved entirely wrong about that when they decided at a later date to remove the tube and try to feed him by mouth again. He *was* unable to swallow. The tube had to be reinserted. And this time it was an ordeal for Joe—in his words, unpleasant, distasteful, and uncomfortable.

Even with the tube, Heller always looked forward to his feedings. One day I was sitting with him as his dinner was being prepared. The method was to mix up everything in a blender, then force it through the tube, which carried it through his nose and to his stomach. As the nurse was about halfway through the feeding, she stopped and remarked that in the event Joe felt like regurgitating, to please tell her. Apparently she didn't know his famous eating habits. He simply shook his head patiently and declared, "You don't understand. Whatever goes into my stomach, I don't give back."

Those of us who visited in intensive care shared the same difficulty trying to fathom what he was attempting to say when he spoke to us, and felt this was due to the damned nasogastric tube, even though his diction had never been that good. Joe seemed exasperated with our inability to understand his speech, berated us as a bunch of deaf old fools, and developed the habit of spelling out the words he knew he could not pronounce, without interrupting the tempo of his speech. He thought this solved the communication problem. What we didn't bother telling him was that this was about as helpful to us as heated suction cups are to a corpse. He couldn't say the letters *m*, *o*, *u*, and *y* any more than he could make their sounds. He could not purse his lips or spread them, and he couldn't clear his throat.

We were able to accept his complaints about our ineptitude cheerfully, since his former grousing was now a rarity. I took to nodding as though I understood, even though I often didn't know what the hell he was talking about. I figured if he was calm, perhaps it wasn't urgent. And even if it was, and because he knew I had a terrible memory, he would undoubtedly repeat it to another friend who might accidentally interpret him correctly. Often, or rather, most times, just as a kind of insurance, he would ask at least three of us to undertake the same task. Since we who attended to his needs were not exactly dopes and were familiar with Heller's ways, we established our own clearinghouse and successfully avoided duplications. We also managed to use his minor problems as a major source of entertainment.

One day Julie Green called George Mandel and asked, "Did you hear what Joe said today?" George, completely off guard, said with a touch of anxiety, "No, what'd he say?" Julie replied, "Nheh dehgrehda waddleta deh nahe nheh!" George laughed appreciatively, but Julie was not quite finished with his heartless parody. He then began to mimic Heller's habit of spelling when we couldn't understand his words and "spelled": "Ghey ghee hav veh gay theh. . . ." We all expected that Heller would shortly be heard berating us in his familiar Brooklyn accent.

I still believed that his doctors were taking extreme measures because they wished to avoid criticism and malpractice suits. They were acting as though it was a serious matter, while we thought it was nothing. In fact, when one of them, who also happens to be a friend of mine, stopped me as we were both leaving the ICU and delivered what I could only describe as a complete classroom lecture on Guillain-Barré, including the latest available statistics relative to the speed of nerve regeneration, the severity of nerve involvement, and the ten percent mortality rate, I hardly listened, though I was impressed and admired his prodigious memory. But what did any of this have to do with Heller or me? Why was this guy wasting our time displaying his superb powers of total recall? I didn't get it.

I realize now that I was oblivious to most of Joe's awful experiences in ICU. I didn't believe he'd be laid up for any great length of time. About ten days after he was admitted, I flew off to Key West with my friends Paula, Cheryl, and Barbara and didn't return until a few days before the New Year.

I saw Joe just before I left for Florida and, though he was unable to do much for himself, he seemed in buoyant spirits and he still looked well. He sent me off with his blessings and reminded me only twice to leave his checkbooks out and to turn over the keys to his apartment and his letterbox to Julie Green, who would be taking over until I got back. He reminded Julie three times to get them.

Julie came to the apartment and I showed him where Heller kept his checkbooks and deposit slips. I was coming back before the first of January, so he didn't have to concern himself with the monthly disbursements. But I asked that he deposit Heller's checks, maintain his balances, and take him his mail and phone messages. Joe could tell him what else to do quite vigorously. We didn't need to worry about that.

Julie conducts a nationwide wholesale diamond business—in fact, he's the only member of our group who has a real job—and his firm has an "800" number permitting out-of-town customers to make free calls. I, therefore, found it convenient, prudent, and inexpensive to keep tabs on Joe's progress by calling daily while I was in the Florida Keys. Green's reports were invariably amusing and gave no clue that Heller was deteriorating. Julie was seeing him almost every day and the daily change, I guess, must not have been noticeable.

As soon as I returned to New York I went to visit Joe and was totally unprepared for the differences in his physical appearance. His usually tanned face was now pale and drawn, and he looked extremely thin—in less than ten days he had lost ten pounds. At first I was alarmed. But Joe's optimism and cheerfulness put me at ease. It pleased him to hear that the weather was terrible in Key West and that some of us had begun to get on each other's nerves. (It's not enough to be happy in the hospital. Your best friend on vacation has got to have a lousy time, too.) He was pleased as well to be indoors during one of the worst winters the city had ever had.

By now he could hardly move without assistance. Whenever I came to visit him in ICU with his mail and messages, he would ask me to fetch his glasses, usually kept in the drawer of the night table, and to stick them on his nose for him. When he wanted me to call someone for him and I didn't have the number, I would have to locate his address book, which was never in the place he thought it was. He no longer had the ability to pick up the book even if it was next to him. He continued to be humorous in spite of his dreadful physical situation, and that was beginning to frighten us.

When I arrived on New Year's Day, I was his only visitor. As soon as I approached his bedside, Joe scarcely greeted me but immediately started croaking out orders.

"Gih bee da sutchin too," he said—or something like that—and I realized he was asking me to give him the suction tube. "Yeah," he mumbled, and then something that sounded like "over there." I handed it to him, and he went on with the rest of the orders. "Now give me my glasses. Not there. There," he murmured, "in the black case. Next to those books. Right." I was getting the hang of his speech. "Now, lift my head. No, not that way. Use the button at the foot of the bed. Not that one, you dope." He was coming through loud and clear. "That's for legs. The legs. The feet—the feet. I want the head, the head. Okay, that's got it." I was going from one side to the other, as he moved his head to point the way. "Now, moisten the swab on the table with water. Over there and bring it here. Moisten my lips with it. Yep. Good. Now, the urinal. It's there. There, you blind fool. Yeah, that's it. Thank you. Lift my head a little higher. Good. Okay, place the urinal between my legs. I can't reach down that far. Fine. Okay. Now, put the head of my cock in."

The volume of the "No!" that issued from my throat startled the ward, if not the entire hospital, and two nurses ran to the bedside to attend to him as I yelled, "I'm getting the fuck out of here!" and stalked out. I have to admit, it was a beautiful Heller maneuver. He set me up for it perfectly. He was grinning when I left.

Away from the hospital, I had begun to fall into a routine of life that was closely associated with Heller's. I slept in his bed. I collected and sorted his mail, listened to his messages, kept his accounts, paid his bills, wrote, signed, and mailed his checks. I visited him daily and kept him abreast of my activities and filled him in on other gossip. My new life, however, did nothing to impair the activity and quality of my old life—it simply added a few good things. I saw all my old friends and found some new ones. I never had to miss a Boz Scaggs, Billy Joel, or Rolling Stones concert, an Elvis Costello or James Taylor club appearance, or a Miles Davis party.

It was my friend Paula Batson who introduced me to the New York contemporary music scene. Attending performances and parties when her artists appeared was part of her job as a publicist with CBS Records. I went as Paula's guest, or, as they say in the business, her "plus one." I could not convince Joe that I truly enjoyed myself at these functions. He thought I was, once again, sacrificing myself for a friend. He forgets that I was always a music lover. As a matter of fact, my writing career began with a record review column for the West Virginia *Daily Athenaeum*, my college paper. The leap (although it took about forty-five years) from rhythm and blues to rock and roll was but a short step for this old jazz buff.

One night I attended a concert at the Palladium to see and have my ears assaulted by a "heavy-metal" group called Judas Priest. I was sitting next to a young man who could not have been more than seventeen. He kept looking at me, shooting glances at my gray hair, then turning away. Finally he found the courage to speak. "Pardon me, sir, but do you really like Judas Priest?" I smiled and answered, "Sure do, man, I think they're intense." He shook his young head in a gesture of awe and disbelief and muttered, "I can't fucking believe it. Oh, boy, wait until I tell Dad about this."

Paula was also my connection to the world of country music, and in the late seventies she introduced me to Bobby Bare, "Sir" Douglas Sahm, Willie Nelson, and Kinky Friedman. I liked all of them immensely, and because Kinky spends a good bit of time in New York performing at the Lone Star Café, we became friends. It was around 1977 when I told Heller about Kinky, and he was so captivated by the concept of a group named Kinky Friedman and the Texas Jewboys that he immediately put the name into the closing pages of his novel *Good as Gold.* When I mentioned that to Kinky, he said, "Ask that sucker how much he's paying me." I told Kinky it wasn't necessary for me to ask. I knew the answer: nothing. Kinky smiled and said, "Shoot, that's okay. Tell Heller he can use my name. Otherwise I'm liable to end up in his damned book as Kinky Schwartz or something worse."

The most serious inconvenience to me during Joe's hospitalization and convalescence was that I saw much less of Ngoot. Living uptown, I began to miss his counsel, wisdom, and, especially, his Oriental delicacies. Mr. Lee's expertise in the kitchen is not limited to Chinese cooking. He is equally familiar with French, Italian, and Middle Eastern fare. In fact, Ngoot is largely responsible for making me a pretty good cook, too. Heller owes him much for that. The rare compliments I've gotten from Joe were for foods that I prepared for him, the results of many years spent as Ngoot's apprentice in the kitchen and countless trips to the best New York markets with the "master."

In the course of screening Heller's mail, I found that he received a good number of requests for autographs. I never before realized the extent of his celebrity and the high regard in which he was held by people who did not know him as well as his friends and relatives did. These requests were many times accompanied by hardcover copies of his novels and stamped commemorative envelopes. The petitioners were invariably respectful and courteous, and they never failed to include return postage. I gave his polite literary groupies my immediate attention. Since I was already signing his checks, I could see no reason why I should not grant his autograph. If the signature was good enough to pass the scrutiny of Chemical Bank, it should be good enough for his fans. Joe complimented me for my consideration to his devotees. He confessed that it had often been a chore to comply with such requests in the past but said he would be more generous in the future, especially if someone else would volunteer to screen the requests, autograph the books, and provide effusive inscriptions, then take them to the post office and wait in line to mail them for him.

One day, because of an abrupt change in the weather, I needed something warmer than I'd brought with me from my place, so I wore Joe's luxurious Eddie Bauer goose-down Alaska Slope parka with genuine wolf-fur ruff. It was simply a matter of convenience. When I arrived at the hospital, Joe, who is by no means visually oriented, suddenly asked, "Hey, Speed, isn't that my coat?" I simply said, "What about it?" It seemed to tickle his fancy, so I figured I would continue to please him with this harmless game. Sometimes it required quite a bit of parading before him until he caught on that I was wearing yet another of his sartorial treasures. It never failed to amuse him when he did. In the past—that is, pre-GBS—it wasn't always so easy to get him to appreciate my jokes. Now I had him laughing over this bit of business with his clothes. This was a changed man! He was somewhat perplexed by the fact that his clothes looked better on me than they ever did on him. Since we are very different in height, weight, and build, he concluded, logically, that he had been buying the wrong sizes. I thought it better to let Joe worry about his clothes not fitting than to think about when he would ever get to try them on again.

Besides, Joe was forgetting about my celebrated flair for looking good in any old thing. I still get compliments when wearing some of his cast-off beauties that really are too small for him now because he weighs a lot more than he did before he got sick. And, thanks to the luxurious life I've been leading since then, so do I.

So there I was, living in Joe's place, all the while making little improvements here and there. I thought he should not be without a gourmet-quality omelet pan and a thick aluminum rice pot. I also bought and charged to him an easy-folding, deluxe ironing board. I got him the best G.E. steam iron, too. After all, what good is an ironing board without an iron? I no longer had to be embarrassed by showing up in his unpressed clothes. It was fortuitous that Charles Gwathmey and I had introduced Joe to our English haberdashers, Turnbull and Asser. I didn't have to be ashamed to wear his custom-made shirts, either.

It seems strange, but I did get the impression that Joe was pleased that I had more or less assumed his identity by living in his apartment, signing his checks, autographing his books, keeping his accounts, screening and answering his mail, talking to his friends and relatives, and wearing his clothes. I even thought I might take a crack at finishing his novel, but, as I told him frankly, I was not altogether pleased with what he had wrought that far.

Within two weeks after Heller was admitted, Mario Puzo showed up in ICU. I know what a heroic act that was, not just because Mario lives on Long Island and will do almost anything to avoid coming to New York but because Mario would rather eat a broom than enter a hospital under any circumstances. He felt he simply had to go for Joe. He may have done it to be sure that Heller was really there, because he shared the skeptical view with the rest of Heller's friends that it might be an elaborate joke. He too considered Joe to be the healthiest of us and the one least likely to get sick.

"If I was in his spot," Mario confided to me after his visit, "you'd have to shoot me! I'd rather croak! I'd have to commit suicide!"

Joe's response when I told him what Mario had said was spoken with calm and indulgent patience: "Ask him how. If you gave me a knife I couldn't use it. I am not able to pull the trigger of a gun. I can't swallow pills. I can't even throw myself out of bed." The swiftness with which he answered gave me the suspicion he'd already been running this idea over in his mind.

After it became clear that Joe was going to be in the hospital much longer than we had expected, Alan Altman, who, as Joe's lawyer, was in a position to know, assured him that he would be able to afford his expensive illness in spite of the fact that his big major medical policy was no longer in effect. "Ever since I've known him, he's always been tense about not having money," he explained to me one day. "Now he's really scared. I don't think he has to be." I could predict that statement would be made by any New York lawyer who sends exorbitant bills to his clients.

Altman became my lawyer, too, after Joe and I received our contract for this book. When we got his bill for services rendered, I was flabbergasted. I thought it was much too high. Joe agreed with me. I asked him if he'd mind if I spoke to Altman myself. Heller gave me his blessing. When I made the call, I expected a big battle and lots of talk, and was almost disappointed when Alan, hearing my complaint, immediately and unhesitatingly agreed to a reduction. I suppose he'll make up for it when he sues me for libel for these remarks.

Another of Joe's frequent visitors was Jeffrey Cohen, who is intelligent, handsome, able, honest, conscientious, sensitive, and a divorce lawyer. I realize this description sounds like a contradiction in terms. Nevertheless, it is true. Jeffrey was unprepared for what he experienced when he hurried to the hospital to visit Joe his third day in intensive care and for what he saw when he kept going there.

"He looked awful," Jeffrey still remembers. "So weak and pale and very, very sick. I figured he was in the right place. But the smell of illness there, you know, is overwhelming. One time I left him and turned right inside the bathroom because I thought I was going to vomit, and that isn't like me at all. He kept telling me he was getting better, and I could see he was getting worse. There was a man right next to him one night who looked better and healthier than he, and the man was dead."

Jeffrey thought Heller was in some kind of euphoric delirium because of his equable geniality, optimism, and humor, and thus joined a small but growing group who privately concluded that Joe had taken leave of his senses.

Even Julie Green, a paragon of patience and equanimity, confessed some puzzlement over Joe's incongruous behavior: he was now exhibiting kindness, gratitude, and unbelievable forbearance. "If it was me, in Heller's spot," Julie said, "I'd get down on my knees, wail like crazy, and beat my fists on the ground." He forgot that Heller couldn't get up on his feet, let alone down on his knees, and no way did he have the ability even to make a fist.

Another mutual friend, playwright Joe Stein, had also been the recipient of curious assignments from Heller whenever he came to his bedside. In fact, Heller was able to find an area in which Stein could be useful even while he was out of town. Stein was leaving over the Christmas holidays for a short vacation with his family. Heller wanted a reaction to that part of his novel that he had on paper, fearing that a time might come when he would have to submit what he had to a publisher to obtain money quickly. Though estranged from his wife, he was supporting her, and his other expenses were not small. I know—I was drawing and signing the checks. He himself, because of his muscular weakness, had been unable to hold and read the first typescript of the long section that had been delivered to him at the hospital, and there was concern about the quality of the manuscript as well.

As soon as Stein got back, about ten days later, he went to the hospital and told Joe that what he had read of his new novel was "simply marvelous. A pure joy," he said. "I was so happy to be giving him this news, and I expected to see a big smile on his face," Stein told me. "Instead, Heller snarled at me: 'Did you have to keep me in suspense? Couldn't you send a cable?' "

All Joe's close friends, regardless of their differences in outlook, gradually began to realize that he was not recovering as fast as we had supposed he would. It looked like it might be a pretty good length of time before he could fend for himself—if ever. Remember, he had never been too good in that area, even when he was in perfect shape. And we were beginning to wonder where he would go and how he would manage.

AT THE BEGINNING of my second week in the intensive care unit, I believe I was still distressed more by my surroundings than by any foreboding considerations of the long-term dangers inherent in my disease. My complaints, as entered in the hospital records, tended to be about disturbing noise and my inability to sleep, about what one doctor's notation characterized as the "ambience" of the ICU. My conversations with the psychiatrist, which began sometime in the middle of the second week, usually had less to do with the future than with the past and present and with the conventional discontents that are the bread and butter of psychotherapy. I was sad and surprised to find myself paralyzed in a hospital. I missed my mother and my brother and my sister, and I missed my wife and my mother-in-law and my father-in-law. I wished that I still had a home and a family life to which to return, and I knew that the wish was hopeless.

I was absorbed in the clock and often felt tormented in the evening by the horseplay at the nurses' station. I could shut the clock and the nurses' station from view with a curtain drawn. I would soon ask to have it opened. I did not want to be isolated. I wanted more privacy and I hated seclusion.

Very early in the morning of the day the item about me appeared in *The New York Times*, which was the Monday at the start of my second week, a nurse surprised me with the message that Dustin Hoffman was on the telephone. He had seen the newspaper and had already been told by the information desk that I was discouraging visitors. Now he had called the nurses' desk in the unit to find out from me if it was all right for him to come. Of course I said yes.

I made certain to be out of bed by the time he arrived; and all of the flushed and fluttery nurses made certain that I'd been shaved, bathed, and otherwise groomed. At that time it still required but two people to move me from the bed to a wheelchair. By the end of that week, when I could no longer assist at all with my shoulders, trunk, or legs, it took at least four, although six generally cooperated in sliding me horizontally from my bed on my bedsheet, at the count of three, to a stretcher-mechanism placed parallel alongside, whose different sections were dropped and raised in order to convert the apparatus into a chair.

Dustin and I had become acquainted about ten years earlier and we would get together for dinner or lunch from time to time if we chanced to meet in the same city. A reason we have remained such good friends is that we have never been close ones. We have never worked together, and that too has undoubtedly helped, leaving each of us with an unmarred respect for the judgment and consideration of the other that is probably unwarranted by both. Between us as the foundation for our friendship are the ground rules I promulgated once only partly in jest: he doesn't have to read my novels, and I don't have to see his movies. When I do go to one of his movies, my attendance is always in connection with the ceremony of a premier, and the film is the price I must pay for the dinner and the party. I think a year or two must have passed since we'd last spoken. But I was not surprised he was so solicitous or that he would hurry to bring me what consolation he could supply.

We greeted each other with the somber good humor of a friendly and resigned philosophical ritual.

"You look terrible," was the way I welcomed him. "What in the hell has been happening to you?"

"I've been having a rough time," was his straight-faced reply.

Dustin was another one of those people of mine who, on first visit, looked alarmingly ashen and grave, fearful, and I could see it was going to take a very heavy effort on my part to boost his spirits. He had already, it turned out, telephoned his own physician, who was not yet at his office, and had left some questions and the message that he would soon call again for the answers. Within minutes of arriving, he requested the loan of a pencil and pad from one of the nurses and went outside to use the pay telephone. He returned in about fifteen minutes with jottings on his pad indicating to me that he had called a medical man for the inside dope on Guillain-Barré, of which he himself, like Mel Brooks before him, was now visibly in terror: I saw the words "peripheral," "paretic," "paresthesia," "self-limiting," and "autoimmunological," all of which were now familiar to me, along with a few that in this context were entirely new, such as "stress" and "triggering factor."

"Most people," Dustin notified me encouragingly, improvising from his notes, "make a good recovery."

"No shit?" I said with a hint of sarcasm that I'm afraid went right by him.

"Yeah," he grunted seriously. "The outlook is favorable, very favorable. In anywhere from . . ."

And here there followed that phenomenon which is often portrayed in imaginative literature as "a voice trailing away."

"Did he also tell you," I kidded him, "that it's catching?"

He ignored this. "There also may sometimes be a triggering factor," he went on like a pedagogue. "Yeah, a triggering factor, you know, something that triggers it. Have you been under any stress lately?"

"Naaah," I replied.

"Really?"

"Haven't you?"

"Who hasn't?"

Then he offered to give me anything I might need.

I shook my head. "Like what?"

"A private nurse, an attendant, a guy just to hang around to wait on you and give you exercise."

"Take a look," I answered, and indicated with a turn of my head the large number of staff members in the unit, most of whom would peek in our direction every chance they could as they continued about their business. "Maybe later on. Right now I've got plenty."

And at just about that second, a "Team 7000" alarm sounded (the code words will vary in different places, but in the Medical ICU at Mount Sinai, it was "Team 7000"). The call was for immediate life-sustaining aid for the comatose woman in the bed opposite mine. Her name was Rose and we were near the entrance of the unit. Suddenly nurses, residents, respiratory therapists, and all else came gathering in full haste, and there were quick comments about such things as blood pressure and pulse rate and commands for atropine and oxygen and God knows what other things. And Peggy Dunne, an able, pleasant woman who was one of the day supervisors, ever so softly asked if I'd mind requesting my visitor to wait just outside until the emergency was past. Dustin overheard and nodded politely and left on tiptoe, looking apologetic and saying he would wait and be back. And as I watched him moving away, I felt for the first time a pang of humiliation and shame at being seen in such surroundings by people I knew.

The emergency was attended to successfully that time and Rose was kept alive. (But I will give large odds that she was not for much longer among the quick.)

"Why did they want me to go out?" Dustin inquired with more interest than petulance after he was allowed back in. Like many of the practitioners of what he sometimes calls his art and at other times speaks of as his profession, he has an attention span that can at times be short; but I know from experience that his curiosity is genuine and intent once it is aroused. "Is there some kind of rule? Or did they think I wouldn't be able to take it?"

"It could be," I answered with a playful irony that I knew would not be wasted upon him, "that they had no part for you."

He smiled wryly at this and inquired again if there was not something he could get me, give me, or do for me. I could think of nothing. He was better here than I was. Dustin is smarter and more inventive than many of the people he deals with, which may explain the occasional conflicts with motion picture producers and directors we hear about, and he came up with a suggestion now that hit the bull's-eye: a Sony Walkman. To me, this was that kind of pure inspiration one thinks of as genius, and I would have leaped to my feet with delight had I possessed the power to. I had never listened to a cassette player of that kind, but I knew what a Walkman was and what it could do for me in my present straits. Here was a gift that would bring me the music I missed and also shield me somewhat from the distressing commotion intrinsic to the functions of the place, which included not merely the noise of machines and the comings and goings and natural conversation at the nurses' station in the late evening but also the insufferable din from the radio there.

What recordings would I want? Dustin's pencil moved rapidly as I rattled off the compositions that came to mind: concertos by Brahms, Beethoven quartets, anything and everything by Bach. Dustin had an assistant named Julius working for him then who knew what to do. The package arrived no more than three hours after. Much of the music I'd asked for was not available on cassettes, but Julius had filled in admirably. Here, along with much else, was the Archduke Trio. And here also was more, much more, than I or anyone could have hoped for, the St. Matthew Passion, almost four hours of choral music as soothing and sublime as anything ever conceived by the mind of man. Toward the end of my third week there, I generously loaned these cassettes of the St. Matthew Passion to a new patient in the bed next to mine, a woman younger than I whom I had met once before on a much sunnier occasion. She was as conscious as I was and there to be monitored for several days for some kind of erratic cardiopulmonary complications. She was the wife of a man for whom my daughter had worked in her first job with an advertising agency, and she was finding unbearable the shocking environment to which I, a veteran now, had grown resigned, if not exactly acclimated. (I was beginning to feel that if one lives in a hospital long enough, sooner or later he will run into just about everyone he's known. My lawyer was in at the start with his gallstones. The daughter of a friend of Speed's turned up in my unit. My father-in-law came into the hospital, for surgery, just a few days after I was admitted, which meant that my daughter had at least two patients to visit each time she came and that my wife was somewhere on the premises almost every day. I repeatedly refused when told that she asked to come see me. What would we say to each other? She was sorry I was sick? I was even sorrier. My preference was honored and probably, as I knew in my heart each time the question was presented to me, at deep-felt emotional cost to both of us.)

I had never listened to a Walkman before and was enchanted by the engulfing clarity of the sound. None of the nurses on duty then had ever listened to one either; nursing is not a high-paying occupation and buying one would have meant more than a day's take-home pay. One by one they came to sample the experience, their faces brightening as they donned the headset. On the evening shift, in one of those eerie lulls that settled in regularly, the headset was tried on by a nurse who was thrilled as much by the music as by the quality of the transcription, and she let out a cry of delight to one of the other young nurses working with her. I suggested she put it on the cassette player on the radio at the nurses' station. There followed an extraordinary ten minutes, both charmed and unreal, in which everyone present was brought to a standstill by the bars of music flowing out suddenly that seemed so melodic and ethereal, of a different world—everyone sentient, that is. The other three patients in the unit with me that evening were on their backs unconscious (they indeed did seem part of a different world), and one or two of them, perhaps all three, were attached to the mechanical respirators or to other pieces of pumping and suctioning equipment that huffed and puffed in the background night and day. The music on the cassette chanced to be the andante from the second Brahms piano concerto, and Misha Dichter has never sounded more beautiful to me or to the others in that small body of rapt listeners who heard him that night in those macabre surroundings.

The shortcoming in this otherwise perfect gift was that by the following day I no longer had the strength and dexterity to handle the cassettes securely or even to manipulate the tiny controls, and I would have been as embarrassed to ask a nurse more than once to hand me a cassette as I would have been to request her to turn the pages and hold a book if I had wanted to read one.

True to the promise he made me as he left, Dustin returned in the morning two or three days later, bringing a present that again was an inspired choice. This time he arrived with a newly purchased electric toothbrush, an appliance with which he was not acquainted, and he did not hesitate to plug it into the outlet he spied in the panel of equipment on the wall in back of me. Curious as to its application and potential usefulness to me, which turned out to be enormous for almost a year, he could not wait to learn how it worked. I had owned one before and instructed him, and he began brushing my teeth.

Now here is something that was like a scene from a movie, to me and to those there with me: Dustin Hoffman brushing my teeth—and in that place!

When Dustin is working at anything, he knows all that he is doing at every moment, and he was no less conscientious brushing the teeth of a friend in an intensive care unit than he would have been in a different role on stage or before a camera. He took seriously what he was doing. People stopped to watch. I was as fascinated as the rest as I listened to him relate without affectation that one of the first jobs he found upon coming to New York to seek his fortune as an actor was in the psychiatric division of a local hospital, where his principal duty was to press down firmly upon the knees of patients as they received a charge of electricity as part of a prescribed program of electroconvulsive therapy, which is more popularly known as shock treatment. This was an intriguing surprise to me, and a line of work I had never heard of before. I did not believe him then, and I do not believe a word of it now.

He was going off with his family for the Christmas–New Year holidays, he informed me, but vowed to come again promptly on his return. I was out of the intensive care unit and in my private room when next he did show up. This time he was accompanied by the playwright Murray Schisgal, who also is a friend of mine. It was another one of those gloomy, bleak, black, frigid nights that often give a New York City winter the appearance of a hell in which the fires have been turned off. The evening nurse, a foxy, short, and very bright young lady named Donna Mirabello, applied, it seemed to me, a good deal more eyeliner for the occasion than she normally wore and perhaps a slightly stronger dose of perfume.

My disease had run its course and reached its "plateau" by then; that is, I would get no worse in the degree of paralyzing effects it would cause. But I looked no better. If anything, I must have struck Dustin and everyone else who came to see me as cadaverously thin, for the weight loss resulting from muscle atrophy had progressed with ravaging speed in the two-week interval. I could not eat and I could not exercise, and the loss of muscle tissue was continuing still. I myself was oblivious to the change—until six months later, when I was out of the hospital and able to study myself in a mirror as I sat in my wheelchair in bathing trunks and a short-sleeved shirt. I was appalled by the extent to which I had withered. And by that time I had regained more than fifteen pounds of the thirty or forty I'd lost.

The visit was short and rather formal. Discreetly, as he was ready to leave, Dustin contrived to hang back and remain alone with me long enough to inquire again if I needed any money. I gave him the assurance that I would contact him when I did.

"Please do that," he stressed, looking down with some modesty and almost mumbling. "I may not have much talent, but money is something I do have a lot of."

"Subtext" is an actor's term which I had first heard, and still have only heard, from him. The subtext of what he was telling me, I teased gratefully in reply, was that he really thought he had a very generous supply of both.

From a medical standpoint, my second week in the hospital was the worst. I could tell I was declining by my diminishing ability to perform the seemingly endless repetitions of uncomplicated muscle tests to which I was subjected by just about every medical visitor who came to see me—my own physicians, visiting physicians from other parts of the hospital who dropped by just out of curiosity, residents on training duty in other areas who were coming to look, professors from the medical school with their pupils, other specialists with other residents to whose training they were contributing. Sometimes no more than ten minutes would elapse between my having the soles of my feet scraped roughly for reflexive response by people I might not see more than that single time. It did not occur to me that I could say no. I did not know that often these strangers had nothing to do with my care.

Dr. Adam Bender, a pleasant, young-looking physician who was both a professor of neurology and director of the Neuro-Muscular Clinic and Laboratory, was always a welcome exception to what I had come to regard as a daylong series of invasions, interruptions, and assaults. He himself was a cheerful, tactful, and sympathetic person, and the small group of medical apprentices he came with were chipper and exuded the agreeable manner of having come on a social visit. It was Dr. Bender who cleared up a lifelong mystery for me by explaining that the absence of a reflex was usually not in itself of much significance. And once he had joined Dr. Sencer in a diagnosis of Guillain-Barré, he invariably left with a grin and reassuring words to the effect: "You're going to get better, you know. Sooner or later you'll be able to do everything again."

I thanked him cordially, while reciting to myself a line I would use in my novel if I ever was able to get back to it: "From your mouth to God's ears."

I soon grew tired of being asked to try to perform the same actions so repeatedly by even my own doctors. I reflected in morose secrecy that both Richard and Mortimer Bader were internists and asked myself why they could not simply look at Dr. Sencer's notes to find out precisely which things I could not do. If Morty or Richard came in the early part of the day and the other appeared later on, I took to going through the procedure vocally, stating irritably, "I can't sit up and I can't lift my head, I can't raise my arm from the shoulder and I still cannot straighten either one or keep it bent against the pressure of your hand. I can't raise my knees and I still can't touch my thumb to my pinky the way you want me to. They listened to my lungs just a little while ago, but you can listen too."

By the middle of the second week I could not smile with a straight face (my mouth and cheeks on one side would be different from what they were on the other) or say the letter *e* with both corners of my mouth spreading equally, I could shrug my shoulders but I could not move them forward or backward, I could no longer raise or lower my eyelids against the gentle weight of a finger, I could not wink my right eye without also closing the left, I could not wrinkle my brow. I could not whistle or bare my teeth. Not one of these actions seems especially important in itself, and I did not miss any until I was out of both hospitals and trying to speak and eat like an ordinary person. These increasing deficits, however, gave evidence that my cranial nerves too were undergoing inflammation. I was coughing more and more. The suction tube and the nasal tube were clogging.

I learned about my cranial nerves from the spoken observations to the resident by Dr. Sencer, whose examinations I did not mind. Dr. Sencer, of course, leveled upon me the closest scrutiny of all. He did not, I believe, miss coming to me a single day in that critical two-week period at the start and often showed up two and even three times on the same day.* Occasionally he was there in the evening, to continue charting the stages of my decline and surmising what they might portend. He was always aggressively optimistic, though no longer invariably convincing, and I wonder now how much of his belittlement of the dangers I faced he truly believed and how much was contrived to sustain my morale.

What I learned from listening to Dr. Sencer was that I do have cranial nerves and that my cranial nerves V, VII, XI, and XII were giving unmistakable evidence of expanding impairment. For the benefit of those of you who have never had Guillain-Barré syndrome or any other serious polyneuritis, or those of you who have had it and have forgotten, the cranial nerves are those nerves outside the spinal cord that go directly from the brain to the muscles of the jaw, face, and tongue they innervate; in conjunction with specific nerves in the cervical plexus, they contribute to certain of the movements of the head, neck, and shoulders. The effects of the disease upon the spinal nerves controlling the rest of my body were self-evident and did not require much elucidation: the effects were paralyzing.

The resident on duty days then was a doctor named Barbara Hirsch, with whom I did not always get along as well as I might have. What began to annoy me about her were the examinations she imposed upon me herself. Sometimes these occurred very shortly after Dr. Sencer had concluded with me and departed, and they seemed merely to be duplicating his in academic and more extensive detail. I did not know then that the resident was required to prepare a comprehensive daily report for each patient under supervision, summarizing all of the data of importance recorded by everyone caring for the patient and including also an

* Neither the Baders nor Dr. Sencer charged me for more than one hospital visit a day, and I was not presented with a bill from either of their offices until I had been out of Mount Sinai several weeks and was a patient at Rusk. Speed, who was still making out my checks in his handwriting and signing them in mine, paid these bills at his own pace, without harassing my troubled soul with any of the particulars.

account of personal contacts and of conclusions derived from direct observation. I began to believe I was being used by her merely to practice upon. I did not like that, and one day I objected vehemently as soon as she approached and made ready to start. She reacted in kind, accusing me of ingratitude and asserting that, though I did not seem to know it, she was then the most important person in my life. I believe now that we were both overstating our positions a little.

I never did apologize to Dr. Hirsch for that outburst, so I'll do that now. I'll thank her also for administering those three spinal taps without inflicting an instant of pain or any other kind of discomfort, and for finding on the first try the proper blood vessel in my wrist for yet another arterial blood gas test, after a pair of eager and repentant nurses had been stabbing around for nearly ten minutes and striking only veins.

It was only in perusing the records much afterward that I gained an appreciation of the large area of responsibility of each of the residents under whose care I found myself. For every day there is that summary of precise technical information, complemented richly by such significant personal findings as "very agitated and depressed," "awake most of the night until 04:40," and "mental status significant for 'ICU' osis." For every day there is a report of the range of my temperature, pulse, and blood pressure and of my respiratory capabilities. There are evaluations of motor ability in each of my upper and lower extremities, as well as of my trunk, face, and everywhere else. From the report for December 29, when Dr. Hirsch was rotated away from ICU service to a different area of training, I learned that my respiratory "parameters declined to a nadir on 12/20–12/24" and that on "Christmas day patient showed real turn around."

I did not need access to the records to know that my respiratory parameters were deteriorating. I had only to watch the needle on the gauge and hear the numbers spoken by the nurse each time I filled my lungs to my maximum and emptied them or inhaled with all the force I could muster from a tube whose opposite end had been stopped up by a thumb. The tests were administered punctually every three hours. In the beginning I faced these two tests with an attitude of competitive excitement; it was a spirit that carried me back in memory to those trifling games of skill in the penny arcades of Coney Island. Sometimes I asked for a second try when my expectations were frustrated, if I performed disappointingly in these demonstrations of what I thought of as "lung strength." (What I know now is that there is no such thing as lung strength. The muscles of the chest and diaphragm do the work of breathing.) I ceased being combative with these two tests when the numbers slid from the thirties to the low twenties and dipped occasionally even into the teens. I was dimly aware that there had to be a bottom somewhere if something serious was to be averted. If my breathing powers were not important, why would they measure them?

The third of the tests, one that measured the "tidal volumes" during normal breathing, became all but useless once I knew what it did measure and saw I could alter the results at will. Normal breathing became impossible once I knew my normal breathing was being measured.

I did not know the figures with which I began and the level to which I could sink with safety. I know now that more than half the people with Guillain-Barré would die from respiratory failure if action were not taken to re-create mechanically the process of breathing. The figures show that in the twelve days between my admission and my low points before Christmas, my capacity to breathe diminished more than half. At no time, though, did I experience any sense of these changes, did I feel any signs of labored breathing or shortness of breath. In fact, my respiratory functions were indeed "still adequate" in the records, and my case was described as atypical for Guillain-Barré in having stricken only moderately the nerves in the thoracic region, which control the musculature of breathing, and afflicted much more severely the cranial and peripheral spinal nerves above and below.

I was therefore very far from fully prepared when one of the

Baders told me early one morning that both brothers had decided I was going to require a tracheostomy. I nodded in silence. He must have been filled with admiration for my stoic poise, taking as heroic courage what I can now unerringly identify as petrified ignorance. The procedure was simple, he told me, and could be performed at my bedside by the resident. There would be a small scar at the front of my neck, but women didn't mind it much, so why should I? I nodded again and inquired when. He answered there was not at that moment any rush. Now I know why he looked so solemn. I was agreeing to have my throat cut.

Dr. Alvin Teirstein is a widely known pulmonary specialist who seemed at that time to be exercising in an unobtrusive way some kind of overall supervision of the Medical Intensive Care Unit in which I found myself. He was mild-mannered, confident, and soft-spoken, exuding the air of someone who is cosmopolitan and contented. Every weekday morning he made the rounds with a group of younger and very respectful doctors who were learning from him and with whom he would discuss briefly the condition of each of the patients. At my bed, when we had finished talking, he would have the nurses sit me up and then would listen himself with his stethoscope on my chest for sounds of any abnormality. Dr. Teirstein seemed stunned for an instant when I repeated to him casually what I had been told by Dr. Bader just a short while earlier. I was wrong in taking for granted that he already knew, that all of my doctors were in touch with each other constantly about me. I have no doubt he showed more surprise than I did, and he appeared to disapprove.

"The numbers are way down," I heard myself arguing with him defensively in something of a whine, as though in justification of the Baders' decision.

Dr. Teirstein responded softly, smiling. "We treat patients here, not numbers," I remember him telling me in a calm and reassuring manner which I began to perceive was second nature to him. "Don't worry about it yet."

It had not occurred to me to worry at all until he urged me not to.

Wally Sencer had not been told either when he showed up later that morning. He also seemed a bit taken aback. Frowning, he directed that my hospital gown be unsnapped, and he stared down at my chest for a long time without uttering a word, studying me more closely than usual. I began to wonder what in the hell he was doing.

"The intercostals are starting to move," he spoke up at last in decision, pointing. "See?" he remarked to the resident and the nurse. "I'm going to try to get them to wait," he revealed to me by way of encouragement. "I'll bet my life the numbers will change with the intercostals and start to go up."

You can bet your life that by now I was rooting for him.

There are muscles running laterally between each of our ribs on the inside and on the outside, and these are called the intercostal muscles. They enlarge the rib cage and they depress the rib cage. Until reflecting upon the contents of this paragraph in sullen anticipation of the need to write it, I harbored a naive conception of the mechanics of human respiration. It was my erroneous notion that breathing, particularly deep breathing, began in the nose and/or mouth with a sucking down of air that inflated the lungs and thereby expanded the chest. They tell me now it is the reverse that occurs. The chest cavity is enlarged by a lowering of the diaphragm and a lifting of the rib cage, and the air then flows in of its own accord, in obedience to the law of physics holding that nature abhors a vacuum. In my case, although I did not know it, just about all of my breathing was being done by the diaphragm. My intercostal muscles had been paralyzed, and on this particular morning, Dr. Sencer was all but certain they were starting to work again.

He was right, thank God. The decline in my respiratory measurements stabilized, and on Christmas Day there was that turnaround already mentioned, with the numbers rising significantly. They did not go much higher in the several days more I was tested, but that danger of respiratory failure had passed, and there was never more talk of a tracheostomy.

And on Easter morning months later, when I had been at the

Rusk Institute awhile and could handle a telephone again, Mario Puzo called to tell me:

"Joe, I gotta come clean with you. It may be a sacrilege to say so, but I really believe you've come back from the dead."

It was in the middle of that second week that Mario, to the excruciating chagrin of us both, made his short, obligatory pilgrimage to the intensive care unit to visit me, led there no doubt by his close friend Carol Gino, who had herself been a nurse before deciding that she would rather write books about nurses than continue working as one, and who had come there for a very long visit, one very much longer than Mario would have liked. I do not believe I am exaggerating when I state that it was as painful for me to look at Mario as it was for him to look at me. In the more than thirty years we have been friends, there has always been this scrupulous reluctance by each of us ever to impose an unwanted social duty on the other; and both of us knew that I no more expected him to come see me in the hospital than I would have wanted to go visit him. Yet here he was, filling us both with guilt and remorse, moved by the dictates of a conscience that his intelligence told him was irrational and by at least one person he knew, Carol, who was better responsive to the amenities of proper civil behavior than either one of us.

You should have seen how sickly he looked. I don't know how he pulled through. I don't know whether it was he or Speed or Carol who first coined the phrase that Mario would rather eat a broom than visit a hospital, but I find that image extremely graphic. I do not know what it is like to eat a broom. I myself would rather *be* in a hospital than ever have to find out, although I do concede that in matters of eating there is much room for individuality.

It would be metaphorically incorrect to depict him as hanging back in the distance, for there was no distance in that confined area for him to hang back in. It would be hard, however, to conceive of his having remained farther away from me than he did, and from the moment he entered he gave the impression of being impatient to leave.

Carol, on the other hand, breezed right up to my bedside on a bubbling crest of animation, folded her elbows on the rail, and began chatting away without inhibition, to me, to Kim, my steady staff nurse, and to others who stopped by just out of interest for minutes at a time. Not before or since have I seen Carol so happily at home. She reminded me, I told her then, of a thirsty cowboy after roundup striding into a saloon, or more precisely, I added, of a hooker who'd made it big on the outside returning to the brothel from which she'd graduated, just to talk over old times in the setting in which she'd spent her most gladsome years. She asked and answered questions about new and old equipment and procedures and dilated freely on her own experiences in hospitals and hospices. And Mario, all the while, waxed paler and paler in the background as he waited for her to finish and depart and, with an aspect of agony, ran his forefinger around inside the collar of a shirt within which his neck appeared to be shrinking with each minute that passed. I knew this much about Mario: There were no more than three restaurants he looked forward to going to on those infrequent occasions he was forced to come into Manhattan. On this occasion, he soon found himself dining in the hospital cafeteria, along with the two nurses Carol had invited for their dinner break in order to prolong as much as possible her exhilarating plunge into this orgy of reminiscence. And to let Mario know, perhaps, that she was having more fun here with Kim and the other nurse than she did at the Cannes Film Festival, to which it was his habit to drag her annually.

While still in my room, Carol declared emphatically that she did not like the look of the secretions I was extracting from my mouth. What I suctioned was drawn through a transparent flexible tube into a receptacle fixed in the wall behind me, which was emptied and cleansed when enough of the viscous waste I was exuding had collected to appear revolting to the average naked eye. I could not turn to see it, but to Mario's naked eye it looked "like a bottle of used phlegm." Clear and colorless at the outset, these secretions had turned white as the amounts grew "copious" and were now described in the records as "thick and creamy yellow." What I could see in the tube was a rusty brown. Kim did not like the look of things either, and she and the other nurses had been making notes of the changes in the daily records.

The misgivings of both were well grounded. The next time it was taken, my temperature, which had been normal, registered 99.8 degrees. The time after that it rose to just about 100 degrees. Immediately, there went into operation a system of examination and treatment that all at once justified the routines of close monitoring which I fatuously had come to scorn as officiously technical and bureaucratic, an administrative defense at Blue Cross's expense against potential irresponsible charges of malpractice. (I'm still not all that certain this assessment is *entirely* amiss.) Every day, in addition to everything already mentioned, there was a chest X ray and an electrocardiogram, both of which I had come to resent as annoying distractions. I was still hooked up by wires to the cardiac emergency warning unit, despite a heartbeat and blood pressure healthier than that of any of my doctors. To the rattling annoyance of all of us, the alarm went off a thousand times a day, just about every time I coughed or heaved a sigh or was moved by one of the nurses. Now, within minutes after the thermometer registered more than a hundred, technicians were there for blood samples and throat cultures for proof of infection. The latest X ray was developed and inspected and showed clouds in one lung where there had been no clouds. I was given injections of an antibiotic. A plastic bag of other antibiotics in solution was hung above me on a pole to drop into me intravenously, alongside the plastic bag of glucose in solution that had been there dripping into me intravenously for about a week, and there was a significant increase in the rate of facetious allusions from people like Bob Towbin, Barbara Gelb, and Mel Brooks relating me in likeness in this new condition to a personage in a work of fiction who is known to them only as the soldier in white. I had contracted pneumonia in the lower lobe of the left lung. It had been discovered straightaway and was treated immediately.

Pneumonia and constipation, I am now in a position to inform you, are complications ever-threatening to people bedridden for a sustained period, the former all the more menacing when there is difficulty in swallowing. Thanks to prompt recognition and response, my pneumonia was over in just two days, and a regimen consisting of chest pounding and the deep inhalation of medicinal vapors was instituted to help keep my lungs clear of secretions that can accumulate there as easily as in the receptacle integrated in the suctioning machinery. My constipation took months longer to be rid of, and I promise right now that I will say very little more about any of *that*.

Mel Brooks was back to see me in that very low period. He was to leave for Europe the next day, and he was greatly depressed by the steep downtrend in my physical state since he'd seen me the first time and by the ironic phenomenon that his newest movie appeared to be doing better in Europe than here. We did what we could to cheer each other up.

This time he arrived with one or two of our closest friends and Speed was there with me already. All of those lousy bastards were going out to dinner in Chinatown without me. This was a group that normally went out to dinner together about once a week—sometimes more. This Gourmet Club really consisted of a herd of gluttonous pigs who ate Chinese food ravenously and disgustingly and among whom I, in my prime, and a very short composer named Hershy Kay, now deceased, were the outstanding performers. Mel could begin eating more viciously than any of the rest of us, but he lacked staying power and would be sighing aloud for dessert and bigger box-office receipts while Hershy and I were still mopping up what remained of the beef and spinach, roast pork, stuffed bean curd, and lobster or crab in black bean sauce, maybe both. And panfried smelts or butterfish.

Mel is made of sterner stuff than Mario and did not hem and haw about coming close to touch and stare and to fire at me whatever questions were burning in his thoughts. He boasted without joy that, from the looks of me, he probably could triple whatever scores I was making on the breathing tests he watched me take, and disdained to try. He was angrily affronted, almost deeply personally insulted, that I could have pneumonia and just lie there in bed like a person who didn't have pneumonia. He fell into contemplation of my left shoulder muscle, appalled by my inability to raise the elbow from the mattress even the tiniest bit. He was glum, shaken, and he clucked his tongue.

"Life hangs by a thread" was pretty much the observation he made to me in a choked voice. He promised to telephone me from the airport on his return from Europe when he changed planes—putting smiles on the faces of those of us acquainted with his compulsion to telephone everybody from any airport while he waited for his plane. Buttoning his heavy winter coat as he turned to leave, he was discoursing in brooding soliloquy on the frailty of human health, and on the fickleness of an American movie audience that was not for this latest masterpiece by the creator of the film *Springtime for Hitler* (released as *The Producers*) smashing the astounding attendance records set by his previous ones, while patrons in Munich, Vienna, and Luxembourg were charging down from the mountains and coming out of the forests in droves the size of which had never been seen in movie houses before.

"Fame is fleeting" was pretty much the observation I made to him in response. The others—Speed, George, Julie Green, Joe Stein—expressed sincere and sorrowful regret at leaving me there while they went down to Chinatown. Who could believe them? Those liars, those hypocrites! They looked so eager.

EVEN THOUGH BY NOW none of us was happy about the way Joe looked, his bedside was still a most convivial place for us to meet.

I missed Mel Brooks's first visit there, but I was present, by appointment, for his next appearance. I had spoken to Julie earlier in the day about a meal. He'd told me that Mel was in town, planned to visit Joe at the hospital, and would join us for dinner. Julie said he would contact Mandel and Stein, and maybe Ngoot. I was standing next to Joe's bed when Mel walked in with Julie. A couple of others showed up in minutes. After a short, friendly greeting, Mel went right to the nurses' station to check on Joe's condition—and perhaps his own.

Not one of us even raised an eyebrow. We knew Mel as a certifiable hypochondriac, as informed as most physicians (and the funniest man alive). It was good to have him around again. Since he now lived in California, I did not get to see him often enough. Mel and I were close friends before I met Joe and before they met each other. In fact, I introduced them.

I first encountered Brooks in the early fifties at a small bash thrown by my friend Stanley Prager. I knew there would be a roomful of bright and funny people. Maybe Zero Mostel would be there or Jack Gilford, maybe both. But I was unprepared for Mel, who was then unknown—at least to me. That night he was the Queen Mother of England admonishing her son, the king, not to leave the palace without his warm cloak and heavy crown: "It's vinter and you go *oon* [Yiddish for "without"] a cloak, *oon* a crown, *oon* a scepter! It's a frost in stritt! I'm not letting you out of the palace!"

I did not see Mel again until the following summer, when he rented a house close to mine on the dunes of Ocean Beach, Fire Island. We saw a lot of each other that summer, and one of the very few arguments I had with my first wife was over her accusations that I was neglecting my family and my business in favor of show business, staying up till all hours playing poker, and hanging out with bums. I was guilty on all counts and sorry about none.

After my wife and I separated, I moved to a studio apartment at 103rd Street and Central Park West. Shortly after, we divorced, although we continued to be business partners. Mel and I remained close friends. Coincidentally, it wasn't long before Mel and his then wife, Florence, began experiencing marital difficulties themselves. Many nights I found myself walking the streets with Mel, a notorious insomniac, listening patiently and sympathetically to his complaints and staying carefully noncommittal. I was extremely fond of Florence and had thought they were happily married. What did I know?

On one fateful evening as we marched around town, Mel told me that he wanted to leave home. He also said that Florence had repeatedly urged him to go. I stupidly dropped my guard and suggested that it was rather demeaning when your spouse asks you to leave more than twice. . . . Mel jumped in with, "You're right. Will you bring your car and help me pack? Can I move in with you?"

I should have bitten my tongue, but of course I said, "Sure." The Brookses' behavior was not what I expected. They acted more like a couple of lovebirds than a couple busting up. They kissed and cuddled and giggled as I did the packing. I was mystified. I was certain the whole thing was a charade and they would be back together in no time. I was wrong.

Mel and I remained roommates for longer than I dreamed possible—three months. He was the worst. We were living in rather close quarters, which did not improve matters. Mel's insomnia didn't help either. He had a blood-sugar problem that kept us a scintilla away from insanity, and his brushstroke of paranoia had me on the verge (more than twice) of calling Bellevue to come and collect him.

Mel once answered a phone call from my office. The studio was my workshop, and I was sculpting a horse at the time. Still, I was startled to overhear him saying: "Mr. Vogel can't speak to you now. He's working on his horsey and he cannot be disturbed." I grabbed for the phone, but he had already hung up.

Then one night Mel went truly berserk. He claims it was because I kept him up with my snoring. In the morning I awoke to find graffiti all over my white walls. It was not "Mel loves Speed." What I saw, splashed on with my best Winsor & Newton paints, was: "You snore, you son-of-a-bitch! Yes, that's what you do! All night! Snore! Snore! Snore! You fuck!" That was pretty bad, but it was unforgivable that he'd begun wearing my best button-down shirts and favorite made-in-England shorts and took them with him on a trip to California. Mel was in L.A. when I finally realized that something had to be done about our ridiculous arrangement.

I had a brainstorm. He was not yet divorced. I called his wife. "Florence," I pleaded, "forgive me. I should not have done it. A friend should never intercede. I should not have helped Mel move out. While he is in California, I would like to make amends and move his things back, and you guys can do whatever you think best without me in the picture."

Florence was completely silent until I finished my long speech, and then she opened up with, "Are you crazy? Where did you get such a dopey idea? If you can't stand him anymore, throw him out. What do you want from me?"

I perceived that I wasn't getting too far with that plan. I had some rethinking to do. I believed that it might be the end of our friendship, but I knew there was no other way. I had to get him out. I decided to confront him even before he got back with my shirts and shorts. I picked up the phone and reached him at the Beverly Hills Hotel.

I began with, "Hiya, Mel, I gotta . . ."

He stopped me before I could continue. "I know. It's your bat, ball, and glove and your ballpark, too," he said. "You want me to leave, right?"

I was stunned but managed a weak "How'd you know?"

He laughed and said, "Will you help me pack and move?"

I said, "Sure! *This* time it'll be a real pleasure."

I was delighted not to have lost him as a pal. And if this sounds like some version of *The Odd Couple*, it's no coincidence. Neil Simon told my friend David Zelag Goodman, the screenwriter, that the stories he had heard about my life with Brooks had been his inspiration.

Several years later when Joe Heller showed up on Fire Island, I was remarried. I had sold my old house and had bought Carl Reiner's lovely oceanfront house in fashionable Seaview and was living happily there with my young bride, my children, her children, and our child. I was sunbathing when an attractive woman approached. It was my kid sister's friend Shirley Heller, formerly Held, and she brought me over to meet her husband, Joe. (It was the summer after the publication of *Catch-22*.) Joe somehow managed to squeeze all the juicy gossip embedded in these recent years of my life out of my curiously obliging mouth, and we became friends, too. Although I felt, intuitively, that they might not be crazy about each other, I put Heller and Brooks together, and they developed a fondness that grew into a friendship.

This evening in the hospital Mel was so busy being a consulting physician, he overlooked the time. But Julie was issuing subtle but unmistakable signals that he hadn't had much lunch. He kept saying he was famished, and his distress served to remind the rest of us that we were ready to eat, too. So no one raised any objections when Stein started putting his coat on, even though we were having lots of laughs with Joe and it wasn't really that late.

It was hard to see Joe lying there with food being shoved down his nose while we were taking off for a huge meal. We felt guilty. Mel eased our consciences by reminding us how Heller would behave if the tube was down another's nose. Brooks echoed others who know Joe well and had seen him recently, saying that even though he looked like a refugee from Dachau, he was a wonderful sick man—maybe the best—and as far as Mel was concerned, Heller could keep that distinction for himself.

It was not surprising that Joe's most frequent visitors at the hospital were also members of what we referred to (with tongue in cheek) as the Gourmet Club. Actually, we were a bunch of gluttons. For two decades this peculiar mixture of males bonded at the eating fields of Coney Island and Chinatown. When we, his friends the Gourmets, recalled Joe's incredible food consumption of the old days and then saw him unable to swallow, we still felt pretty uneasy. We could not even begin to entertain the thought that he would not get back this ability. There had to be limits to fate's cruelty.

One night while Julie, George, and I discussed this over dinner at our then-favorite spot in Chinatown, George told us that he had consulted his brother-in-law, a physician, who was familiar with Guillain-Barré. George warned that there was no way to predict which of the damaged nerves would regenerate, and that Joe might never be able to swallow again. Green, well acquainted with Joe's appetite, broke the silence that greeted this bit of news, saying, "I'll bet on him!"

Our so-called Gourmet Club has gained a reputation of sorts over the many years of its existence. It would be immodest for me to add "for no good reason," because we have had a considerable amount of publicity. I believe that in the process it was inevitable that there would be some misinformation, distortion, oversights, and plain lies. I would like to set the record straight.

Heller, interviewed by *People* magazine in October of 1974, was quoted as saying that he likes to hang out with Mandel, Puzo, Brooks, Vogel, and Stein, and that we get together for dinner in Chinatown once or twice a week. Then Mel, in a *Playboy* interview several months later, mentioned our names somewhat gratuitously in answer to a question about "egg creams." Later that year, Heller was also interviewed by the same publication.

> PLAYBOY: How did the Gourmet Club start?
>
> HELLER: Thirteen years ago, Ngoot Lee, the famous Chinese advertising man, began cooking dinner for a group of us once a week. Then Ngoot became successful and decided cooking put him in a subservient position, so we began going to Chinese restaurants instead.
>
> PLAYBOY: We didn't know there were any Chinese admen.
>
> HELLER: Ngoot cunningly hides his nationality by speaking Yiddish.

A few years after that, Mario Puzo, who really shuns publicity, was seduced by *Time* magazine, which did a cover story on him. Puzo got into the act by speaking fondly of dinners in Chinatown with his "closest and oldest friends, novelists Mandel and Heller, diamond merchant Julie Green and a retired clothing executive named Speed Vogel."

Mario is an extremely shy and gentle man who not only avoids public attention but who also agonizes about inconveniencing his friends. He and Joe share pretty much the same attitudes about social demands, and it was interesting to see them together at the hospital. Obviously, each knew what the other was thinking. Joe understood that Mario wished he were anywhere else, and Mario felt certain that if the situation were reversed, Joe would have found some way not to appear—for which Mario would have been grateful.

Once Carol Gino wanted to have a simple surprise party for

Mario; she invited only her entire family and his, all his friends, lawyers, agents, and most of the literary world—just *The Godfather* wedding scene. While I was at the party, Joe was home formulating his lame excuse for not attending. He was about to call to apologize when Puzo phoned to thank him for not coming. In fact, Mario confessed to a wistful envy that, because of Guillain-Barré, Joe now had the perfect excuse for turning down everything and everyone. "I only wish I could get that lucky," Mario said. "I guess once a guy has Guillain-Barré he never again has to go to anything he doesn't want to, does he?"

The same year the *Time* article about Mario appeared, there was a profile of Mel by Kenneth Tynan in *The New Yorker* which contained an in-depth portrait of the Gourmet Club. I would declare it a fairly accurate picture, but it still bears some correcting. For example, Tynan quotes Carl Reiner as saying, "The members are very polite. Once I had a seat facing the kitchen door and I looked through and saw a rat strolling across the floor. They immediately offered me a chair facing the other way." Well, Reiner is a dear man, the nicest I have ever met in show business, but this had nothing to do with politeness. We switched because we just don't like listening to complaints.

Reiner also told Tynan: "I would put that group up against the Algonquin Round Table and bet that, line for line, they were funnier. The speed of the wit is breathtaking. It just flies back and forth." It was a safe bet for Carl. By that time, most of the Algonquin crowd were dead.

In a *New York Times Magazine* feature piece titled "Catching Joseph Heller," Barbara Gelb wrote the following: "He [Joe] sees the same old friends week after week, never seeming to tire of the basically boring, second-rate Chinatown meals (from which wives and girl friends are barred) that he shares greedily with a basically unglamorous Gang of Four. The gang expands to include Puzo and Brooks and one or two others when they are in town, but more often consists of just Heller and three old buddies named George Mandel, Julius Green, and 'Speed' Vogel. Green is a successful small-businessman, Vogel is a retired textile manufacturer and a former itinerant herring taster for Zabar's, and Mandel, who grew up with Heller in Coney Island, is a novelist and magazine writer."

I can overlook the bit about the "same old friends," and readily agree to "second-rate" because if there were "first-rate" in Chinatown we'd be there, but since when by them is an itinerant herring taster for Zabar's not glamorous?

Our Gourmet Club was born in the early sixties, shortly after I became friends with Ngoot Lee and figured out that the delightful odors that were wafting into my studio were emanating from the Oriental dishes simmering on Lee's stove. I was not bold enough to invite myself, but it required all my powers of self-restraint not to. Within a few weeks, though, I was rewarded for my patience. Mr. Lee graciously invited me to partake of his "humble fare." It was the best food I had ever eaten. The first dish he set before me was a huge plate of rice on which he piled a mixture of pork and lamb with vegetables, herbs, Oriental spices, and sauce. It sounds terrible, but it tasted delicious.

After my extravagant praise, Ngoot began inviting me often, and I never refused. The food he prepared was marvelous. I could not, for very long, contain my enthusiasm, nor could I control my big mouth. One night I told Mel about Ngoot's cooking and he wanted in. When I asked, Ngoot said, "Sure." A few days later, I spread the word to Heller. He, too, wanted a taste. I was not surprised. Ngoot, always generous, said, "Why not?" The thing snowballed. Mel had to tell his friend Julie Green. I said, "I like Julie. Let's include him." Joe wanted to bring George Mandel. Mel said, "By all means." Almost ten years later, Mandel mentioned it to Mario Puzo, and Heller said, "Who could leave him out?"

Here, then, we had the nucleus, the charter members of the Gourmets. Others found out about the club and wanted to join. We refused all requests. We allowed good people, like Carl Reiner and Joe Stein, visiting privileges. Magnanimously, we sometimes permitted Joe and Carl to bring guests, but all guests were screened and a single "no" from a member could keep them out. A few real celebrities wanted to eat with us and were, for the most part, turned down unless they had one specific talent: the prime requisite for inclusion was that the candidate have a good "mouth." This had nothing to do with eloquence. "Mouth" referred only to appetite.

Joe Stein has now been eating with us regularly for more than ten years. Try though he may, he still cannot obtain membership. The late Hershy Kay, the shortest man in show business, a composer and the orchestrator of such Broadway hits as *Evita* and *A Chorus Line*, ate with us for fifteen years and was not a member either. For one thing, poor Hershy was much too short for full membership. (As Mel expressed it, "Except for Joe, all of us are quite short. Some of us are very short. Hershy is *too short.*") For another thing, Hershy had broken one of our sacred laws. He ate from a member's plate. This was forbidden. Instead of standing up like a man and reaching, or even climbing up on the table and crawling to the center where the platters were, he chose to break the law. It was, by the way, the same law for the tall, short, or the lame, the same law for the lion and the lamb—admittedly, it was unfair, but eating from another person's plate, or serving spoon, or mouth, was breaking the law. We did eventually forgive Hershy for his shortness—after he died. Then he was unanimously voted a full membership. Joe Stein, however, is still only a mere trainee (and usually not mentioned at all in stories about Brooks or Heller).*

Joe Stein's son, Harry, who writes for *Esquire* magazine and is the author of the books *Ethics* and *Hoopla*, was at one time asked to do an article on our famous Gourmet Club. The editor of a

---

* Since Heller has moved to East Hampton, Stein thinks he's become a bona fide member because we invite him to join us just about every time we eat in Chinatown. He is not. The basic law he broke, which cannot be overlooked, was that he complained. Not about the quality of the food or the service, which would have been fine with us, God knows. His big mistake was to say, "I think maybe you guys ordered too much." And he repeated that outrage several times. Our first statute, Green's law: "Better to have too much than not enough," wisely provides that every member has the right to order any dish he wants.

national magazine had heard of the Gourmets and surmised that we were a modern Algonquin Round Table, with discussions that were astute, witty, and fascinating. Harry, who had once attended, refused. "It's just a bunch of old guys stuffing themselves," he told the editor, "and talking about girls." What Harry didn't appreciate was that we had been talking about girls only to put him at ease. We feared that our usual topics would have been too heavy for him to absorb during a big meal. With Heller setting the pace, we were quite used to weighty discussions. Harry would have leaped at the chance of doing a piece on us if only he had been with us the night we discussed the currents of the Hudson River, or why ice flows upstream. At another time we talked about the good fortune of the human race to find itself on a planet that happened to have water. (Both these conversations turned up later in *Good as Gold.*) Other important dialogues focused on the perfect melon from "Harry the Fruit" (owner of the all-day, all-night, every-day-of-the-year fruit shop we used to frequent), and the night Chinatown ran out of lobsters.

When Master Chef Ngoot was at the helm, making a meal for us in his apartment, we were well organized. Julie Green and I acted as Lee's shoppers as well as his sous-chefs. At about six, Julie and I would meet, drive to Chinatown, buy at least twice as much as Ngoot had ordered, drive back to the studio, and wash, sort, and chop under the inscrutable eye of Lee. This was a real quid pro quo arrangement. Julie and I learned how to cook; Joe, George, Mario, and Mel learned how to get fat. And Ngoot could practice his Yiddish.

Zero Mostel had actually been Lee's first instructor in that wonderful language, but we were obliged to make a few corrections. For example, we found it necessary to explain that the four-letter words our good friend Ngoot learned from Zero were not Yiddish. After our careful deprogramming and two years of instruction, Lee was still not able to say, *"Se schver tzu zein ah yid"* ("It's hard to be a Jew"). Maybe he does not believe it.

Mr. Lee became a smash hit at our birthday and anniversary

parties, to which he was always invited, not merely because he could be persuaded to cook a few dishes but mainly because of the Ronald Colman manners he would adopt in the presence of what he considered the "uptowners" and his charming trilingual speech.

The Gourmets, after several years of weekly feasts at Lee's studio, were finally approached with an unusual request: "Was-sah matter with you fucking guys, you got no fucking class? I'm cooking my fucking ass off for you fucking guys, not once not any of you fucking guys got the brains to take me out to dinner? You schmucks!"

Ngoot made us feel like the greedy and unfeeling brutes we were. We voted that the following week be "Mother's Day" for Ngoot Lee. Furthermore, we decided that we would have a banquet in his honor at the restaurant of his choice.

At the end of that night out, when one of us inquired whether the evening was to his satisfaction, Ngoot replied: "No!" We were stunned. "Not one of you fucking guys thought to bring me one *farshtunkener* flower for Mother's Day!" We promised not to be so forgetful next year. On the way uptown the car stalled at a traffic light. Heller, a man noted for a certain kind of wit, rose immediately to the occasion. "Hey, Ngoot, get out and pull it."

We continued having great Gourmet Club dinners, either prepared by Mr. Lee or ordered by him in Chinatown until that sad day when he announced with embarrassment (and swore us to secrecy besides) that he had become advertising consultant for a prominent department store and he could eat with us only now and then. Anyway, he said, he was getting tired of cooking for a bunch of "hot-dog eaters." We vowed to keep his dirty secret and not tell his other bohemian artist friends, provided he continue to find good places for us to eat in Chinatown. He agreed to this arrangement but extracted still another promise from us that we not tell any of our other "round-eyed" friends for fear the "uptown trade" would popularize his finds, consequently spoiling them with fancy menus, doubled prices, lousy food, and overcrowding.

We remembered that was exactly what happened to a restaurant called Mon Sing, which we prized for a few years because we liked the food and because we could always get in. One infamous night, Hershy Kay, in betrayal of our commitment to secrecy, brought his neighbor, Craig Claiborne of *The New York Times*, as well as what seemed to be the entire ballet corps of the City Center Opera. We found out about this treachery through a featured article about the restaurant in the *Times*. Mon Sing was ruined for us forever overnight. It was crowded, the food soon deteriorated. The restaurant even started accepting credit cards.

After the "uptown trade" destroyed our favorite spot in Chinatown, security became tight and Mr. Lee wisely kept his knowledge to himself. He suspected that there were members of the club who couldn't be trusted. He was absolutely right. But he did not reckon with the genius of Heller, an interrogator so skilled he could extract blood from a stone . . . if he could not get soup and was hungry. On one of Joe's nocturnal excursions, he chanced upon Ngoot and, after plying him with whiskey, managed to get Lee to reveal his latest discovery. This led to the famous "Night of the Lobsters."

I could describe this event in detail, but I have been sworn to secrecy. However, I am one of those who cannot be trusted. Here goes.

The hard core of the Gourmets, namely Julie, George, Joe, and I, were walking along the Bowery section of Chinatown trying to decide where to eat. Mon Sing was crowded and we couldn't get in. Julie said, "Geez, but if that blabbermouthed midget Hershy hadn't ruined it for us at Mon Sing, maybe Ngoot would give us a new place to eat. The stuff we've been getting lately is awful."

"Yeah, right." "You said it," we all brilliantly echoed. All, that is, except for our boy Joey, who said, after not much soul-searching, that Ngoot had actually just taken him to a wonderful place, but of course he was sworn to secrecy and could not take us there. The news he imparted was received by us with the customary derision it deserved.

Who knew better than we that nothing that Heller ever said could be trusted? In our world he was more famous as a put-on artist than a novelist. We each hit him with a witty remark: "Come on!" "Stop kidding." "Tell it to Sweeney."

Joe didn't stop. He kept saying how marvelous the dishes were, how succulent the pork, how delicious the house soup. . . . The most extravagant praise he saved for the lobster—cooked in a way he had never tasted before. We just kept walking and mumbling "Yeah, yeah" and "Sure, sure." Now the problem for those of us who still remain his friends is that we can't believe a word he says, even when he's lying. So when he walked us into a joint that looked like an ordinary luncheonette, we marched along without another word and sat down. Joe whispered something to a smiling waiter, which I later learned was, "Bring us the identical meal that Ngoot Lee ordered for me last night," and before two minutes had passed (which is precisely the way we like it) food appeared. The soup was superb, the braised crab perfect, the pork tender, crisp, and most delicious, and then, what we thought the *pièce de résistance*: the lobster, steamed in lemon oil and other exquisite spices. Marvelous. Joe summoned the waiter and, with a frown that puzzled us, told the poor man that it was not what we had wanted. We sat contentedly sipping a fine tea when, behold! another dish miraculously appeared, and when uncovered it turned out to be another pair of lobsters. They were Cantonese style with minced pork, egg, scallions, and black bean sauce, but executed to perfection. It was hard to believe our taste buds. These last two were even better than the first. Absolutely the best we'd ever had. We left nothing but the shells, and these were picked clean. But Joe shook his leonine head unhappily and said, "Just take it easy, guys. It's not the right dish."

He called for the waiter and explained that, though the food he'd served was very good, it didn't seem to be the same meal as the one he'd eaten with his young, gray-haired Chinese friend. "Don't you remember?" he asked. "It wasn't with black bean sauce or steamed. It was something quite different." The waiter's eyes suddenly lit up with recognition and he disappeared into the kitchen. I foolishly remarked that I could not possibly take another bite of anything. And Joe replied, "Yeah, just wait till you taste this." It was quite a while but they finally arrived: lobsters, and they were better than the best. With a big smile and mumbling, "Oh boy. That's the one I meant!" Joe started snaring the best pieces with his forks and spoons. (Joe never used chopsticks as the rest of us did. He always asked for and received, without argument, three large serving spoons. He was once asked why he never bothered to learn how to use chopsticks. His answer: "Too slow.") Though Joe got his usual head start, we soon caught up and, despite the frenzy, even voracious eaters like us could recognize the superb quality of this excellently prepared dish. It was called "baked lobster" and seemed to be simply prepared. Sautéed in chicken fat and very little else. (However, I suspect that "very little else" is an essential ingredient that I'll never figure out.)

The very next morning, Joe got an early call from Mr. Lee. "You Judas prick," cried Ngoot. "I take pity on you, you animal. I take you this best place in Chinatown, you *gonif*," he sputtered, "you swear you would not betray me. I'll never trust you again, you *dreck!*"

Heller was absolutely dumbfounded. "Who told you?" he gasped. "Was it Speed? Or Julie? Then it must have been George."

"None of them fucking guys. You schmuck," Ngoot exploded, "by now all fucking Chinatown knows about four crazy round-eyes, two with beards, two without, that ate up all the lobsters in town, you dumb fuck. Even my little girl, Jen, called first thing this morning. I knew right away. All Chinatown is talking about the four guys that ate six lobsters after all those other fucking dishes. They even sent out to another restaurant for the last two. How fucking smart do you think I have to be to figure out it was you? On top of everything else, you insult my intelligence!"

In the years since, New Sun (a most appropriate name for this incredible restaurant) disappeared. We have tried desperately and failed to find a chef who can duplicate the taste of baked lobster. Ngoot says he can but won't. Ngoot, by now, is no longer interested in impressing us.

After Ngoot took his department store job and we began eating out on a regular basis, it was not at all unusual for us to finish a huge Chinatown meal, like the one at New Sun, and then walk to Little Italy for large paper cups of lemon ice. The lemon ice emporium we found on Mulberry Street looked like a small, ordinary bake shop, but the proprietor, Valentino Sorrento, was an extraordinary man and we judged his ices the best in the world.

Valentino had a dark and handsome Italian face that closely resembled Marcello Mastroianni's, but there was a sadness to him that masked a comic soul, one akin to Henry Armetta's. A *Pagliacci* in reverse. Valentino would tease us mercilessly about eating Chinese food when there was so much good Italian fare in the neighborhood, and he thought we were insane to ask for ices after September's San Gennaro festival, the traditional cutoff point for making ices. "Gelati? Okay. But ices . . . you crazy! Who gonna want ices in cold weather?"

"Us!" we urged.

"Nah," he intoned, "you couldn't buy enough. You nice guys, but I ain't going broke for you. Forget ices."

We pleaded and finally he agreed to a compromise. Before he stopped making ices for the season, he said he would freeze up and set aside a big batch for us in pint containers so that we could get ices in his bakery or take them home. It wasn't as good as getting fresh because we had to wait until they thawed before we could eat them, but once they softened, they were almost the same. Patience, however, is not Heller's strongest suit, so he developed a better way. He began phoning beforehand to tell Valentino to take a few pints out of the freezer so they would be ready by the time we finished dinner in Chinatown and walked over to his shop. If we got there too soon and the containers were still hard, we simply munched on Italian cookies, chatted with Sorrento, and waited. The pints would thaw enough so we could plunge a spoon into them by the time we were ready to leave. This wasn't exactly protocol. Ices should be squeezed out of a pleated paper cup without using any utensil, but since we were already compromising, we had it his way. By the time we got to the bottom of the container, it was slush—the *crème de la crème* of ices. Naturally, we fought like tigers to take command of the container then. Only the strongest and greediest succeeded. (Once, as a joke, Heller told Sorrento when ordering a batch of lemon ices on the telephone to stick a couple of pints under his arms while he waited on his other customers. That way they would be nicely softened for us by the time we arrived. Valentino didn't think it was that funny, either.)

On another occasion, I recall a lively argument between Valentino and Ngoot about the relative merits of pasta and Chinese noodles. Each was, of course, violently defending his ethnic bias when Ngoot raised his hand to interrupt the controversy and said, "Okay, take it easy. You guys didn't invent noodles. We did! We eat noodles for long time before your paisan Marco Polo showed up in China and took back what the goombah thought was the recipe. What we give him was *chazzerei.* From Column B. We kept all that good stuff for us. We also left a coupla ingredients outa the recipe he took."

Many evenings, after the Gourmets left Sorrento's, we'd stop in the Village for a slice or two of pizza, buy a couple of bags of roasted peanuts, then wash it all down with a real New York egg cream.

I remember one night in a new restaurant when it was just

Joe, Julie, George, and I. Ngoot could not make it, which meant we were without an interpreter. Heller was curious about the side of our menu that was in Chinese characters. The waiter told him that it was a banquet for ten people, very delicious—not for just us. Joe said, "It sounds good. We'll have it." The waiter thought we were either joking or insane. Heller persuaded him we were serious and that large quantities were not a problem. We were moved to a big, round table and shortly thereafter the food began arriving. In the middle of this meal of many superb dishes, we slowly became aware that our table was surrounded by waiters, chefs, customers—even the cashier. We could not be sure, but it seemed to me that the mutterings in their native tongue were bets for or against our survival.

We left nothing.

The Gourmet Club became a kind of ritual meeting that gained importance and took precedence over all other social functions in our lives. Our wives displayed various degrees of annoyance at our priorities but avoided making dates on Gourmet nights in deference to our wishes. All wives, without exception, said the club was an exclusionary, male chauvinist enterprise. They were absolutely right, but what did that have to do with it? We had our rules, by-laws, and traditions. One of the charter members—I am not at liberty to mention which one—declared, "Ladies kill a meal!" We took that sensible statement as our slogan and stubbornly refused to mend our ways. Actually, we did not exclude wives; our attitude was straightforward and equitable: "It's okay for you to bring *your* wife, it's just not so okay for me to bring *mine*."

The wives were once, en masse, invited to join us for a meal in Chinatown. They accepted. And afterward, their unanimous response was to request that, in the future, we continue eating without them. "Is this all you do?" they asked. "Just eat and talk?"

One night in the hospital, I asked Joe a serious question. I wanted to know if he had at any time during his ordeal turned to prayer. He confessed that he had. But the prayers were not to win lawsuits, make a complete recovery, or finish his novel.

"Someday in this life," he said, "I would like to eat another baked lobster, like the one at the old New Sun."

So would I.

BY THE TWENTY-SIXTH of December my respiratory parameters were no longer deteriorating and I was described in the medical records as "clearly stable as far as Guillain-Barré" was concerned. On the twenty-ninth, I requested for the second time of Morty Bader that I be moved out of the intensive care unit, since the medical danger was ostensibly over. He was not unsympathetic. His resistance on this occasion was based on the calendar and on my continuing need for special nursing attention. An extended New Year's Eve holiday weekend was looming, and he knew there could be serious staffing problems at the hospital. Only in the intensive care unit could he guarantee the close supervision I'd grown used to and whose sudden lack, he warned me, would be more upsetting to me than I could imagine. Could I not stick it out for an additional five or six days? For me to go to a private room without a private nurse would present problems. Another powerful inducement for remaining was that Blue Cross was paying in full for certain costs in the intensive care unit that I would have to begin assuming for myself once I left, and it was now no secret to anyone that there were going to be plenty before I was finished. I surrendered to his persuasions with such alacrity as to evidence even to me that I was still harboring repressed agitations about leaving that were more extreme than I was allowing myself to realize.

My first demand to leave the intensive care unit (the first of what I could call my two seizures of overwrought desperation) occurred, curiously enough, in the aftermath of Dustin Hoffman's first visit and his uplifting gift of the Sony Walkman. So much for the reputation of music and the permanently healing effects of Beethoven, Bach, and Brahms. I don't know what brought about this reversal in spirit during that night. The number of nights I'd already spent in that place could have been enough. And, of course, most of them were sleepless. (As all of my doctors would point out, they would have been sleepless for anyone there in his right mind.)

It was the nurse on that 10:00 p.m. to 7:00 a.m. shift, a woman whose signature I cannot decipher, to whom I apparently first made known my decision, formed some time during those haunted hours, to get the hell out of there the very next day, regardless of the risk, to whom, as the record states, I "c/o [complained of] need to leave the ICU." I must have made it clear to her that I would not stay there even one day longer to placate anyone, not even myself! And that was it.

I announced this arbitrary determination to my day nurse as soon as she assumed charge of me at 7:00 a.m. (Good God! To be at work at seven a person has to be out of bed at least by six, I'd realized with pity.)

I fear I must have broadcast this same bathetic decision to everyone that morning, as though to emphasize through repetition the immutability of my resolve and to bring that much nearer the moment at which the transfer would be accomplished. Nothing would deter me, it was useless to try. I had lawyers visiting me every day.

Dr. Hirsch wrote of me then as "very agitated and depressed about the ICU setting" and that "Pt's mental status significant for ICU disturbance." And Wally Sencer recorded that "between the MICU ambience and the lack of sleep, the patient has become very agitated." Even Kim Kudzin, who reported for work in the afternoon, noted that I was still "verbalizing frustration c̄ [with] depression related to prolonged hospitalization" and lack of sleep. The crucial meeting, of course, took place with Morty Bader. Morty and I talked in subdued tones, as the two of us did typically. I declared to him, tearfully and heroically, that I would rather be dead than remain there. I told him frankly that I would have to go mad if I stayed. I could not bear being there.

Morty did not belittle me. Instead he acknowledged my protestations with the same respectful sobriety he had shown me from the Sunday I had called him on the telephone with my recitation of symptoms I was more than half sure he would ridicule. He was silent until it was time for him to reply.

"You'll get better treatment in here than anywhere else in the hospital," he told me straight out after the slightest shake of his head in disagreement. And immediately I felt a tremendous relief that I was *not* going to leave! Can you imagine? He went on, "And you still need it. There's nothing unusual about the way you're reacting. I'm surprised you haven't complained about this sooner. Look where you are." Suddenly I knew I wanted more than anything else in the world to remain right there. Now I was frantic at the prospect of being anywhere else. "Let me send a psychiatrist around to talk to you and see how much of a strain you're really under," Morty continued. "You'll feel better after you talk to him. Wally thinks so too."

I felt better already. I know ambivalence when I can no longer shut my eyes to it and I can recognize repression when it smacks me in the face. Now if I still felt myself trembling, it was because of how narrowly I had just escaped separating myself from the safety of this abhorrent unit on which I had come unconsciously to believe everything in my life depended. It was not just the atmosphere and the noise there that were keeping me from sleeping but an immense fright that I had been only partially successful in hiding from myself. I felt both blissful relief and a dejected, infantile shame. A couple of more days had to pass before I succeeded in untangling my confused feelings and the psychiatrist sent to me could write:

> Alert, friendly, optimistic. Now adjusting to prospect of move to single room but expects it will take a few days to get used to the idea and glad it isn't taking place today.

I didn't want to stay and I didn't want to go.

Dr. Arthur Peck is a psychiatrist affiliated with Mount Sinai Hospital. He served as a soldier in the same war as I did, if I understood him correctly. He had gone to medical school afterward, and he had trained in psychiatry upon discovering about himself that he had not much taste for sickness and blood. Now he was specializing just about exclusively in the emotional problems of hospital patients, many with illnesses more traumatic and relentless than mine. This told me he did not often engage in programs of long-term therapy. It hinted also, I think, of a peculiar ambivalence of his own.

There would be no way to overstate the comfort I derived from him. Within ten minutes he assured me that I was not in a state of psychosis and that I was not showing signs of any other kind of mental breakdown—I was merely in misery. Only a person already far gone would respond any differently to that unnatural environment and my unnatural condition. (From a source other than Dr. Peck I found out that one of my regular physicians had been a patient in that identical unit a few years earlier, and after three days had started pleading more fiercely than I had to be taken out.)

Recording his impressions of me in those first few meetings, Dr. Peck wrote that I was "voluble, with good affect . . . alert, talkative, pleasant . . . and very friendly."

Is it any wonder we got on so well?

He also found me "severely distressed at being unable to sleep in the unit" and noted that I was well aware of my illness and the need for care but that I was "avoiding the slow passing of time by ruminating in numbers and trying *not* to see the unit clock." I was also "apprehensive re uncertainty of Dx. & Dx. for recovery."

I had good cause to be apprehensive about the diagnosis. If it turned out to be anything other than Guillain-Barré, all bets on my eventual recovery were off. Surprising to me now is that not one of my friends ever made a comment to me, or even to each other, about my suddenly having a psychiatrist seeing me there every weekday. Could it really be they did not find that strange? As strange as I did?

Very often, because of a flood of interruptions by the nurses and doctors or by the arrival of the physical therapist who had been ordered for me, there would be an antic quality to our bedside psychotherapy sessions that caused us both to chuckle. By nature helpful, Dr. Peck would instinctively become an eager part of the lifting team transferring me back to bed from the stretcher chair, or join with a nurse to position me for the chest X ray or to roll me on my side as a preliminary to rolling me back onto the canvas sling of the bed scale, a contraption astounding me still by the sheer simplicity of concept and application. I am not good at puzzles and have no mechanical imagination, and it would have taken me a thousand years before I gave up trying to figure out how to change the sheet of a bed while someone was in it. The method is the same one employed to mount a patient on the stretcher of the bed scale in order to hoist him mechanically and weigh him while he is suspended. It's lucky for me the problem was given to someone else, for here the sheets were changed every morning and my weight was measured and recorded every few days.

Dr. Peck was of help to me in ways I could not have foreseen, and I found him useful even when discussing such trivial problems as the Oedipal complex, repetition compulsions, the impact on children of the death of parents, and the character and psychology of some of my other doctors. When I pined for the homes and the people of the past, it took little more than my saying so aloud to him for me to be reminded that I had lapsed into another spell of regression and that these relationships were extinct.

Only twice did Dr. Peck surprise me. There were male nurses on the staff, three or four, I think, all of them foreign-born, and they seemed mainly to work on the night shift. And of course, I had to rely upon them too for assistance with things like the urinal and bedpan and with the suction tube when it fell to the floor, and to uncross my ankles for me when they were hooked or adjust me to a different position on my side from the one which only ten or twelve minutes before I was positive would remain comfortable for at least an hour or two.

The first time Dr. Peck surprised me was by giving a visible start when I revealed to him something I had discovered about myself that *I* thought innocuous: that I was embarrassed and therefore more reluctant to call upon the males for the things I needed than to ask for aid from the women. And I, in turn, was startled by what I took to be his unexpected sharp reaction to what I lackadaisically had assumed, and still do, was a sentiment acknowledged to be almost universal among men. That instant is a mystery to me still. My other surprise from Dr. Peck came when I asked him his fee. He agreed to lower it if my medical insurance was not extensive enough to cover his charges along with all my others. It wasn't and he did.

It was to Dr. Peck that I outlined serenely the rational plan I had formulated for coping with all of the demoralizing experiences of living in the ICU. He was more laconic than I and wrote in the record that "patient states he decided to acclimate himself to his environment."

And why not? Why had I not thought of that sooner? Much of my anguish, I had deduced coolly, was rising from my failure and frustration in attempting to live normally in an environment in which the usual rhythms of normal activity were impossible to maintain. Why was it necessary to get my sleep in one unbroken stretch at night? I could accommodate myself to the idea of indiscriminate noises all night long as easily as I had gotten used to the nightly pandemonium of the trucks and subways and sirens and shouts in the streets of Manhattan, to all of which I had long grown just about oblivious. I could accumulate the sleep I needed in bits and pieces—why did it have to be all at once and only at night? If people died, they died; they would have done so without me, and they weren't doing it there now just to spite me. What business was it of mine? And I could have been very much worse off, I told Dr. Peck: I could have been a doctor or a nurse there. It was mainly a matter of attitude, I concluded sensibly. What could be easier?

That's what *I* thought.

The empirical fallacy in all this positive thinking was that it did not make the slightest difference. I *still* could not go to sleep at night when I was tired and felt it was time to. When I did drift off it was always from an exhausted stupor, after hours of struggle. And I was very soon jerked awake by a sound or thought.

One night that second week I was allowed a common antihistamine often used as a sleeping potion, Benadryl. I was given a dose about eight in the evening and dropped right off without knowing I was doing so. At twelve-thirty I came wide awake to find a small group of residents at the foot of my bed. I had none of the customary feelings that tell us we have been asleep. The shock was bewildering. And I was again at a loss—here it was, just a little past midnight and I was not now in the least sleepy. What was I to do with the rest of the night? At four in the morning I was given a second dose; I went right off again without knowing I was going, and I came wide awake at seven without realizing I'd been gone. And again at the foot of my bed I saw a group of six or eight or ten who were talking about me in voices raised to normal level. Again I was aghast: Why had I not had an inkling this was going on? And after that initial dazed and disoriented moment of incomprehension and confusion, I felt humiliated and exposed, mocked, pathetic, vulnerable, and indignant. I was almost overcome by a powerful impulse to mourn.

I was pleased I had slept, I admitted to Dr. Peck. But those abrupt changes back and forth between consciousness and insensibility were too intimidating for me to go through. I refused the Benadryl after that. I preferred the dolorous chagrin of insomnia. I decided to wait and to labor for my sleep until the needs of body and soul grew too strong to withstand.

But when the day came, on the afternoon and evening of December 30, when I felt again that craving for sleep, felt it more profoundly than ever before, and this time knew I could have it immediately and in immense abundance, I found myself fighting it off, and I went into a state of terror more horrible than anything I can recall ever having experienced before.

Between about four in the afternoon and ten at night, I thought I would die from the intensity alone of the fear I was suffering in secret as I struggled between a need for sleep so enormous it could no longer be staved off and a mortal dread of succumbing to it, the petrifying foreknowledge that if I drew that one more breath that would take me into dreamland, it was going to be my last.

I can recall the details. The day was dreary and overcast, night was still falling early. My bed was raised, as I usually wanted it, to a position halfway between sitting and reclining, and I was on my back. From there I could watch what took place. My mind was keenly alert, like someone trapped. The suction tube was there, first in one hand, then in the other. I could not raise my head, but I could turn it from left to right, and I watched vigilantly every person who moved and every single thing that happened. I looked at it all. I could not stop staring at things I did not want to see. What I longed for most in the world was sleep, and what I began to dread most was getting it.

I was sucking in air deeply like someone in thirst. I could hear myself breathe, feel the air flowing in and spreading through me. My lids would lower, my vision would dim, my eyes would nearly close. Air was like ether to me, frightful, pervasive, and overpowering. And when that moment came that I was just about unconscious, when I knew I was already sucking in that ultimate one, I began to fight with all the willpower I could command against completing it, strived as hard as I could to resist inhaling that final wee bit more that would mean my going to sleep (and "dying," Dr. Peck stated in his note the following day). In a peculiar inversion of logic, breathing had become lethal, sleep deadly. No wonder I could not make head or tails of much that was happening. I would check myself at the last instant, I would snap my head up with a violent shudder, I would force open my eyes, and I would stare at all about me anxiously with paranoid hostility, alarm, and suspicion. I distrusted every object and living being my eyes fell on in that ghostly, small world. And in a very few minutes that restful longing for sleep would come stealing over me once more and I would feel myself drifting downward into darkness contentedly again, welcoming and cherishing that soothing repose that was coming—until I remembered with a gasp where I was heading, and that critical need to pull back and save myself took hold of me again.

In this way did the hours crawl and my feelings of terror increase until I began to think I could not much longer bear this frightened state of conflicted indecision. I could not come to grips with what I wanted. I felt I would suffocate from air and die from lack of sleep. This, I told myself, was hysteria. And soon I was wondering how much longer a person could suffer such painful stress and still survive. I felt myself in danger of dying just from that, until my lids grew heavy again, my breathing deeper—and I caught myself just in time to pull myself back again from the very chasm of destruction. I felt that something ameliorating had to happen soon if my heart was not to stop.

At last it was night. At last the new shift of nurses had arrived. And among them I saw one who might mean my salvation. I prayed to God she would be assigned to me. I watched in apprehensive suspense, calculating the odds, to see which two of the four now coming on duty would be delegated to my unit, which one of the two would then be mine. When I saw my prayer was answered, I knew I was saved, and I sighed and lay back with relief. In World War II, I was a bombardier on sixty combat missions. There was a minute in one of them when I thought my plane had exploded, and I was scared on the next twenty-three more missions required of me after that one, which included a couple to the bridge across the Po River just north of Ferrara and one to the very heavily defended Italian harbor of La Spezia. That day in the hospital was the worst in my life.

Her name was Jean Genova and I doubt she was much older than twenty-five. If my memory is reliable, she was of pale complexion and had dark hair and very dark eyes. We had talked before. She impressed me from the first as shy, dignified, and reserved, and extremely competent and intelligent. Like another of my favorites, Lori Meiselman, who worked on the day shift, she was of short and slight build; this made their skill at lifting and turning me all the more remarkable. Both these young women possessed the marvelous, priceless knack of moving me as though I were of one piece, without any sharp poking of fingers into flesh to get it done or any tracking back for a pelvis or a leg that had not been brought along with the rest. But Lori Meiselman, with a crowd of coworkers flying about on that hectic morning shift, was much more the extrovert. Jean was single and worked by choice on the night shift, a preference releasing her, I inferred, from the pressures of conforming to a New York City social life which is, to many, pointless, onerous, and obnoxious.

She did not boast or probe. The daughter of a physician, she had already applied to medical school, and it was with many qualms that she looked ahead to the personal interview required for admission. I've wondered since how she made out. She was reticent, and most doctors and medical students I meet are not reticent, with the exception of psychiatrists, who have secrets to keep. It is as easy to make glib generalizations about doctors as it is about book writers and book reviewers, and one of the feelings I have now about the doctors I've met is that, excluding surgeons, they are scandalously underpaid. Their fees are too high and they don't earn enough.

In this somewhat darkened chamber in which I lay I now had a trusted person I felt I could talk to, and I did—I began right in urgently, pouring out to her in a lowered voice all I had been feeling and thinking.

"I've been having a very scary time of it these past few hours," I confided, as soon as Jean came to my side to ask how I was doing, and then, perhaps even smiling a bit in self-effacement and wonder, calmly related to her at great and unashamed length all I'd been going through.

I felt right back to normal as soon as I started. (The celebrated "talking cure" of Sigmund Freud does not solve certain problems and does solve others, and fortunately for me this one was among the latter.) I slept well after that, for perhaps four or five hours. And in the morning all that was left for me to talk about was the striking, almost whimsical memory of my fear of my fear.

I was alert and in good spirits when I awoke in the morning, according to the nurse on duty then, although she reported that I spoke to her "about bad dreams" I'd had "related to not breathing."

When Dr. Teirstein appeared on rounds with his group, I informed him with almost boastful excitement of my dramatic adventure with hysteria the day before, from which I had barely escaped with my life. All of them let me talk without interruption. Then, as though they had not heard a word of everything gripping I'd said, Dr. Teirstein put his stethoscope to my chest. A young female doctor in the group commented favorably on the fact that in the respiration measurements my ability to inhale against resistance had improved to a minus 30. "Yes," said Dr. Teirstein, agreeing quietly with his mild smile. "But you could probably go over fifty without even trying." They were not all that riveted. Maybe I was telling it wrong.

Arthur Peck was more attentive and communicative. He pointed out, almost diffidently, that it was anxiety I was describing, not hysteria. A person with hysteria would not suspect he had it. And he gave me his guarantee that people, even when asleep, do not suffocate themselves—*cannot* suffocate themselves—from anxiety (even if he wanted to, a person cannot stop himself from breathing) and that humans do not die from unhappiness. Then he directed my notice to something obvious that I resolutely had been blocking out: the respirators to which the other patients there, all of them unconscious, were connected and the noise that came steadily from these machines. It was not so surprising that I'd been afraid to sleep from the day I arrived or that my concerns had coalesced so densely on the matter of breathing. Of our talk that day he wrote:

> Although he is calm and not especially afraid this AM, reports severe anx. yest. aft. and evening re. falling asleep and therefore stopping breathing, hence dying. This persisted until he repeated it to a night RN. Then he slept and awoke without anxiety. He reports he almost asked for me to be called, so I will leave my home telephone. . . . Also, if this problem recurs, I am ordering Valium. I doubt he will request it at all but he appreciated having it ordered.

I did not ask for Valium and I did not use his home number. I did request him to continue seeing me after the weekend was over and I was moved to a private room. I did not yet want to think of letting him go.

I spent the several days of that long holiday weekend in the throes of another severe separation conflict, for I did not want to let go of the intensive care unit either. By now I loathed everything about the place except the personnel and the continuous medical reassurance they provided, and I detested myself for being there; yet my worry now was that I might be forced out by a ripple of true emergency cases before the holiday weekend was past. It would not take many. The beds in both halves of the unit totaled only eight. In sneaky self-concern, I kept greedy inventory of the number of beds and patients and alertly fired questions whenever I heard mention of another new telephone call from the emergency room. A young black girl was admitted (wheeled in on a stretcher) who was close to death from anaphylactic shock incited by something she'd eaten at a quiet family party. Her life was saved and she was moved out to the hospital proper after a couple of days. A foreign-born woman was wheeled in who was almost gone from asthma; she dwelt by herself in a small flat in the city, where she had no friends or relatives, and she was susceptible to severe attacks of asthma each holiday season. (Overhearing the bedside consultations of others was part of the noise I could not turn off.)

I can tell you more stories! Some time around here, a stocky, pugnacious young drug addict who'd nearly died from an overdose was brought upstairs and put into the bed beside mine. As soon as he could talk, he demanded to be let out—he had good knowledge of his legal rights. As soon as he could stand, he climbed out of bed and tottered here and there with clenched fists, insisting threateningly in tough street language that the person with authority to release him be brought there without delay. Now and then he would stagger heavily against the side of my bed, jarring it. My daughter stopped by while he was still there, and both of us were spellbound as we gaped and listened to him. I wanted him out of there even if he dropped dead. I was less humane than the doctors. What would happen if his anger fell upon me? I wondered why the nurses did not ring for the police to hurry to protect me. And yet, perversely, his belligerent intransigence brought joy to my heart. I was all for him. He wanted to leave. I wanted him to leave. "Get him the fuck out," I was rooting for him, silently. He got his way and the bed was empty.

Oh, can I tell you stories? On one of these mornings an elderly woman died. Before the day ended, her bed was taken by another elderly woman. And for a day and a half after that, my favorite morning nurse kept addressing the second woman with the name of the first—until I finally felt forced to correct her. (Nurses talk even to unconscious patients, addressing them by name, talk more loudly to them, in fact, trying to get through.) And when I did remind her, she looked blankly at me for a minute, disbelieving. "Don't you remember?" I repeated. "You were the one right there taking care of her. You were the one who gave the alarm." It does not surprise me that most nurses seem to choose to discontinue working there before they are even thirty.

There was a noticeable slackening of activity in that long, last week. I was not wired to the cardiac monitor anymore. Poor Speed—he did me the signal favor of going to Key West on vacation and, because of dismal weather I relished hearing about, having an oppressively unpleasant time; two who'd left as best friends, he predicted, probably would hardly speak to each other again. He was mistaken. I've wondered in reconsideration, knowing the good-natured fellow he is, whether he was not inventing that part of the tale simply to fill me with happiness. (I should explain that the man named Quilp in Charles Dickens's *The Old Curiosity Shop* is, to my mind and to my good friend Julius Green's, one of the most lovable characters in all literature. Scrooge is another, until he undergoes that lamentable change of heart toward the end.)

Playwright Joe (*Fiddler on the Roof*) Stein went off to Barbados for the holidays with his wife and her daughter and took the three hundred and twenty-five pages of that draft of *God Knows* with him to evaluate for me. I couldn't read it, but he could, and I wanted to know if he thought it was good enough to submit to a publisher in that form. He was definite that it was but took his sweet time telling me. I expected him to telegraph. (There was selfish cause for jubilation on his part too, for at that time I already owed him ten thousand dollars.) But Joe seems to like everything I write, I took cynically into account. So a little bit later I went for a second opinion to my good friend Barbara Gelb, who doesn't like any of the writing I do but somehow manages to be more or less pleased with each finished work, despite its inevitably being too long. Barbara, who has the ruthless soul of a first-class copy editor, believes that every sentence, paragraph, chapter, and novel I've published is much too long. In her estimation, everything ever written by anybody is too long, except the commendable, comprehensive biography of Eugene O'Neill that she did far back with her husband, Arthur Gelb, which would be a much more commendable work if it weren't so long.

One of the directors of nursing for the entire hospital dropped by to say that three experienced private-duty nurses had been found who would stay with me in my private room for as long as they were needed and who'd agreed, since I could not write checks, to be paid once a week instead of after each shift, as is customary. (This woman, by the way, and a codirector in the same office were the only two people in nursing I met in both my hospitals who had ever read a word I had written.) Valerie Humphries, about whom we shall hear more, was one of the three nurses, and the only opinion she had formed of me as an author prior to my becoming her patient was that I was "someone who looked like Norman Mailer." (By now she has read all of my books, and she does not think they are too long, and she knows I am far, far better-looking than Mailer.)

Morty Bader ruminated about the advisability of my going to a rehabilitation facility like Rusk when my hospitalization was over, and he offered to set in motion the paperwork necessary when he saw I did not protest. Richie Bader told me, not for the first time, that nerve tissue regenerates at the minute rate of one millimeter a day and repeated the rather warming anecdote of the method by which that measurement had been ascertained.* Both, I realized only later, were gradually getting me adjusted to the idea that my recovery was going to take much longer than I dared admit. With Morty I had more than one discussion about poetry too, especially Tennyson's "Ulysses," whose closing lines, with their message to the aging, he seemed to be suggesting, might have exceptional personal application for both of us.

Wally Sencer, ever the aggressive optimist, took a contrary view to the defeatist prospect of a rehabilitation hospital. "With a crazy disease like this," he pretty much declared, "you might feel like jumping out of bed in two weeks and go right home." I did not want to mention that I no longer had a home I really cared to go to.

Behind Sencer's back one day a staff neurologist with a theo-

* Dr. Stephen Head, an English surgeon, with that goal in mind, intentionally slashed the nerve in his own forearm and every day kept track of the extent to which sensation returned below the point of incision.

retical bent of mind requested permission to search my body for the presence of a tick. I was all for his finding one. A tick as the source of my ailment would kick off the process of full recovery simultaneously with its removal. He did not find any. Sencer snickered when I told him. "With the toxin from a tick," he said, "you would keep getting worse. You're getting better."

Better? I was still coughing a good deal and suctioning "copious" secretions. But I was able to hold a paperback book again. I could swallow Jell-O now and then when I tried, but I had trouble maneuvering my tongue and my "posterior pharyngeal wall and superior pharyngeal constrictors" were still paralyzed. I could raise my right hand to my face and comb the hair on the right side of my head. My grip was stronger and my biceps were improved, wrote the nurses and the physical therapist. But if they didn't tell me, I would not have known.

The daily half-hour physical therapy sessions were a pleasant distraction, mainly because of the therapist, Ellen, a vivacious, attractive young woman with an outgoing personality that might easily have been misconstrued by some men as flirtatiousness. There was kidding around when she was there. The sessions were prized by me more as a diversion than for any deep faith I had in their efficacy: I could not genuinely believe benefit would ensue from hip and shoulder exercises in which I could not feel myself participating and she *could* feel my muscles working. But I did find being sat up on the side of the bed (with "maximum assistance") challenging and fun. I could maintain my balance for more than fifteen minutes. This did not seem like much of a feat to me, until I tried to lower myself back to the mattress gradually, and dropped like a sack of potatoes. My head would go down like a rock if it was not held. Bent forward while sitting on the side of my bed, I had no trouble sitting back up. If I tilted myself rearward even an inch, I would drop all the way over, just like a sack of potatoes. (My back muscles were working, my abdominals were not.)

By now I was really starting to lose weight. One of my medical manuals observes that the onset of Guillain-Barré is so rapid that paralysis is there before atrophy can begin. I weighed in at Mount Sinai at 165. In the second week, when the process began, I went down from 162 to 155 in one week, and from 155 to 147 in another. I estimate I was under 140 when I left Mount Sinai. I have to estimate because I was not weighed again after leaving the ICU. Weight was no longer significant to the doctors. I was suffering from muscle loss, not malnutrition. And there was not much they could do about that.

By the end of the second week my atrophy was "general." Now I could listen to the medical tour guides calling attention to the evidences of muscle waste. For those of you who don't know, the erosion shows up most conspicuously in the temples, where holes the size of half dollars appear, in the back of the hands between the thumb and index finger, and in the palms of the hands at the base of the thumb, where hollows show and for a long, long time, perhaps forever, remain.

On New Year's Eve there was a small champagne celebration in the unit as midnight approached, and a couple of the nurses thoughtfully offered me some through the tube in my nose. I thought it wiser to decline. I did not want to risk finding myself pondering any new variations in function or sensation that could have been induced by alcohol as well as by pathology. Besides, I never could abide the taste of any but the best champagne. I have still not been able to say this to my very good friend A. Robert Towbin, who, because he himself is not much of a drinker, does not always serve the best champagne to the swarms of people he habitually invites to drop in for lunch or dinner or anything else whenever they want to.

Bob Towbin was an English major at Dartmouth and, when younger, a talented artist whose luck it was—bad, good, or very much of both—to succeed on Wall Street as an investment banker. He is a person who seems to enjoy everything, including his own misfortunes, and mine too. His apartment was near the hospital, and from the start, he'd been coming to see me most mornings, on working days in an overcoat and three-piece suit on his way downtown to the financial district, on weekends in a jogging suit and a grin, with a flushed and perspiring face. What tickled me about him even then was a mind-boggling affability that transcended everything, an indestructible conviviality that was unaffected by the hospital or the reasons for our meeting there. Never once were his spirits any less cheerful or his subjects of conversation much changed from what they would have been were we at a garden party or on a pleasure boat chartered for the Cannes Film Festival on which I was to request him to accommodate Speed Vogel that spring. (Bob Towbin's good feelings did not falter an iota several weeks later when I broke the news to him that I was indeed going to need the twelve thousand five hundred dollars I had mentioned I might have to borrow from him. The check was there by messenger that same afternoon. Poor Speed endorsed it, with my signature, of course, and picked up my telephone to give him my thanks.) Towbin's early-morning joviality helped brighten the day for me, and, once I'd been moved to the private room, he was one of the first of several unusual influences to inspire my day nurse, Valerie Humphries, to wonder about this new patient she had and to cast a charismatic patina of macho attractiveness upon the limp and shriveled figure I presented.

The five days of that weekend crept slowly to conclusion. I was not kicked out. I did not die. One afternoon, to alleviate my monotony, a nurse kindly took me for a ride in my wheelchair through the halls on the floor outside the ICU. This was the inside of a hospital as it normally looked. I did not like the way it looked and was not keen to go again. There were so many more sick people there than I had imagined, so many more in the hospital than I could envision, more than I wanted to see or know about.

Very late one night a Filipino nurse I had never seen before looked in on me for a minute from her post in the other part of the unit and whispered in a very thick accent, "You going to get better. Did they tell you that?" I was deeply touched and fell in love.

On one of those days shortly before I was moved Adam

Bender appeared again with his peppy young group, told me once more I was bound to recover, and brightly proposed that I take another EMG test, just for the heck of it, to see what differences might turn up. There would be no charge, he pointed out. I was not seduced by his largess.

On Monday morning I was ready early. I did not go until late afternoon. Julius Green arrived with a fresh supply of new Jockey shorts and took back his dinky little radio and a few other small possessions I would not need. He or someone else gathered up my electric toothbrush and Sony Walkman, the electric shaver and the address book I had brought with me, Norman Cousins's *Anatomy of an Illness* and Jane Austen's *Emma*, along with what few other things I had. (There was room for hardly anything there in the space allotted each patient.) I forget what friends were with me when I moved. Six members of the staff took hold of my bedsheet, one supporting my head with a hand and half of them on each side, and at the count of three, lifted and slid me from the bed to the stretcher that was then transformed to a wheelchair. I said good-bye to such people who were there. An aide wheeled me. I had come in lying down on the mobile stretcher three weeks before. I was leaving sitting up. Here was progress. (Not really, for I was in better shape the day I was admitted.)

I still could not stand, swallow, or sit myself up. Seated, I could not raise either foot. I could not raise my head or my left arm or turn myself over in bed. I would soon find out that I could not support the weight of a telephone receiver. I could not maneuver my tongue or reach my groin, and no one could tell me when I would be able to. I had not the strength in my jaws to bite my fingernails and I had been biting my fingernails contentedly for more than fifty years. I had no stocks or bonds to speak of. I was very low in cash and had not much coming in. I was out of danger. I tolerated the transfer well.

JUST FOUR DAYS AFTER the New Year, Joe was wheeled over to his private room in the Klingenstein Pavilion of Mount Sinai. The change from ICU to this room was like transferring from hades to paradise.

What a difference. The room was spacious and quiet, with a view of Central Park and the West Side skyline. He had his own bathroom and telephone. He could use neither, but we could. His private nurses were probably assigned for their ability and dedication to their calling. It did not hurt that the two we saw during the day and evening happened to be young and pretty. It made visiting him a real pleasure. Joe can and surely will speak for himself now, but in this new environment, I felt that things were looking up for us. In Joe's room, the only depressing sight was Joe.

I was told that economic considerations were partly responsible for the Bader decision to keep Joe in ICU longer than was medically indicated. After I saw how much better the private room was in every way, I felt like telling them they were wrong and cruel to have kept him suffering in ICU just to save a bit of money. But I'm glad I held my tongue. I was soon signing checks for twenty-one hundred dollars each week just for Joe's private nurses. I would later, silently, thank those smart Bader boys for their concern.

Joe was still behaving as though nothing much was wrong with him. We chalked it up to courage and gallantry in the face of adversity. I know now that he talked to others about feeling weak, ragged, and anxious and about his inability to sleep and his fear that he might not awake if he did. But he did not render these complaints to any of his friends. Maybe he was acting on his own dictum: "A friend in need is no friend of mine." Or perhaps he feared that if he did not provide us with cheerful news and laughs we would stop coming around. I knew Joe was seeing a psychiatrist regularly. It did not occur to me to ask him why. None of his close friends said anything to him about it, nor did we discuss it with each other.

I would find out later that Dr. Peck, the psychiatrist, actually told Heller he was sane. Joe's nephew, Paul, his lawyer, Jeffrey, and several friends had their doubts. Joe's friend Marvin Green, a prize-winning yachtsman and business tycoon, told his friend Stanley Cohen, an American lawyer then practicing in Paris, about his visit to Heller. "He looked as close to death as anyone I've ever seen in my life, and he was lying there chatting away like there was nothing wrong with him!"

I met almost all of Heller's nurses, but I got to know Valerie Humphries and Donna Mirabello the best, since they covered the times when I was most likely to visit. Joe told me that his late-shift nurse, Willie Mae Grasty, was also "crackerjack" and perfect for that particular shift when he hoped to be able to sleep. She was inclined to be silent yet alert to his needs if he happened to wake in the middle of the night. I have seen good-looking nurses before, but felt Valerie and Donna were outstanding. I confess that Donna was more what I considered to be my type: Mediterranean, dark, short, and well rounded. She was also witty, intelligent, personable, and, unsurprisingly, engaged to be married. Valerie seemed too slim and too tall for me, but she was single by preference, cheerful, and appealing.

Valerie looked like she could easily eat apples off my head, but I was wrong. She was not quite that tall, although given a bigger and more varied menu, I'm certain she could have stretched for the occasion. With the possible exception of Heller, Valerie Humphries is the biggest eater I have ever encountered. Joe, who admires a good "mouth," positively glows with loving approval when Valerie sighs, "I'm so full I can't take another bite"—and then takes several more. Valerie has somehow fathomed that the way to his heart is through *her* stomach. Since she has been hanging out with us, Nurse Humphries and her former patient are not as thin as they were. And neither am I.

My first view of Nurse Humphries was from the rear. She was bending over her patient, adjusting the pillow under his head, and making funny noises. It sounded like cooing. When she stood, I realized she was simply giggling. She was also blushing. I don't know what Joe said to make her laugh, but I surmised that it was either a probing, personal question or a lascivious remark. Or both. Joe introduced us and she chuckled when she heard my name was "Speed." She has a pleasantly musical lilt to her laughter, so we tried to be amusing. (I know that's like trying to be charming. It usually doesn't work. With Valerie it never failed.) She was an appreciative audience for our banter and good-natured teasing. Somehow she could understand Joe's garbled speech and illegible scrawl. She invariably laughed at his jokes, thought his friends were adorable, and enjoyed nursing him. She could anticipate his need to urinate or be turned or have his pillow plumped, and God knows what else when I was not around. (Heller doesn't tell me everything.) It was obvious that he enjoyed having her attend him. What more could anyone ask? I soon decided she was absolutely the perfect nurse for him.

Joe appeared to be less helpless in his new quarters because he had some use of his hands and control over his arms. He still could not move his torso and had to be turned. I was often pressed into service to help move him from one place to another when there were not enough professionals around. I found out what a "pull sheet" is and how cleverly it is employed to transfer a patient from one place to another. I enjoyed my role as medical assistant. Actually, I was almost a doctor way before I was a herring taster.* I'm sure I would have been a pretty good doctor, too, but I'm not sorry in the least that I'm not. I can stand the sight of blood (somebody else's), yet I have no patience at all for the sick unless they are close friends. I would have had a very small practice. As a herring taster I would have made a better living.

Before he contracted GBS, Joe used to be addicted to Stim-U-Dents, those soft toothpicks designed to massage the gums. Not a bad habit for one's dental hygiene, provided one confines their use to the privacy of one's bathroom. It was quite another matter and thoroughly obnoxious when that little orange stick of wood was seen hanging out of Heller's mouth all the time. Now in the hospital, Joe developed a new form of oral gratification. He used moistened toothbrushes to soothe his parched lips and a suction tube to remove the accumulation of phlegm from his throat. He often held one in each hand, like a scepter and orb. I guess he was glad to be able to do something for himself. That nasogastric tube must have been very uncomfortable, and I was entirely sympathetic to this particularly awful feature of an otherwise horrible circumstance. I would have hated it. Joe never complained. He continued to behave with the dignity of a king. He was bathed frequently and was always well groomed. His nurses helped him with urinals and bedpans. They transferred him constantly in order to change his linen. He accommodated himself to these procedures with an attitude that was beyond mere acceptance. In ICU, he had been cheerful. Now he was positively joyful, practically ecstatic. I suspected that Nurse Humphries might have had something to do with it.

---

* I volunteered my services as a taster to my friend Saul Zabar one day when he was incapacitated with a head cold. Saul, one of the three owners of Zabar's, the famous food store, found my taste to his and suggested regular employment. I was delighted. The hours were short and worked out well with my regular routine. We not only tasted herring; smoked sturgeon, salmon, and other delicacies, including the best caviars, had to be sampled, too. I've done many things in my life, but this was the best job I ever had.

Now, when I arrived with his mail and messages, Joe would ask me to "please" wet his toothbrush and hand it to him, so that he could apply it to his lips. He never failed to say "thank you" when I did. I could not help but compare his present manifestation to the pre-GBS Heller. In the old days, his favorite reply to any civil question, such as "How are things?" was a gruffly uttered: "What's it *your* business?" Now he gladly answered anyone with patience and consideration and his requests were always polite. Predictably, his friends Julius Green and one Speed Vogel, otherwise a couple of gentle types, had been heavily influenced by Joe. Now they adopted his old habit of saying rudely: "What's it *your* business?" to each other, a habit they find hard to break even now.

One day Valerie happened to tell Joe that she loved the Lone Star Café, was a fan of country-western music, and was crazy about Kinky Friedman and the Texas Jewboys. Nurse Humphries was astonished when he told her that I knew Mort Cooperman, the owner of the Lone Star, and that Kinky himself was a friend of mine and a fan of the author of *Catch-22* (not to mention his cameo appearance in *Good as Gold*). At that bit of news she was now really impressed with us and got, even for her, quite excited. Joe told me all about this when I arrived at the hospital during Valerie's lunch break. Heller asked me if I would, as a favor to him, take her to see Kinky at the Lone Star. I said I would be delighted to oblige. At this time, Joe was either playing it cool and didn't want us to know that he was romantically inclined toward his nurse, or perhaps the "lovebug" had not taken a bite yet. I still thought Valerie was a bit tall for me, but she was good-looking, and from what I remembered hearing about nurses from my older brother, the doctor, I thought it might be an interesting evening.

Val was thrilled when I suggested an evening out, and she accepted my invitation without hesitation. I called Kinky and told him I was planning to catch his act with Heller's nurse as my "plus one." Kinky was glad to hear that Joe was out of ICU and that I was coming. He said he would be sure to put me on the "hit list" (music talk meaning "no admission charge").

My friend Cheryl once did a story for *People* magazine about the famous Wyoming defense lawyer Gerry Spence, and he had given her his wonderfully aged Stetson as a souvenir. It was much too big for her and she generously passed it along to me. I was crazy about that hat. It had just the right number of stains and moth holes. But it gave me pause when a friend suggested that in New York City only real cowboys or assholes wear hats like that; I acknowledged the truth in what she said and tucked that Stetson away. However, I knew that Valerie would get a big kick out of it, and I was wearing the authentic ten-gallon number when I picked her up.

Actually, the evening turned out even better than I had expected. When I gave my name at the door, the hostess flashed me a smile of recognition and passed me through with a nice little flourish, while others had to queue up and pay. Nurse Humphries was impressed when we were hailed from the bandstand. "Here comes my good friend Speed Vogel, and with him is Joseph Heller's beautiful nurse, Valerie Humphries," Kinky said. I was astonished that Kinky remembered my message. He'd sounded hung over when I phoned.

Valerie had a fine time. She couldn't sit still. She twisted and bounced to the music, and laughed appreciatively at the outrageous ethnic jokes. Kinky even dedicated a song to her. When he finished his first set, he came to the table and chatted with us until it was time to go back to the stage. Even though Valerie had the early-morning shift, she wanted us to stay for the second set. By the time we left, I'd had one beer too many and was a little woozy—but, always the gentleman, I escorted Joe's nurse to her doorstep. She invited me in for a nightcap. It was now about 2 a.m. Valerie was wide awake and full of pep and I was winding down and getting sleepy. I managed to polish off a bourbon, then I picked up my raunchy Stetson and staggered into the night, the door slowly closing behind me.

The next morning, while I was still in my bed, peacefully

asleep, Valerie was entertaining Joe with a description of our evening. He was still giggling when I showed up with his mail and he thanked me for squiring his nurse for him.

Heller was not the only one overpraising me for self-sacrificing kindness. Many acquaintances and a few misguided friends were making that same mistake. I could hardly take my workouts at the gym without having somebody ask about Joe and remind me with moist eyes and imbecilic smiles what a wonderful friend I was to attend to him. Only Julie Green and Heller's impertinent nephew saw through my "selflessness" from the beginning. They knew how much I was putting myself out and how much I "suffered." As Paul said, "Speed isn't inconvenienced one bit. He was always hanging out with my Uncle Joe, only now he's hanging out with him in hospitals."

Kinky Friedman called several times after Valerie and I saw him at the Lone Star to ask about Joe's progress and to find out the best time to visit. I indicated that it might be better to wait until Joe was stronger. Kinky was understanding and said he'd keep in touch.

Just as Joe was getting used to his private room, I was well settled in his apartment on Eighth Avenue. After reading the *Times* and eating a leisurely breakfast, I would check Joe's mail, sort his bills and checks, answer his correspondence, make some calls, go to the bank, then continue by bicycle through Central Park to Mount Sinai. I always arrived in time for Joe's lunch—and mine. The hospital kitchen provided apples, various fruit juices, yogurt, and coffee for the patients. I managed with that. Valerie, however, could not. She had to have a real meal. After a bit of banter, she would excuse herself, slip into her coat, and leave, asking me to attend Heller in her absence, promising to return soon. She always did, even though I had no urgent need to leave and told her she could take all the time she wanted. I suspect she hurried back so as not to miss any fun we might be having, particularly if other visitors showed up while she was away.

My favorite mode of transportation is the bicycle. I stubbornly refuse to use anything else, regardless of the weather. One day in January it snowed heavily. The next day was warmer and the snow began to melt. Another weather change brought winds from the north, and the streets turned to ice. Dauntless, I hopped on my bike and started on my way to the hospital. By the time I reached Central Park, which was only about seven blocks, I realized that riding my bicycle under these conditions was pretty dumb. Yet I was determined to continue on my path to deliver the mail and a few other items Joe had asked for. The wind was against me and I was skidding all over the place. I was almost halfway there and reasoned that it would be silly to give up at that point. Fortunately, there was no other traffic in the park. (Nobody else was that stupid, but I just couldn't make my-self turn back.) When I finally reached the 103rd Street exit, a combination of deep snow, icy crusts, a steep downhill terrain, and heavy wind made my chances for survival minimal. The bike skidded out of control and shot out from under me. I landed on my skull. I saw stars. My first thought was of Joe. I could hear him say: "You schmuck! You don't even have major medical!" I had a headache but was only slightly bruised. The bike seat was twisted and the hand brake bent. Joe's coat, his good Eddie Bauer, was smudged. Otherwise, we were intact. I thanked the God that looks out for children, old people, and idiots, being glad that I qualified for all three categories.

Rubbing my head, I walked the bike the rest of the way to the hospital and locked it to a parking meter. I never told either Joe or Julie about this incident. I was too ashamed. In a way I was lucky. Yael, a friend of Valerie's who was working in the room next door to Joe's in Klingenstein, did not have my good fortune. On the same day that I escaped practically unscathed, she slipped on the ice coming to work and broke her hand. I was back on my bike in an hour, she was out of work for a month.

I was not the only one who appreciated Joe's change in venue. Julie Green and George Mandel liked it much better as a hang-out than the ICU and they began visiting frequently and staying longer. As Julie put it, "You know, it's not bad here. We could do worse." George claimed the atmosphere of Joe's private room was similar to the old SAC (Social and Athletic Club) in Coney Island, which would prompt him to ask, "Did I tell you guys how we always used to kick Joe's ass out of our clubhouse because he was still just a kid?" Green and I smiled at the picture of young Joey Heller being kicked out by George whenever he conjured it up, and it actually got a laugh from Valerie every time.

By this time, Valerie was so enchanted by Joe and his friends that we could have recited the phone book and it would have pleased her. She was obviously crazy about Julie, whom she called a "little munchkin," and it sometimes looked as if she was about to pick George up and hug him because he was "cuddly and cute." When Joe Stein joined the group and we horsed around with Heller in our customary fashion, Valerie behaved as though she had never heard anything like it. I guess it was bizarre hospital deportment, but her reaction to our antics was immoderate. She was having too much fun. There were, however, others who supported her view that Joe's room at Mount Sinai was the place to go for a good time. Joe's son, Ted, would phone first and ask who was around before he would commit for a visit that day. If Joe indicated that he was either alone or with people his son didn't find funny, Ted's response was, "Nah, I think I may go to a movie instead. Maybe tomorrow. Let me know who shows up. . . . Is Dustin coming again?" And Alan Altman, a very busy lawyer, came often and confessed, "It was not like visiting any other patient. It was sheer entertainment."

I TOLERATED THE TRANSFER well and was delivered to the room in good condition. Alert and oriented, judged Donna Mirabello, who was equipped to know. Several days a week she did double duty at the hospital, working the morning shift in surgery as a staff nurse and coming from there directly to a private case like mine. She would soon be married to a man she'd met as a fellow student at New York University, who was completing his training as an oral surgeon. Hers was a family history to evoke envy in many a contemporary parent and child, a background from which her common sense and solid commitment to purpose undoubtedly derive. The daughter of a retired New York City fireman who'd supplemented his income by doing television repair work in his spare time, she had two older brothers who'd been through Ivy League professional schools, one at Harvard, one at Columbia, one in medicine, the other in law. She was Italian and of less than medium height, with a family home in the Sheepshead Bay section of Brooklyn, which is not far from Coney Island. Much in her speech reminded me of Mario Puzo's, and much in her speech also reminded me of my own. Hearing of an extensive orthopedic surgical procedure in which she had assisted that morning with a child as a patient, I did not feel entitled to make great claim on her pity. I don't think I asked for much. But when she took at least one day off on each of my three weekends there, I was hurt and scared, and I resented it bitterly. I did not understand yet that she was working every day at her real job as a staff nurse in one of the operating rooms and that her optional employment was with me. If I *had* known that then, I *still* would have been hurt and scared and resented her bitterly.

Just about the first thing to affect me strongly when I looked about the private room was the absence of suctioning equipment. In intensive care, the unit had been built in. Here it was not. They told me none had been ordered. Would I need it? I sure as hell would. Donna did some talking and the omission was rectified quickly with the delivery of a small unit on wheels with a manual switch.

The second thing to impress me was the quality of character necessary for a good night nurse, the temperament to sit in endless patience from midnight to dawn without making a disturbing sound. With me it was Willie Mae Grasty, and she was there for all of the twenty-two nights I was. Donna introduced us shortly before twelve. They had worked before on successive shifts with the same patients.

Willie Mae Grasty was a sturdy black woman with a husband and grown children. She spoke gently and moved carefully, exuding a maternal watchfulness that was protective and commiserating. I was amazed: she spent that first night in a chair with her hands clasped in her lap beneath a dim lamp, never moving or making a noise unless I spoke first to ask for something. Then she responded alertly, always wide awake. What food she ate during her meal break she brought with her and consumed outside in the hall at the nurses' station. Probably, the hospital cafeteria was closed, and there were no all-night eating places in the neighborhood to which she would choose to go. She'd remind me I could press the call button and talk out loud through the intercom system installed in back of me above the headboard if I wanted her. She was seldom gone more than half an hour and I don't think I ever had to call her. I don't know how it came about, for her hours were such as to preclude contact with any of my friends, but she was soon spending part of each night reading signed copies of the novels of Edie Green, Julie's wife. Edie is a woman who one day decided she could write better novels than many of the poor ones she found herself reading, and she has since published more books than I have, under her full name of Edith Piñero Green. Willie Mae had ministered to sick people by the score, but she'd never, I believe, run into one who knew a woman who'd written books. She always reported for work early and did not keep Donna waiting. This was a courtesy extended by all three of my nurses to the others. She did not keep me waiting either. She was due at midnight and I could not see much point in even trying to go to sleep for the night before she arrived.

There really was little for a night nurse to do with me except to turn me from one side to the other every two hours, or sooner if I was uncomfortable and asked to be moved, and to provide relief for any specific need that arose. I was not in pain and my condition was stable. My only medication was an inoculation of the anticoagulant heparin, which was administered during the day in the flesh of one part of my waist or another; from about the first week on, I had been wearing elastic stockings, another measure taken to reduce the danger of blood clots. The formation of embolisms, which occurs most frequently in the legs, is an additional threat to anyone immobilized.

Our nightly routine hardly varied. As soon as she settled in I would ask for my Isocal, a concentrated solution of proteins and other nutrients I was taking on my own in my futile efforts to maintain my weight, along with whatever medicines I also chose for myself, all given me through the tube, of course. Soon I was taking the sedative chloral hydrate every night in the never-realized hope I might once sleep until morning. Unlike my experience with the Benadryl, the effects here were so subtle that I never could be positive there were any. (At Rusk, on my own initiative, but with the approval of Keiko Marchand, the Japanese nurse, I discontinued the chloral hydrate with no discernible change.) Then I would say good night and start out facing away from the small lamp, and she would not have much out of the ordinary to do until about six or six-thirty, when the hospital came astir.

Then Willie Mae and I would chat lazily awhile, most commonly about the cold room and the icy drafts coming in off the park through the loose-fitting panes, and then, with a sigh, I would say, "Okay. Let's go." And while I switched channels on the television set for the morning news, she would begin making me ready for the morning nurse. After the urinal once more, there would be the bed bath and back rub, a change of hospital gown and bedsheet, and then the range-of-motion exercises, movements by the nurse of the upper and lower extremities of the patient unable to move these limbs alone. These were done, I'd heard say, to avert "locked" or "frozen" joints and shrunken ligaments. At times I felt severe stiffness in my arms and shoulders during these exercises, so there could have been some truth in what I'd heard them say. I would squeeze out toothpaste and use the electric toothbrush, principally to massage my gums, although not for a couple of more months did I have the strength in my thumbs, even in both combined, to force in the button to turn the unit on and off. The switch on my electric shaver, which slid, was easier. Next, if we were early, I might ask for another can of Isocal or a glass of apple juice while I waited for the night to come officially to its end. Willie Mae would then slowly assemble her things, her coat and scarf and hat and gloves, and her novel by Edith Piñero Green. After writing her brief report, she would stand near the door until the morning nurse arrived and my day officially began, and then she would give me a cheery good-bye and leave to go home.

At midnight on my first day in this new setting, Donna told me as she was leaving, and Willie Mae nodded in accord, that I had a treat in store for me the next morning when I laid eyes on my day nurse. She spoke of Valerie as sexy, tall, and pretty, beautiful enough—and here I quote—"to be in one of those daytime television shows like *The Nurses.*" I had no idea what she meant by this last. But I do know the image invoked in my fancy by her depiction, and I also knew that neither Valerie nor any other woman on earth could measure up to it. When it comes to the visions of the male sexual imagination, or of *my* sexual imagination, the female flesh is weak. Besides, from the value Donna was attaching to height, I was already supposing that she was another one of these short women convinced that taller ones have an insurmountable advantage in the competitive arena of attractiveness. Women are not good judges of feminine beauty. They envy models, don't they? And unsurprisingly, it turned out that from Valerie's point of view, Donna, with her richer complexion and shorter, shapely figure, was blessed with a sultry allure she herself could not command.

From my point of view, which was the hospital bed, I saw a tall, rather slender-looking, dark-haired woman appear abruptly just before eight the next morning, dressed in a long down coat with a tubular collar still rolled up to cup a red-cheeked face. This woman who came hurrying in was wearing too much rouge, eye shadow, and lipstick for my taste, and she still does. (Lipstick gets on her front teeth, and I and Sydney Gruson are the ones who have to call that to her attention. And she is still giving me answers to questions I asked four years ago.) Only when she removed the coat and disclosed her uniform did it register upon me who she was.

"Hiyah, Valerie, welcome home," she remembers my calling out to her in boisterous greeting, surprising her. And she remembers feeling glad.

Nurses tend to evaluate patients as jobs: by the seriousness of their illnesses, their dispositions and personalities, their pain, visitors, relatives, the amount of medicines and urgent procedures and supervision required. By all of these standards, I was a saint, a dream come true, the answer to this kind of working girl's prayers. On just about that same day a nurse named Yael Herman went to work on the same floor for a Belgian who'd flown to

New York for the surgical removal of a cancerous section of his throat. He was in pain, needed injections of morphine and other medications on a fixed schedule, had fluid collecting in his trachea that had to be suctioned out almost hourly, was watched every minute the first few days by his wife or a nurse, and neither he nor his wife understood English. I was much better off. So was Valerie, compared to Yael; she was practically on vacation, apart from having to rise early. Valerie Humphries was in luck.

And so was I.

Joe Stein let me know she was a very kind person. Julie Green, after asking me her age and hearing I didn't know, informed me, "Never mind, you could do much worse." Sydney Gruson told me she was pretty, after glimpsing her but once for less than a minute at a moment when she was greatly flustered and anxious to get back to me in the room in which I lay, in order to complete an indelicate procedure to which a vain and tasteful man would be averse even to allude.

Then there were a number of other things about her that I was able to see for myself.

She was punctual in arrival and punctilious in performance. She took an inordinate pride in doing her work well, especially in her attendance to details. With me, this soon entailed seeing to it almost officiously that I did as much as I could for myself, an attitude, Speed could have told her, foretokening trouble. She would have me comb as much of my hair as I was able to reach before finishing the rest, and it was (and is) of importance to her that my hair be combed. The same was true of my electric shaver; with my elbows resting on a surface, I could get to much of the right side of my face but to hardly any of the left. Once, when we were already at Rusk, she sternly instructed the new nurse relieving her to make me eat as much of the regular dinner as I could before feeding me my blenderized meal, and neglected to add I might not be able to swallow any of it. The impasse that ensued as a consequence after Valerie had gone lasted close to half an hour and was all the more exasperating because the poor, blindly obedient woman understood little English and I was finding it infuriating and impossible to try to explain the distinction between what had been said and what had been meant, only that I should *try* eating the meal first. I might have been a saint, but I was not made of stone.

From conversations in the days, and weeks, and years that followed, I learned from Valerie that she had never been married, not even once or twice.

She remembered Pearl Bailey but not Pearl Harbor, which to my perspicacious intelligence put her age somewhere between thirty-five and fifty. She was a woman who kept busy: she took bridge lessons one evening a week, figure-skating lessons another, and she went to movies, plays, concerts. She was a person who, unfortunately, to my way of thinking, was interested in just about everything, with equal and nondiscriminating curiosity and enthusiasm. She could enjoy without inhibition things it was not fashionable to enjoy (e.g., the Mike Nichols production of *The Little Foxes,* the Elizabeth Taylor performance in the role of Regina). She liked Vivaldi and Handel's *Water Music Suite,* but that could be corrected. To her credit, she had fallen sound asleep the year before at a presentation of Handel's *Messiah,* which is no easy thing to do when the libretto is in the mother tongue of the auditor. On the other hand, she could hear operatic music for the first time and distinguish Beverly Sills from Joan Sutherland and both from Leontyne Price, Maria Callas, and Shirley Verrett, whereas I, who have listened to so much more and can hum just about all of the melodic lines of almost everything I've ever heard, can barely tell Frank Sinatra's voice from Mario Puzo's. She knew the names of champion golfers, figure skaters, real estate developers, tennis players, rock stars. For ten years or so, she had worked as a secretary, mostly in the offices of Union Carbide and Manhattan real estate firms, before deciding to have a crack at the more appealing occupation of nursing. Like Browning's "Last Duchess," she tends to like whatever she looks upon; she enjoys meeting people, and her reigning and repulsive vice is a warm predisposition to give almost everyone the benefit of the doubt. She is solicitous about her patients to an extent not entirely practical and remains on cordial terms with many of them long after the circumstances of their meeting have been resolved. Soon she would be calling the nurses' station one or two evenings a week or the room to speak to Donna if something about me had been left in doubt when she'd gone for the day. She liked reading British and American thrillers when she found herself with time to read and, almost incongruously, was enchanted with the legend of George Sand, whose works she'd not only collected but read.

"Never mind," I could remember Julie Green repeating, leaning back contentedly in my wheelchair and gazing out over Central Park with that kind of smile that comes with the introspective knowledge of having found one's proper niche in life, "you could do much worse." (He was not that contented in his own room in a different hospital in the spring of the year before, when he suffered his episode of coronary insufficiency while taking a stress test recommended by his physician to find out how good a condition he was in—he and his physician did not have to wait long for the results. But his room was not as colorful as mine and did not have an outside view. And I did not find him nearly as pleasant to visit as he found visiting me. As an altruistic alternative, I would escort his two children, who could take care of themselves at home but were too young to drive, to their house at the Fire Island beach on weekends, leaving to his wife the luxury of spending hours in his drab quarters making certain he did not slip away to the bathroom for a secret smoke, as both of them knew he had been doing for years, just as now they both know he will occasionally slip away for a whole glass of pure unadulterated cholesterol. Valerie was finding Julie Green, too, odd, intriguing, generous, and amusing.)

Valerie Humphries took horseback-riding lessons also with her younger sister two hours outside of New York, in a community misnamed Pleasant Valley, when she went to visit. God knows where she found the time or energy or zeal for so many lessons, or the money. (She is now being taught to knit by Rosalie Gwathmey, who is the wife of the artist Robert Gwathmey and the mother of Charles Gwathmey, the architect—all of these Gwathmeys have been friends of Speed's and mine for many years. On the island of Saint Croix, where we went for a month that first winter while I was still recuperating, she took sailing, windsurfing, and tennis lessons and was almost inconsolable because waterskiing had been temporarily discontinued.) When we met in the beginning of January, Valerie already had a share in a ski house in Vermont and had made plans to travel there that coming weekend. She recollects that I looked so stricken when she mentioned she might not be with me Saturday and Sunday that she knew almost at once she would have to change those plans.

That isn't exactly the way I remember it. But Valerie does not lie or dissemble, *yet,* and she didn't go to Vermont that weekend to that house in which she had rented a share. Or the next weekend. Like my night nurse, Mrs. Grasty, Valerie did not miss a day taking care of me during my entire stay. In fact, if the truth be told, Valerie never went back to that ski house again. She had skis that have not been used since and some nifty new ski outfits that have not been worn, and one of her fellow tenants saw to the return of her things to the city. In fact, if the truth be told, and she tells it still with a kind of incredulous amazement, she was having a much better time in the hospital, with a patient so different from most she usually could expect, whose visitors were so different from those she normally encountered, and different from each other.

I was always in good spirits on her shift, if you can believe what she wrote in her daily reports, and you can. That item appears every single day, and it was true, even on days when I was not in good spirits with anyone else because of emotional concerns or trying physical experiences. She was in good spirits too and began arriving for work earlier and earlier. She was impressed by my friends, by their number and variety and by the length of many of the friendships, and she was eager to know more about them. I knew all about them and was eager to learn more about her. Of course, I was in good spirits when she was on duty. Why wouldn't I be? By the end of that first week I already was flirting with her with all my might!

A very wise lady I'll never forget once tipped me off to something I have never forgotten: A man who can talk interestingly to a woman, she said, and especially who can make her laugh, she added, can win her heart.

God knows I talked plenty to Valerie and did my best to be interesting. Luckily, I could continue talking away to her a mile a minute even while she was feeding me my breakfast and lunch through the tube, and she could speak to me in turn. (My wise woman could also have added that it helps if the man is willing to listen, but I think that's implied.) Valerie, I was to discover, is a person inclined to refer to the day on which the championship game in the National Football League is played as "SuperSunday"; to be perfectly fair to her, she did that with me just once. She calls the woman Charles Windsor is married to Lady or Princess Di and tells me, or used to, of the things that go on in Di's life. She has an uncontrollable tendency to read aloud to anyone present from *The New York Times* items that are of special interest to her, even when that person to whom she is reading aloud has already been through the paper. (We were not exaggerating by much in that reference to me earlier as a saint.) And in the matter of holding her attention and making her laugh or smile, I had effortless and gratuitous support from many of the people coming to see me. Gregarious and jolly instinctively, she soon was displaying a rapt and warm affection for just about everyone she met there through me, and she still does.

The emergence of Kinky Friedman into our casual chatter was an unexpected stroke of fortune! I could not believe my ears when I heard her mention his name.* Here was this woman who could distinguish Placido Domingo from Luciano Pavarotti on

---

* I could not believe my ears the first time I heard *anyone* mention Kinky Friedman and his Texas Jewboys, now billing himself as Kinky Friedman, the Original Texas Jewboy. I'd learned of him first from Speed Vogel and a young woman in the record industry, Paula, with whom he was then, so to speak, keeping company. Immediately, I wrote him into a chapter of *Good as Gold,* citing him twice favorably in comments

first note saying without self-consciousness that one of her favorite night spots in the city was the Lone Star Café and that her favorite performer there was the country-western singer Kinky Friedman. Like a bolt from the blue came to me the idea for the first in a series of cunning actions ultimately constituting a plot both Mephistophelean and successful.

Another duty for Speed. By that time, as well I knew, Speed was on the friendliest terms with the owner of the Lone Star, Mort Cooperman, and with Kinky too, and I did not feel I was demanding too much of Speed to go out on a date with Valerie for me and take her there. And of course he did, that same or the next night.

It was easy to see right off when she reported for work the following morning that the effect upon her was precisely as calculated, a mood of thrilled elation, and one of gratitude too. Kinky, tipped off by Speed, had even dedicated that song to her and later had come over after his show and been flatteringly attentive. The effect upon me, as I listened to her excited report, was one of shocked perturbation. The specter of disillusionment arose when she repeated the opening lines of the song, "Old Ben Lucas," and proclaimed the song one of her favorites. The work goes this way: "Old Ben Lucas/Had a lot of mucus/Coming right out of his nose." I was appalled by this evidence of a sharp divergence in our respective tastes. That she found this funny was alarming. (I can't believe she prized it because it reminded her of me.) Surely, this was gross (and I am not), it was vulgar and insensitive, a steep falling off from that popular, spiritual work of Kinky's which I consider to be among his sparkling masterpieces: "They Ain't Making Jews Like Jesus Anymore."

But nobody's perfect, I had to tell myself, and cripples, as Speed and Julie Green reminded me often, can't be choosers. And the die had been cast; I had launched myself on a course of conduct too irresistible to forsake. A chance observation from

---

made by a former governor of Texas modeled on the real John Connally: once in a comparison with Gold ("Kinky's smarter, but I like you more") and once in a comparison with Henry Kissinger ("Had hair like Kinky's, but Kinky is smarter").

one or the other of us about the play *Amadeus* inspired me to ask Joe Stein to obtain two house seats for me to employ as a lure to keep Valerie in town the next weekend, and I was too much the sophisticate to probe into the identity of the person using the second one. I later charmed her again with two tickets to the Broadway production of *Othello* with James Earl Jones and Christopher Plummer. That too went over well. I was painting the town red, tripping the light fantastic. Kinky, Mozart, Shakespeare—with what could I equal them? Next came Tchaikovsky and *Swan Lake,* this time with her mother, Lillian. Lillian was coming into the city to see her daughter, who was now working too many days a week to make a filial visit to the suburbs. Valerie is familiar with the names of prima ballerinas too, and thinks as much of Natalia Makarova as she does of Donald Trump. Her eyes popped at my glittering invitation. Because her mother had never been to the Russian Tea Room, I recommended they dine there and saw to the reservation. Then, without a hint from this Lothario of what I had in mind, I arranged for the meal to be paid by me and for them to be told, only when they requested the check, that the dinner had already been taken care of by Mr. Heller. Let me tell you, I was wining and dining her royally while lying inanimately in my bed like a wilted weed. I had never thought it possible to make someone so happy without lifting a finger! Both of us were in very good spirits almost all of the time.

Sadly, it usually was a much different and less lively story most afternoons and evenings with Donna Mirabello, who, rather more quickly than I would have found credible, began to find me boring and said so bluntly and frequently, complaining mainly because I didn't even want to watch television. To accommodate her—after all, I was both gallant host and paternalistic employer—I tried. I put the set wholly at her disposal. I sat out of bed in my wheelchair—to which she and a pick-up gang of four or five other nurses from the floor had moved me on my "pull sheet"—and I let her select the programs. Whatever channel she wanted to watch I let her, and I even endeavored to watch along with her. If I could not connect at all with what was showing, I said nothing and tried continuing to read *Emma.* We failed at television together. There was just no pleasing her. When the truth at the core of the matter finally hit her, she gave up like a good loser, denouncing me wryly, "It's just no fun watching with you!" And she did not try again.

What was I to do? I wasn't ailing enough for either one of us to be dramatic to the other. The shortfall in this curiosity I sometimes have about other people is that it's usually quickly surfeited, and dramatic new facts do not accrue to any of us at a daily pace to make us more fascinating than the evening before.

There really was not ordinarily much for Donna to do for me each day in those last three or four hours at the end of her shift. Early each evening my dinner tray would come up. I would do the best I could with the soup and Jell-O or ice cream, while she, her eyes upon me in case I should start to choke, ground up the rest of the meal in the blender, liquefying all. This was a blender Speed had brought from the apartment he had furnished for me, where he was now living and entertaining his friends and some of mine, occasionally giving dinners, for this Paula he was dating was a superlative cook. In the private room the choice was between blenderizing the menu meals on our own or living on a liquid formula from the kitchen. I preferred the roughage, for all the good that was doing me. Soon after my feeding, Donna would leave for her dinner break, which was supposed to last one hour but often went on a few minutes more, never one minute less. One night she was ten minutes late returning and I was sufficiently distraught to criticize her, and she did not forgive me for that. Neither one of us understood that I did not want her to go at all, that I did not want to be without her, and that I certainly did not want to be alone. On the days she did not work she handpicked a very able and agreeable Filipino replacement named Tessie, but it was not the same. I felt abandoned without my Donna, as monotonously unexciting as we frequently found each other. If a visitor was there, which seldom happened at that hour, I was not so lonely when she was gone, but I watched the clock anyway, awaiting her return.

That was the worst part of each day for me, when Donna or her replacement went to dinner and there was no one with me. Talk about time crawling! It was already dark outside (in the daytime it was not that bad when Valerie left for lunch for there was a continual bustle of activity in the hall). As she prepared to go, we had to make sure that the call button was at hand, that the telephone was right down there with me at lap level or below once I could lift and hold the receiver, that the switch for the television set was in reach. Because I was alone, I did want to watch television. Ted, my son, had purchased for me a decent FM radio, but music did not suffice in that void. And on television all I could find worth watching was the news—and that was worth watching for only about three and a half minutes.

I was able to measure the progress of Donna's dinner hour by the passage of the evening news, those two thirty-minute programs, one of local news, the other covering the rest of the world, and each of them shortly after the beginning made me feel that she had been gone a quarter of a year. I was dismayed to discover that there is not even ten minutes' worth of authentic television news to be reported every twenty-four hours, and a good portion of that has to do with fires, record colds and snowfalls, gruesome homicides, and plane crashes that could have been excerpted from the newscasts of the week before. In the absence of official scandal or national catastrophe (mere national tragedy is no longer enough), there is just about nothing visually absorbing ever going on in any government anywhere, and I cannot think of a duller group of people than those prominent in our own government when they are going about the business of government, until they've been found out in a scandal or caught up in a national catastrophe. Even the newspapers have a tough time breathing life into these bureaucratic automatons, who are so much alike from one administration into the next. It may be that these people attracted to public service are no duller in their occupations than are the rest of us in ours, but the work of the rest of us is not the lifeblood of daily news reporting. And then there are those previews on one newscast of the headline stories to be featured on a later one! There are worse things to being hospitalized than having nothing better to do than watch a television show you'd rather be dead than subjected to any longer, but it was sometimes hard to keep that in mind as I switched in increasing wrath from one newscast to the other without relief and finally turned the damned thing off. And then I would turn it back on. Oh, how I blamed Donna! Or finally, perversely, I would roll over to my back and give up, knowing I would have to remain there like an upset turtle until Donna reappeared.

Each time she left for dinner, I was filled with forebodings that she would not return. This was grist for the mill of Dr. Peck, but on the tenth day after my transfer, neither he nor I could see any need for continued psychiatric consultation. Besides, Dr. Peck was leaving for a week, and we both expected I would be going to Rusk a few days after that. And even I could tell that this reaction of mine to Donna's going out to dinner for an hour was a reverberation of something remote that was not of crucial importance to unravel at that time.

Once she was back, we joked and talked a bit of this and that when we could think of something new to say, easing jointly into a kind of uneventful domestic tranquillity as we waited for the rest of the evening to pass. Rarely would a doctor drop by that late unless sent for. As much for sport and variety as for anything else, I would ask to be moved out of bed again. With Donna and four or five other people transferring me on a bedsheet, and with me in a hospital gown unfurling everywhere, and with one of them reminding another to take hold of my head, the wisecracks and puns were ribald and obvious. At about ten-thirty she would give me through the tube the dose of chloral hydrate that might or might not help me to go to sleep after Willie Mae was on the scene to relieve her. And that was about it. Is it any wonder that Donna found me boring as a patient and often joked with me about that and other things? (My urine, which was measured and looked at, was invariably described in the nurses' reports as amber and clear. I was voiding in gargantuan floods of five and six hundred cubic centimeters because of the huge volume of blenderized food and other liquids I consumed. One day after I had voided a record 700 cc and she was holding the container up to the light, I asked how it looked. "Beautiful," she answered. "You ought to bottle it and get rich selling it as souvenirs. You could call it *Good as Gold.*" I indeed was lucky in the selection of my nurses.)

When visitors came with whom Donna was already familiar, she fit right into the friendly social atmosphere. With others, she could sense that the conversation was going to be of a personal quality and tactfully withdrew. There were a number of very private conversations with Barbara Gelb; we had lived for years in the same apartment building and the friendship of the adults in both families had been close.

Sydney Gruson stopped by the first time on one of the darkest and coldest nights of one of the darkest and coldest winters; I made him a facetious apology for canceling my plans to come to his house for dinner the Wednesday after the Sunday I'd gone into the hospital. Morty Bader looked in while he was there. I felt proud of myself introducing them, for each had heard of the other. Sydney knew of Morty and Richie Bader as identical twins *and* excellent physicians (with the Baders as family doctors, you have the economic edge of getting two opinions for the price of one, although the two opinions you get tend to be identical opinions); and Morty instantly recognized Sydney by name as the former foreign correspondent, former foreign editor, and current vice-chairman of *The New York Times.*

I had a visit at night from Stanley Cohen, a boy from the Bronx who is licensed to live and to practice law in France, as well as in New York. He came with his best friend and wife, Toby, and with the encouraging rumor of a person he knew of who'd gone into the hospital with Guillain-Barré six months before and was already back at work with no observable indications of aftereffects. I wondered why both of them looked so very sad.

(I know now that I was continuing to lose weight at that same rapid rate, and by then, of course, my glowing suntan had all but vanished. People seeing me for the first time were no longer telling me how good I looked.)

Stanley mentioned that a friend of mine, Marvin Green, would come by after work the following day; indirectly, Marvin and he had met through me, and now they occasionally came together on business matters about which I myself knew practically nothing.

I was already troubled by coughing when Marvin arrived the next evening. My old friend Marvin Green was now the president and major stockholder of the company called Reeves Communications. He and I had met back in about 1955, when I was a copywriter at *Time* magazine doing texts for slide shows intended to aid the advertising-space salesman in bringing in more advertising revenue, and he was the salesman for a small visual-arts company called Visualscope, which hoped to do the artwork for these shows and to provide the projection equipment and services as well. I was already writing *Catch-22.* Not many years after the novel was published, which was in 1961, Marvin was a partner in Visualscope and soon after that, the owner. Then Visualscope acquired Reeves Communications, and Marvin was still the boss.

He is a large man with a hearty appetite and can put on a gigantic amount of weight easily. Marvin is a Protestant with austere forebears. His great-grandfather, a Christian Scientist, had made millions back when a million was more than a million, out of the Conestoga wagon, and had left almost all of his money to the church. His grandfather, having accumulated a personal fortune entirely on his own, made the same bequest, and his father, who in turn had amassed *his* millions, had made known his determination to preserve that tradition, each directing an opulent inheritance away from his descendants to the church as a matter of moral and religious conviction. Enough money for a house and a college education for each child had been the inflexible rule. (It is my chilling nightmare that Marvin might employ the same ascetic discipline with his own children—and leave nothing to them or to me. I do not have his puritanical principles and I've told him he need endure no remorse that his money would weaken *my* character.)

We had much to chew the fat about. It was clear from his face that he was upset by my appearance. He wore a black overcoat, and I remember he didn't take it off. He too had not been sick since childhood, he confided solemnly when I reviewed my excellent medical history as a contrast to the suddenness of the change. Marvin was the first person I'd ever met who had a love of sailing. (I have gone sailing several times since I first met him and the only drearier day I've ever spent at sea was the one I went fishing.) I chided him on a goal he'd once expressed, to have a million dollars before he was thirty-five, cease work, and spend the rest of his life on a sailboat with those members of his family who wanted to live that way with him. Now he was much past thirty-five and worth more than one million, and he was spending as much time at business as ever. He was a failure, I kidded him between my seizures of coughing, while I was the success.

The night he was there, the fits of coughing I had begun to suffer would last a minute or two, and we would have to pause, because I could not talk or pay attention to what was said. He was with me an hour and we covered much ground, speaking casually and rationally about our children, work, attitudes, plans, and all other things that came to mind, and Marvin grew convinced that I had taken leave of all my senses. He told that to Stanley Cohen the very next day in a voice shaking with emotion Marvin does not often display. There I was, so obviously close to death, and I lay in my bed babbling away idiotically with him about people like Steve DeClerque and others we'd known at *Time* so far back, as though I could not see a thing was wrong! (He thought I was crazy, he thought I was dying, nevertheless he lent me twelve and a half thousand dollars and offered more. Now which one of us would *you* say is crazy?)

The coughing would begin very late in the afternoon or early in the evening and, growing worse for three consecutive days, last past midnight, with Donna departing and Willie Mae staring at me mournfully until I conked out from sheer exhaustion finally. It would not bother me when I awoke during the night, and there would be no remnants of it in the morning or sooner than late in the afternoon of the next day. Go figure. It was not related to the secretions I was suctioning; I was using daily something called a nebulizer, inhaling deeply medicinal steam produced in clouds inside a rubber mask fitted tightly across my face, and my lungs were clear. I had no fever. Valerie would telephone once or twice each evening and receive the grievous news that I was coughing again. If there was a remedy, it was not deemed vital I be given it. The only trick that did seem to help was one I devised myself: the bed lowered fully and the pillows removed, my head and throat on a level no higher than the rest of me. But the relief, if it came at all, was dilatory in arriving and only temporary, and the method was not successful every time. I can remember Joe and Elisa Stein looking down at me a long time with expressions of woe and sympathy. I couldn't talk and I couldn't listen, and I thanked them for coming and sent them away.

Per Gedin, my publisher in Stockholm, flew into New York on his annual scouting trip for new American manuscripts he liked by people he liked. (Per maintains he can determine an author's character and personality from his writing and that he will not publish a work by someone whose company he feels he would not enjoy immensely. He could have guessed wrong about that when he published Alexander Solzhenitsyn.) The high regard in which my books are held in Sweden is due more to him than to any other man—even me. When he came to the Swedish firm of Wahlstrom & Widstand many years ago as manager and partner, *Catch-22* had been published, enjoyed a noble, small success, and was out of print. Per reissued the work with the energetic zest and fanfare that characterizes most of his actions, and the book has been a lively commodity there in at least two editions since (paperback, book club, regular, what have you), paving the way for the generally successful reception of my later novels in that country.

Having learned where I was and why, he phoned first and came to see me at dusk of the day my coughing was worst. He told me a year later of the mournful dread he'd had to overcome in order to force himself to step into my room. I could well imagine him cowering at the doorjamb, for I know how sensitive and sentimental a human he is. And I know how I would have felt about him had our positions been reversed. He is one of the dearest people I know in the world. He knows I feel that way about him.

Each year on his trip to New York, there would traditionally be at least one long and late dinner at a good restaurant with lots of whiskey and wine for which he would pay. On the day of his departure, we would again meet as a tradition for a leisurely lunch at the Russian Tea Room, for which I would pay, and we would sit when finished and continue sipping vodka until it was time for him to hurry away to the hotel for his luggage and a cab to the airport. This year we were not going to do that. Here is a measure of the generosity and gracious imagination of the man, the manner of his gift to me two years before of the sheepskin coat he was wearing for which I had paid him a compliment: when leaving the restaurant, he simply handed his coat check to the employee at the door with directions that it be given to me fifteen minutes after he had gone. And that's how I found out that Per Gedin had given me the sheepskin coat off his back.

He is, even at his jolliest, a man of many nervous mannerisms. Now he was more fidgety than ever and he looked, even while attempting to smile, as though he were going to cry. I lay on my back with the bed lowered. The wind was blowing in gusts and a heavy wet snow was falling, as though the shadowy atmosphere in the room were not melancholy enough. Outside the window the twilight sky was already turning black. I don't think I was able to stop coughing for as long as thirty seconds. I allowed him to stay only until I felt the obligations of hospitality had been satisfied—he had made the trip through a snowfall, after all—and then I waved him away and commanded him to do me a big favor and leave, telling him I couldn't stand seeing him look that way and that I was well aware there were places in the city where he could be having a much better time than he was having with me. We both felt easier when he rose to go.

So affected was Per by this meeting that he went back home with the report to friends of ours in publishing in Copenhagen and Oslo that I was close to death and would certainly be crippled for life if I was unlucky enough to survive.

When Per was back in New York the following winter, we returned in a way to our old routine, with Valerie along to help me on with my sheepskin coat and because I knew that Per *would* enjoy *her* company immensely.

What in the world had possessed him the year before to make him so pessimistic? I joked. Wasn't it obvious I was going to make a full recovery? Hadn't I told him that?

I know it was one of the things I hastened compulsively to repeat to everybody. And here is another one for the book: I did not feel any more the invalid because of the coughing, felt nothing different from the extreme annoyance and frustration that a normal person with a bad cold and a bronchial cough would feel and deplore. I did not associate it with sickness. And here's one thing more: I never once throughout the entire experience thought of myself as weak, which to my mind always meant sleepy, lethargic, not strong. I was paralyzed, not weak. And in truth, *I* wasn't weak. My *muscles* were weak. *I* felt just fine during the day, with as much mental energy and playful zest as ever. It was the rest of me that was lousy and lying down on the job.

For Donna and me there was not much room for tedium the three or four evenings the coughing went on. I have no memory of what she did for her dinner hour. (It's hard to believe she would leave me alone in that state for her dinner breaks; it's even harder to believe she would give them up!) Here is how she wrote of what I complained of that last and worst night, at 10:00 p.m.:

> c/o irritation in throat, coughing from $4^{\underline{pm}}$ on without relief. Dr. Bader's office called at $6^{\underline{pm}}$. On call Dr. returned call at $7^{\underline{30}}$. Ordered NG tube to be removed and reinserted in AM if necessary. Dr. Cohen, med. resident, came up to see pt. at $8^{\underline{pm}}$. Tested gag reflex. Tube to be removed after pt. received sleeping medication and hydrated with fluid. Valium at $9^{\underline{pm}}$ for anxiety.

Sleep medication was given at 10:45 p.m., she recorded later, along with 500 cc of apple juice, all of it through the NG tube, which was then removed. The removal of the tube was "tolerated well." The tube is long and limp, about eighteen inches, I'd say, and mine was coated on much of its middle with globs of clotted, discolored mucus, which I suppose is what we think of as phlegm.

In between the phone calls and the removal of the tube, Donna was busy at "$5^{\underline{pm}}$" and again at "$8^{\underline{30}}$ PM" with a problem unrelated to this main one, to my complaining of a "need to defecate" that I was unable to relieve. The record is brief but as explicit as we'd want it: "No BM 3 day. Received glycerine supp. $5^{\underline{pm}}$ without results. Fleet enema $8^{\underline{30}}$ PM with poor results." I am speaking metaphorically when I tell you I had my hands full. I am speaking literally if I say the same about Donna. At 11:10 my temperature was 100.1 degrees, orally, and Dr. Cohen, the resident, was notified. He returned to take a blood culture and to examine me for evidences of infection.

The blood tests all were negative, my neck was supple, my chest was clear. From midnight on, with Willie Mae Grasty doing the reporting, and with the tube out, I suffered no further from coughing and there was no excessive need for suctioning. At 2:00 a.m. my temperature was down to 98.9, at 4:00 a.m. to 98.3, and at 7:30 a.m., it was back to a gorgeously normal 98.6, in time, mercifully, for Valerie Humphries's arrival less than thirty minutes later. But . . . no BM. Willie Mae wondered in her report if my "elevation in temperature could have resulted from excessive coughing and any anxiety that caused." Inasmuch as the tests were negative, her guess was as good as any. Certainly, I was not a victim of neglect that night, by nurses, doctors, or hospital.

In the morning, the NG tube was replaced by a doctor associated with the Baders, so swiftly and adeptly that there was scarcely a moment of more than mild discomfort. (Nevertheless, I did not want to go through that again if I could avoid it, and I was spared the necessity at Rusk by Speed's deft application of a needle and thread when the cap of the one I had was accidentally torn off.) There was no more coughing.

Every morning now after feeding me my breakfast and sprucing me up for company, Valerie would produce a tray of semisolid foods from somewhere for me to experiment with as I sat in my wheelchair. A piece of banana proved the easiest consistently; soon, with Valerie urging me onward, I could manage a boiled egg if it was very soft (and with salt, it was as delicious to me as anything in the world I had ever tasted). Cooked the least little too long, bits would adhere like gravel at the rear of my palate and on the rear of my tongue, and I was lacking the power and the know-how to deliver them to whatever muscle group farther back would normally carry them down into the esophagus and allow gravity to take over and do something good for a change—were it not for those damned secretions thickening and rising to prohibit an easier passage, and the flow of these secretions often seemed to be stimulated by the flavor of the food itself, even of baby food. I would use the suction tube to clear these bits away in order to try again with a very small part of another spoonful.

One morning, Dr. Sencer, who often was as discontented as I was, grew so enraged with these secretions that he took hold of me by the shoulders, dangled me upside down over the side of the bed, and shook me roughly, pounding my back with the flat of his hand. This, I learned later, goes into the books as postural drainage; "a small amount of thick dark phlegm was expectorated" with the rest and this violent approach did the trick—until the next time I tried to eat. Jell-O and ice cream were easy too, but nothing was predictable, and there were no guarantees from one time to the next. Clear liquids were the hardest—well, they were liquid and they spilled and flowed all over my mouth, were impossible to retain in one position long enough for me to swallow them.

Because it was taken for granted I'd be going on to Rusk, a general feeling set in that I was merely marking time while waiting to transfer from a place in which I had been sick to one in which I would smoothly recover fully. Day-to-day developments were no longer individually significant, except for episodes like the coughing. And except for my difficulty with swallowing, which suddenly became of tremendous importance when it unexpectedly endangered the transfer to Rusk to which I now was so much looking forward.

Grace Neil, a social worker at the hospital, was processing the application, my physical therapist, Ellen, who had trained at Rusk, was following it up with people she knew there, and an orientation booklet had arrived that was turned over to Speed. There were things to be bought and money to be advanced. From the start there was a certain amount of administrative confusion. For example, it proved impossible to learn how much of the cost, if any, Blue Cross would pay; and I could not find out for sure until presented with my first monthly bill. (For those of you who follow in my footsteps, I will tell you now that a Blue Cross policy like mine will pay for half of only one month of care in a rehabilitation hospital that does not also meet the criteria for a medical one, and Rusk does not.)

My physical therapy sessions with Ellen continued every weekday, with Valerie watching avidly in order to learn to administer some of these same exercises herself. By now, with Speed writing out checks for so many new things, I began to wonder who was paying for the physical therapy. It turned out that Blue Cross was paying the hospital for Ellen's services but that I was paying for the periodic bedside evaluations by her superior, a physiatrist overseeing all of the rehabilitation work at the hospital. (Who knows why?) I learned from Ellen that it required only one person with a knowledge of the techniques of lifting to transfer me to the wheelchair or even to hoist me onto my feet, and that I was able to stand by myself with my knees locked, and even move forward and backward a few inches, for as long as five minutes without tiring. However, we ordinarily stand with our knees not locked but at least a little bit flexed, which means that the involved muscles (quadriceps) are working all the time, and my quadriceps were not working at all. So I also learned I would fall like a boulder if my knees buckled, and we were very careful after the first time we found that out.

Every daily report of Ellen's spoke of improvements. And of course I was improving and everybody who was with me much could see it. People like Sydney Gruson and Toby Cohen would be rendered almost speechless by the drastic change in appearance they saw the first time they came. But my regulars, I began to feel, were paying less and less attention, and they were utilizing my hospital room as a convenient meeting place evenings and weekends, as a hangout, and me as a justification for spending time in this home-away-from-home instead of in the homes to which they belonged. At times they would stay longer than I wanted anyone to, and I would pretend to be sleepy, wishing they would take the hint and go, because I *was* sleepy.

"Hey, I think he's sleeping," I can remember hearing Joe Stein warning in a hushed voice one time when I lay there faking it. "Maybe we'd better go."

"Nah," George Mandel answered him with authority. "Don't worry. If he wants to sleep, he'll sleep. Yesterday he dropped off right while I was telling him a story. We won't bother him."

And Julie Green had a theory about my swallowing that he kept reiterating from his favorite place—my wheelchair (a choice of perch that did not fail to horrify Valerie, who is tensely superstitious about illness and prayed he was not jinxing himself): "Never mind, listen to me, do you hear? If they want you to swallow, better get them to bring you a good soy sauce chicken from Chinatown—you'll see—or something good from an Italian restaurant. Why would anyone want to swallow that stuff they're giving you?" (And it could be that he was on to something, for only when my daughter, Erica, arrived at Rusk one evening with a meatball in a container of sauce from an Italian restaurant did the swallowing instincts that babies are born with all return in a rush and begin working in concert. I did not have to try to remember *how* to do it. I *was* doing it.)

There was no doubt that my motor abilities were gradually returning. The increments of gain were minuscule, but the effects were cumulative, and I was doing things I had not been able to. By now I could hold the telephone without trouble, even lift it (flexing my biceps) if the unit had been placed below shoulder level and I did not have to rely on my shoulder muscles (deltoids). Among the first people I telephoned were my brother and my sister, to prove to each of them that I really was still alive and to display how hardy I sounded. Had I a clue of how awful I sounded I would have delayed another month or two. I sounded pathetic and barely intelligible, but people were too charitable to tell me—then. I began to catch on as the weeks passed and everybody I spoke to on the telephone exclaimed in a cry of delight how much better I sounded than the time before. In my own ears my voice sounded no different, the timbre no more resonant, the elocution no more Shakespearean, than it ever had.

And I was, now and then, able to swallow food, mincingly, those soft foods I've mentioned, although not as much or as many as my doctors hoped I would. From what Dr. Sencer could observe, he was convinced that I ought to be doing more (and I am convinced he felt this way at least in part because he wished strongly for it to be so. He wanted a full recovery right then and there—God dammit—while I was still under his supervision. To hell with Rusk!). My palate was moving, my posterior wall was moving, my pharyngeal constrictors were starting to come around—what more did I need? I was getting the impression from him at times that he was impatiently dissatisfied with me and just about fed up with my secretions and with every muscle group in my mouth.

There was an evening when, with Donna Mirabello as witness, I put away a whole bowl of wonton soup (American style, from the hospital kitchen) with such incredible dispatch that I swept confidently on to the roast chicken and succeeded in downing "a small amount." Donna grinned with surprise and approval. I boasted about this to Valerie in the morning and called with gusto for a full breakfast tray. And found I was able to eat almost none of it. I did no better with lunch. Into the blender both meals went, and "NGT feedings still continued." What I had not pondered before (and you haven't, either, I'll bet and win from almost every one of you) is that the tongue is a muscle, and that even the lips and cheeks and those several other things inside the face that are employed in eating are also muscles; and just like my deltoids, quadriceps, latissimus dorsi, and my adductors, abductors, and hip flexors, these muscles of mine too could easily be rendered paretic by fatigue and by the failure of my nerve cells to supply adequate innervation. (I'm still a long way from successful in trying to chart in my mind the sequence of all those motions busily performed by the healthy tongue in the actions of chewing and swallowing. You try. Try also with your cheeks, because whatever it is they do, mine still do not. Food will collect on the outside of my teeth and I sneakily have to maneuver it back inside them with my fingers by cupping my jaw in my hand while feigning deep thought. The lips prevent the mess in the mouth from dribbling. Much of this will be familiar to people related to other people who've suffered a stroke.)

At the suggestion of Dr. Sencer, one of my Dr. Baders arranged a consultation with an ear, nose, and throat specialist, Dr. Max Som. (It could be that my doctors were already aware of ominous rumblings of resistance at Rusk, of which I was not yet cognizant.) Dr. Som came in the evening directly from surgery, accompanied by a younger man also accoutred dramatically in green surgical cap, shirt, and billowy pants, to whom he pointed out and dictated his observations. There was a moment in which I feared they had dressed that way to work on me. Because of the surgical garb, I had a distorted image of what Dr. Som looked like and did not recognize him when he stopped in several days later just to say hello when less hurried and to see how I was progressing. Dr. Som is eminent in his field, and he spent almost an hour with me. I felt like a charity patient when the bill he sent was less than half of what I had estimated.

I forget who else was in the room with us during the examination. Dr. Som, I suppose, went as deeply into my throat as it is possible to go into a throat that is not anesthetized. And his very first words to the man assisting him brought a wave of relief.

"There are fibrillations of the tongue." And to me he explained, "That means your tongue is weak. I can see it trembling all around."

He was saying I wasn't nuts—I confess I overstate: He was saying that, aside from other contributing possibilities that could have signified I *was* nuts, there were substantial physical reasons for my inability to swallow. My uvula and vocal cords were moving well, his report went on, I was not to be started on fluids yet, "the outlook for recovery from G-B syndrome was good, the swallowing should improve gradually and return in time."

The problem springing up to confront me suddenly was that I had no time. Without warning there came the shattering news—erroneous, as it luckily turned out—that the Rusk Institute would under no circumstances accept me until I was able to swallow food and liquids, to take my meals without placing extraordinary demands upon a staff already overburdened with the care of patients who were all wholly or partly immobilized by a wide, grim spectrum of injuries and diseases.

I don't believe I had ever seen Mortimer Bader (or was it Richard?) look more glum than when, with Grace Neil at his shoulder, looking equally downcast, he told me that Rusk was not going to admit me until I could do without the NG tube. I was stunned, but probably I endeavored to conceal my feelings behind a mask of worldly fatalism. (I wonder how I really looked to both of them.) I remember predicting almost dispassionately that we were talking about weeks or months. But all the emotions I secretly felt crystallized into the single, unspoken question: Where could I go? Glancing back now, I am moved almost to tears. But I do not believe I felt that way at the time. Instead, I think I fortified myself with that kind of resignation which I imagine overcomes certain other small animals just before, when finding themselves cornered, they give up.

My grief was compounded by the unrealistic dream that only at Rusk would I truly start to get better and that any delay in arriving there would mean a much longer postponement of that state of full recovery in which I would not be physically dependent on anyone anymore. And once again—where could I go?

I could not remain much longer at Mount Sinai: I was quadriparetic, as they call it, practically an emaciated basket case almost six feet long when it came to moving myself, but I was no longer ill. Apart from paralysis, I was healthy as a horse. And I could not face with poise the outlook of returning in so disabled a condition to that small, new apartment on Eighth Avenue and Fifty-third Street, where, even with nurses, I was convinced I would perish rapidly from the combined miseries of loneliness, inactivity, and self-pity. The apartment was close to ideal for Speed Vogel in his circumstances—there was almost enough closet and shelf space for his extensive and colorful wardrobe, and there was sufficient floor space in the living room for even his bicycle. But it was far from appropriate for me. This setback in plans would have left me helplessly devastated had the requirement imposed by Rusk proved impossible to overcome.

Rusk was also reluctant to accept anyone with medical problems that could not be treated by the physiatrists by whom that rehabilitation facility was mainly staffed.

The compromise resolving that dreadful, late-hour crisis was worked out assiduously by both my Dr. Baders and the supremely capable social workers at Mount Sinai. It took yeoman's service on the telephone by Grace Neil to persuade whomever she spoke to in the admitting office that the tube feedings were not complicated or a cause of complications and did not take all that long to administer by my private nurses. It required perseverance by the Baders' office to drive home the fact that I now was sound medically—as it turned out, I proved to be one of the very few patients on a floor of fifty or sixty at Rusk who did not once require a catheter. And it took ingenuity as well to arrange for an internist they knew at the New York University Medical Center, of which the Howard A. Rusk Institute of Rehabilitation Medicine is a part, to keep track of my medical condition, which was good and has remained good to this day. In the end, I was admitted to Rusk with the stipulation that I retain private-duty nurses for as long as my need for tube feedings persisted.

But not until the very end of the week were there promising indications of a possible change of mind. And not until Monday, the day before I'd been originally scheduled to move, was my admission validated, and was Mrs. G. Neil, CSW, able to enter in the record:

> Social Service: Per tel. discussion w. Dr. M. Bader, bed is provided at Rusk for Mr. Heller. Arrangements have been completed for Keefe & Keefe [ambulance] . . . to transfer Mr. Heller at 11 a.m. Tues. 01/26/82. He will be accompanied by his private duty RN. Patient's morale is greatly improved knowing he can go to Rusk w. definite date set. There is some appropriate anxiety w. determination to do well.

And along with the anxiety there were separation blues, strong mixed feelings about leaving Mount Sinai, which struck me ironically as analogous to the widespread ambivalence of children leaving home. (Most people I've met who have a penchant for reminiscing about their childhoods are looking back on unhappy ones.) You would have thought I'd had a good time there! And the boys seemed moody too at the impending loss of so convenient a club room. "You know, it's not bad here," Julie Green would say again and again, each time as though in fresh discovery. Clearly, as if only yesterday, I can remember him leaning back in my wheelchair early in that week before the uncertainty about my going to Rusk arose, clasping his hands behind his head and saying to the others, with his tiny crooked smile and wistful voice: "What are we going to do for laughs when he gets out of this hospital?"

His candid question touched more than one nerve in Miss Valerie Humphries, who was not yet quite used to him and who was thoroughly outraged by the callous disrespect of a remark so entirely hostile to all her experience, but she kept her anger to herself. By the next morning her indignation had turned into something different. She was more than a little subdued at the beginning of the day, not in her usual good spirits, but patently dejected. She soon told me why.

"Yesterday, when your friend in the wheelchair, George, or what's his name—Joe Stein?"

"Julie Green?"

"Yes. When I heard him say what he did, 'What are we going to do for laughs' when you get out of the hospital, I couldn't believe it. I thought it was the most heartless thing I'd ever heard anyone say. I really wanted to tell him off. Then last night, when I was in my apartment, I began to wonder about me. And I asked myself, 'What am I going to do for laughs when you leave?' "

I was touched and I was pleased. And all the more so when she went on to admit that she'd never had so good a time in a hospital as she'd had with us and did not know when she'd have so much fun in one again.

Well, touched and pleased though I was, I could not guarantee her another patient like me, I had to confess modestly. I'd already asked her to make the trip with me to Rusk in the ambulance, promising her a full day's pay if she would agree. She was offended I'd even had doubt, and she rejected my offer of money, saying she'd make up her day's pay by working the afternoon shift.

Now, of course, with this condition imposed upon me by Rusk, I *could* guarantee her a patient *exactly* like me, if she wanted to register there and continue working for me. As you know, she said yes: the hospital was much closer to her apartment.

Just one problem remained that loomed in my turbulent fantasy as a threat to upset everything at the last, as precisely that kind of medical malfunction to make me an untouchable for Rusk. Glycerin and Dulcolax suppositories hadn't worked. Neither Fleet, mineral oil, nor tap water enemas had produced "good results." Castor oil had been given without "good results." For seven days there had been *no* results. (A cruder man might write I was full of shit.) My abdomen was so distended now that I could not sit up in the bed or chair to eat or be sat up for exercise.

What produced good results finally was a young and good-looking gastroenterologist named Dan Present, who came on the eve of the day I was to go. "No wonder," he said in less than a minute after hearing my descriptions, which by then included painful rectal contractions occurring like clockwork every several minutes for the past day and a half. "It's as hard as cast iron." His account in the record of his diagnosis and remedy is a miracle of succinct narration:

Dx. Impaction.
Disimpacted.

Dr. Present returned the next morning to finish the job. By then Julie Green had brought back to me the clothing he'd taken away that first Sunday at the hospital six weeks earlier. (It remains astounding to all of us that only six weeks had elapsed, only three weeks and one day in each of the two places, which seems not that much of a molehill out of which to try to make a magic mountain.) Valerie dressed me, and we were ready to go when the ambulance arrived.

THAT WAS JANUARY 26. Joe had given me the orientation booklet for Rusk, which contained a complete list of clothing requirements—things like shirts, slacks, warm-up suits, socks, underwear, and slippers. A bargain store on Broadway close to his apartment proved the perfect place for filling those needs. Robes and pajamas were articles of clothing he'd never worn before, and I expected he would throw them out just as soon as he left Rusk.

There wasn't enough time to sew in the name tapes that Rusk recommended, but assembling everything and packing his suitcase was fun, like sending one of my kids to camp. I had it all ready and waiting in his room long before the ambulance arrived to collect him.

I was sure he would take this transfer well. He was certainly looking forward to the move. We, his friends, were nervous. We were afraid the atmosphere might not be as congenial for us as that of his room at Mount Sinai had been. When Joe arrived at Rusk, Valerie called to give me his new room number and I biked over to check it out.

All in all, it was okay. The view was not Central Park, and the hospital was not exactly cheerful, but there was a convenient coffee shop and the cafeteria was better than Mount Sinai's. I figured we would tolerate the transfer well. On Thirty-fourth Street and First Avenue, we were much closer to Chinatown.

I noticed almost every patient was in some type of wheelchair. Some were pushed, others pushed themselves. I saw two kinds of self-propelled, motorized wheelchairs. One was hand-controlled, the other seemed to move mysteriously. I found out it was breath-operated, designed for quadriplegics.

I saw one very large L-shaped room for physical therapy that looked like a typical gym with rowing machines, bicycles, parallel bars, slanting boards (which I later learned were called "tilt tables"), and a platform with thick exercise mats. On another floor there was an occupational therapy room with many smaller adjustable tables, machines, and simple games like checkers and dominoes. Some were ordinary devices such as typewriters and sewing machines, and others looked like complicated toys. They were designed to require the use of fingers, hands, arms, and shoulders.

There were no other cases of GBS on his floor when Joe was admitted. The other patients were victims of stroke, oxygen deprivation, or some other form of brain or spinal disease or injury. Many were survivors of auto accidents. All had nerve damage, and physical recovery was limited to the extent damage was reversible. In this regard, Heller had an advantage, and his therapists were aware of it. They anticipated good results from their efforts and, having sweet dispositions anyway, found satisfaction and reward watching Joe's progress.

Because of Joe's full schedule, he was rarely in his room when I came to visit, so I would have to go looking for him. I could usually find him in either physical or occupational therapy. In the beginning, at PT he seemed to spend most of his time working with a therapist on the platform mat. Sometimes he was using the tilt table and later, when he grew strong enough, I might find him walking through the parallel bars. Often as I came in, I'd be intercepted by one of the therapists, who would greet me with a big smile, grab me by the arm, and hustle me over toward Joe, saying, "Speed, come and see what Joe can do on the mat by himself!" In later weeks, they were acknowledging my arrival with just as much enthusiasm, telling me, "Speed, guess what? Joe was walking in the parallel bars before. No kidding." It was like being back with my children again—this time in nursery school. The nurses and therapists were all uncommonly strong, intelligent, cheerful, and good-looking. When Joe's physical therapist found out I was a cyclist, she introduced me to one of her colleagues, who invited me to enter a bicycle marathon with her and her friends that Sunday. Unfortunately, I was already committed—probably on some mission for Joe—but it was a tempting offer.

Because I had been in charge of Joe's checkbooks, I had become familiar with his income and expenditures. And when I signed his name to the weekly checks for his nurses at Mount Sinai, I was perturbed by the drain on his finances. By the time he was admitted to Rusk and we knew that his health insurance was just about exhausted, I was the one who felt sick.

Julie Green had discovered a policy that would have picked up eighty percent of all medical bills in excess of ten thousand dollars had been allowed to lapse just a few months before Heller got GBS. Where was the money coming from to pay for all this? By now I was familiar with the kind of checks he received. None while I was in charge was large, many were for less than a hundred dollars. A typical month's worth of royalties that year looked like this: from Candida Donadio, literary agent, $160.79, $5.51, $47.92, $6.50; from publisher Simon and Schuster, $470.25; from Russell & Volkening, literary agents, $16.69, $18.35; from Lantz, theatrical agent, $103.95—a total of $829.96. He was now spending more than this amount every two days just for hospitalization at Rusk! His monthly bill was over twelve thousand dollars, and this did not include doctors' bills there, which were close to another thousand dollars per month, and his outside personal expenses.

I was once considered a shrewd businessman. At least smart

enough to know that when more money is going out than coming in, you eventually go broke. At one time I maintained an eleven-room apartment on Central Park West, a summer house on Fire Island, a studio in Chelsea for me, and another on West End Avenue for my wife. Making allowances for inflation, Heller's cost of living was still much higher than mine when I was in business and rolling in dough. He was separated from his wife and sending her a monthly allowance—as large, Joe told me, as she'd been getting when they were living together. It was much more than I was sending mine.

Each month I was signing Heller's checks for five residences, and Joe was living in none of them. He was in the hospital. I wrote rent checks for the Heller family apartment, his apartment on Eighth Avenue, and the studio in Santa Fe he'd rented for a year and could no longer use. In addition, there were mortgage payments for a co-op in Greenwich Village (occupied by one of his children) and the house in East Hampton (mostly unoccupied in the winter). There were also periodic payments for lawyers, accountants, certain other relatives, utilities, insurance premiums, taxes, and God knows all else. Now the bills for his medical care were starting to come in from Rusk as well as Mount Sinai. Just in February, for example, I had written checks totaling $17,097.32. What I deposited for him was truly insignificant.

Joe's medical bills from the doctors at Mount Sinai were many and not small. I made partial payments whenever I could, and soon Joe made things easier for me by arranging for loans. He had already borrowed ten thousand from Joe Stein. While I was still secretary of his treasury, I deposited a check for twelve thousand five hundred dollars he had borrowed from Marvin Green and another from Bob Towbin for the same amount. So there really was nothing for *me* to worry about.

By then I was already friendly with Bob Towbin and his family. But my introduction had been arranged through a typical Heller maneuver. One day, several years before GBS, Joe called and asked if I would cook a Chinese meal for some friends he'd met in the Hamptons. Heller knew that I almost never say no, so he was safe when he volunteered my services. Irene Towbin, on the other hand, had been deliberately misled. She thought Joe was recommending a professional, an expert Chinese chef. (Heller had neglected to mention this detail to me.)

Joe and Irene picked me up at my studio on our way to Chinatown. I liked Irene at once. I'd already planned the menu and we were heading for my favorite suppliers when Irene took me aside and quietly asked: "By the way, what is your usual fee?" I was dumbfounded. I looked around for Heller, but he had disappeared. "I have no fee, Irene. What did Joe tell you?" It was her turn to be surprised. "I asked him if he knew anyone who could cater an Oriental dinner and he said he had a friend who was a Chinese chef. Aren't you a professional?"

I told her that I was a good amateur, familiar with Chinese cuisine, and that I'd be happy to prepare some dishes for her party in any case.

Irene seemed unhappy. "I simply couldn't allow you to do that. It wouldn't be fair to let you cook a dinner for thirty people without paying you for it."

"Thirty?" I believe I showed surprise. I recovered enough to say, "Oh, sure, thirty is a cinch if I have some help with the washing and chopping. Sounds like fun. And forget about paying me. I don't do that for money." I could have gladly murdered Heller for his little joke.

THERE WAS NO JOKE! I didn't plan one, and I don't know why Speed continues to believe and say that I did. I didn't tell anything to Irene Towbin to suggest he was a professional cook, and I don't know where she got the idea that he expected to be paid. She apologized to me afterward for what she had said and expressed the hope that she had not offended him. I had nothing to do with *that* one.

WHO ARE YOU going to believe, him or me? Heller or Poor Speed, the guy who cooked the meal for *his* friends?

I mentally revised the menu; we did our shopping, and then loaded everything into Irene's car. The dinner turned out well and I enjoyed meeting the guests (after the cooking, I became one), as well as the host and the rest of his family. And I was enchanted by the Towbins' youngest, Zach, who was about ten years old and utterly winning. Meeting him was worth all the work.

AND HE AND ZACH have been good friends since. It will come as no surprise to anyone who knows Speed that he struck up a friendship with a ten-year-old, for Speed is one of those children from six to sixty-five about whom we occasionally hear who can relate to anything of special pertinence to people anywhere in the ages in between. With him it is not much of an exaggeration. Given half a chance, he will say yes to everyone and everything; he finds that easier than weighing a decision. There are qualities about him that many people find fascinating and unbelievable, and Valerie Humphries was one of those people. Here was this crinkly-eyed, even-tempered man with a gray beard and ten-speed bike who was old enough to be her father and young enough to be a swain, which is something else he is known to be good at. He not only cooks but shops, irons, sews, saws, hammers, and mends just about everything. Twenty years back when he was still a partner in his successful textile firm, Mel Brooks described him as "a Huck Finn floating around Manhattan on his raft," free to meet anyone at any time of the business day for any kind of social appointment. He runs six miles at the gym, while I at my best could do only four. He has roasted his own coffee beans just to learn how, and he has hung raw chickens on my clothesline to dry before cooking them. He cuts my hair—as Valerie witnessed in stark disbelief after the hospital beautician had washed and shampooed my head with her special equipment for the bedridden. No one else has given me a haircut in almost fifteen years, since the day he deliberated and concluded he knew how. I have a sculpture of his outside my house, a large metal bird. And, as you know, I commissioned his first oil painting many years ago. At the Rusk Institute, each of two young female physical therapists separately estimated his age at five years younger than that of their respective fathers; both these fathers were almost fifteen years younger than I am, and Speed is at least a couple of years my senior. He gives to Jeffrey Cohen, at thirty-five, something to look ahead to. As with the painting, he has been able to succeed at least one time with everything he's ever attempted. I did not doubt he would produce an exceptional Chinese meal for Irene's thirty guests if he said he would try, and he had plenty of help with the washing and the chopping, for people were drawn to the kitchen by the spectacle and remained to pitch in.

BEFORE I GO ON, I ask again, Who are you going to believe, him or me? Poor Speed? Or a man like him who commissions paintings from a neophyte mainly to irritate his friends who are professional artists?

Zach was interested in my preparations and stayed with me in the kitchen. I showed him how to slice beef and cook rice, and he told me a story about his huge stuffed bear, "Broccoli," who had mysteriously disappeared from the family station wagon and miraculously returned. Zach took me to his bedroom and showed me Broccoli, the largest and most gorgeous stuffed black bear I ever saw, one that I thought was unique and could see might take a good bit of time to replace. Shortly after the bear "disappeared," Zach received a short note in the mail: "I'm on a secret mission. I'll keep in touch. Broccoli." He then started receiving letters and cards from exotic cities all around the world (arranged by his creative parents through the cooperation of friends while an identical substitute was being made by the person who had crafted the original), describing the adventures of Broccoli as he traveled and with promises to return soon. Finally, after months of these messages, Broccoli was back in the apartment one day, looking good as new.

Zach was very precocious and I was not sure he was taken in by his parents' lovely scheme. On the other hand, he told his story without a hint that he was on to what had really happened. I didn't know whether he was putting me on or whether, because he *was* young, he really thought Broccoli had been on a mission. I felt Zach's tale about the bear said enough about the Towbins' sensitivity to merit anybody's admiration. I developed a fondness for the entire family. I consider them good friends; still I would never have had the nerve to ask the Towbins—or anybody else—if I could be a guest on their chartered yacht in Cannes for the film festival. Heller did. For me.

Poor Speed, therefore, would soon have to go to Europe as a guest on their yacht to attend the festival, eat sumptuously, and have a perfectly marvelous time, while Heller, just out of the hospital, was getting embroiled in serious matrimonial legal action. ("That is the way it is in life," as the judge at his divorce trial was to say about a different matter that touched on me. I spent most of the summer of 1984 in the French countryside in the house of Joe's friends Stanley and Toby Cohen, in the town of Saché. Joe, as he grumbled when I was back, "spent half the summer with lawyers and the other half in a dentist's chair.")

From the beginning I had brought all of Joe's mail to him at the hospital, and now I was delivering it to Rusk. Along with the bills, we had quite a number of letters. In the early days, I had to open them for him. More often than not, except with personal letters, he would take a cursory glance at the sender and say, "Throw it out." That drove me crazy. Sometimes I opened them anyway. Joe indulged me once in a while by letting me read a paragraph or two before he grunted, "Throw it out or take it home and read it yourself." In the room at Mount Sinai, he once ordered, "Throw it in the blender if you think it's so important for me." Green would smile when he was there to hear him and say, "That's our boy, Mr. Gracious. He must be getting better, he sounds like himself again."

My revenge was to taunt Joe about the one-hundred-thirty-two-dollar major medical insurance premium notice that he probably tossed out. He had already confessed that he once threw out some sizable checks by mistake, so it was reasonable to assume that he was responsible for this toss-out prize winner. If that was the true reason the policy had lapsed, his short trip to the wastebasket with that piece of paper was already costing him more than he wanted to think about. One day when I found Heller in occupational therapy hand-stitching a wallet, I could not resist telling him that if he had paid that premium he might have had a few more dollars to stick in his lovely new billfold, if he ever finished it.

Together we decided to reduce what expenses of his we could. The apartment in Santa Fe was certainly unnecessary now. I spoke to his landlady, who was sympathetic and agreed to cancel the balance of his lease. I also ordered the telephone there disconnected, and I asked his friend in Santa Fe, Mary Jane Doe,* to pack his things in some boxes and ship them to me at the apartment. From the goodness of my heart and the bottom of Joe's bank account, I sent her a check for fifty dollars to cover the cost. And this was an act that turned out to have some strange and quite humorous repercussions more than a year and a half later.

On October 19, 1983, Joseph Heller was on the witness stand at his divorce trial and was being cross-examined by the defendant's lawyer. (I don't know which Joe liked less, courtrooms or hospitals.) The lawyer's name was Mr. William Binderman, and he had in his possession copies of all of the entries in Joe's checkbooks. Earlier, in March of that same year, Joe was deposed, and during this deposition he was asked if he had ever written a check to M. J. Doe. Heller's answer, under oath, was "No." Now, with Heller in the witness chair and the bank records in hand, Mr. Binderman was certain he had nailed him in an out-and-out lie.

The issue was one of credibility, as the transcript shows Mr. Binderman insisting to the court. "Credibility is whether or not this man tells the truth," he argued. "Is the man a liar or does he believe in the oath?" Mr. Binderman, confident that Heller's

* The name used for this person is obviously not the real one.

credibility would be impeached, produced a photocopy of the page from the checkbook that included a clear entry for fifty dollars paid to "M. J. Doe" and wanted to know if Joe recognized it. And, of course, it did not all work out quite the way Mr. Binderman had foreseen.

When Joe looked at the page of evidence shown to him, he said, simply, "I recognize that as being from my book. I don't see my handwriting on it."

At this point, Jeffrey Cohen, aware of the facts and savoring the opportunity, asked for and received permission to take over the questioning.

"Do you know whose handwriting it is?" asked Jeffrey.

"Yes," said Heller.

"Whose handwriting is it?"

"Irving Speed Vogel's."

And then, from the judge, came: "Who is he?"

"He is a very close friend of mine," said the witness, Heller. "While I was in the hospital he took over the management of everything I needed done that I could not do myself, including the signing of checks. He was able to duplicate my signature."

Then the matter moved to its conclusion with the judge saying to Mr. Binderman, "Well, you are trying to show credibility and you are asking in the examination before trial if he drew a check to Mary Jane Doe and he said he did not and there is a check registered in somebody else's handwriting with 'M. J. Doe' on it."

"In his account," said Mr. Binderman.

"That was not the question," said Jeffrey Cohen.

And the judge said, "The question is whether he drew the check and his testimony was 'No.' That is an accurate statement as far as I can tell. . . . If you had asked in the examination before trial whether a check on his account was drawn to Mary Jane Doe—the direct question was answered, apparently."

"I can understand that, your Honor," said Mr. Binderman.

And the judge remarked, "That is the way it is in life."

IT WAS NOT UNTIL I went back to Rusk as an outpatient that I began to appreciate the disagreeable place it might have seemed to many of the people who had come there to visit me. At Rusk the patients are not sick, usually. They are damaged, most of them permanently and some very, very seriously. And enough are in view to evidence that the catastrophes they had suffered were common misfortunes that could happen to anyone. Although I came in a wheelchair, I found myself looking away from the others in wheelchairs or on stretchers. When I was a patient, it seemed natural for me to be in a hospital. Now it did not. I felt like an invalid, and I did not enjoy being reminded I was one each afternoon I went. I was a spectator and a spectacle. I did not enjoy that either.

As a patient, I took to the place the instant I was delivered. A nurse named Mary Welch was there to receive me, on temporary assignment in that wing that day, assisted by another named Meryl Farquharson who worked regularly in that section and whose serene, smiling competence and low humming of spirituals as she moved calmly and gracefully about her business gave me inestimable reassurance in what proved to be a long period ahead. Valerie unpacked, sorting the clothing Speed had purchased into the drawers of a dresser and onto the hangers and shelves of the closet just inside the entrance and opposite the bathroom. The second day nurse on duty there regularly was Margaret George, who later coached obligingly when Valerie grew interested in learning to lift me. The nurses lauded the excellent condition of my skin and praised Mount Sinai Hospital; they had never, they volunteered, received a patient from Mount Sinai with bedsores. Valerie liked the relaxed manner and sociable warmth of the women. At Rusk there is a spirit of energy and optimism on weekdays when all of the schedules are in operation that was unlike anything she had witnessed before in any of the hospitals in which she had worked, and she liked that too. She liked me. She liked the location. She agreed to keep working for me there for as long as I needed a private day nurse.

With the other shifts I would have to take my chances. Neither Donna nor Willie Mae would have come that far downtown even had I asked. I lucked out on the night shift with Herman Bryan, who was quiet, experienced, and sensible, and who was with me almost every night for the week and a half Dr. Ragnarsson countenanced my having private-duty nurses twenty-four hours a day. On the afternoon shift there weren't any I wanted a second time. I had been spoiled by my others at Mount Sinai. (As a guru of mine named Speed Vogel likes to remind: the enemy of the good is the better.)

In my second week, when the various professional assessments of me had been completed, Dr. Ragnarsson, one of the two physiatrists in charge of that floor, let me know he thought I would be better off getting used to doing without my private nurses. I reacted with fear and relief, the latter having mainly to do with the reduction in expenses. He was confident the staff could take care of everything but the tube feedings. He proposed that I persuade my day nurse to stay two hours more for the last feeding and that I rely on myself and the hospital staff for everything after that. The apprehension I suffered the first night I was alone did not last long. I had my call button. It is standard practice for someone to come every two hours to make certain each patient is turned from one side onto another. I therefore was never unattended for longer than that, and I could call for assistance sooner whenever I had to.

Inducing Valerie to stay until six each working day was as uncomplicated as I had foreseen. A liberal increase in pay for those two hours was but part of that temptation. She hung around for an extra hour or so most days anyway. I was still courting her with all my might. Speed and I did not forget Valentine's Day. After that, there was a small dinner party at Elaine's, with somebody else, of course, doing the hard work of entertaining her for me. Valerie had been to Elaine's before, but never as a guest of Mario Puzo, who is treated at Elaine's with much respect, as he is at all the other places of which he is a habitué. Mario has a special way of making sure that he is treated as a man of respect. I label that special way "excessive overtipping," and with him it is not a redundancy. (The roulette table at the casino in Cannes is another place at which Mario Puzo is treated as a man of respect, as Speed can testify from experience later if he breaks the code of silence.)

The first time Valerie took two days off to visit her sister, who lives a distance away, she was amazed by a basket of spring flowers from me delivered by a local florist that arrived at the house an hour after she did. Guileless, she could not imagine how I had found the florist or learned the address of the house in that small suburb of Poughkeepsie. It did not occur to her that I simply had telephoned her sister and asked her to do the whole thing for me, including the writing of the risqué note I had dictated. Guilefully, I made arrangements to have Speed make arrangements for a dozen roses to be waiting when she returned to her apartment. When a man lies in bed paralyzed for several months, he has time to devote to being attentive to a woman and the effort to expend in transforming himself into a perfect courtier.

There was a Saturday afternoon Dustin came to visit me at Rusk with Murray Schisgal and Murray's wife, Reene, who was recently out of the hospital herself. ("Reene" is the way her parents spelled it on the birth certificate, and Reene is the name Renée has been stuck with.) The two of us had exchanged compassion on the telephone frequently. This was the first time they were seeing Valerie, but I would guess that Valerie had seen Dustin before on the screen. Mainly for show, I asked Valerie to take me out of the bed to my wheelchair. All of them goggled a moment and applauded lustily when she demonstrated the technique taught her for bringing me to my feet from the bed in order to move me into the wheelchair. Sexually suggestive, it was something to watch—and it still is. In this stand-and-pivot maneuver, we begin with our arms around each other and her skirt hiked over her knees, and we come to rest belly-to-belly and cheek-to-cheek, with her legs parted and her skirt still up, and with our arms still around each other. Both men honored her with the conjecture that if she grew tired of working as a nurse she surely could find other employment as an actress, a model, or a hooker, all of them prospects, though they did not know it, of which she was already aware, having had them laid out for her countless times before by interns, residents, and physicians, and by patients too, even by patients whose prostate glands had recently been excised.

Valerie was eating better also, as I steadily found myself eating more. Julius Green seldom arrived with fewer than half a dozen small containers of Häagen-Dazs ice cream, which were stored in the refrigerator at the nurses' center, and not just for me. Usually he came up with cupcakes too. Once it was known I could gnaw at a bagel, Jeffrey Cohen always called first to learn what kind of spread Valerie and I would prefer that Saturday or Sunday morning. Others brought donuts and cans of cookies. I was trying to put back weight, even with the tube still in, and I began averaging close to five pounds weekly as I rounded into form. There were leftovers from Chinatown, of which the chief beneficiary was the reticent Japanese evening nurse named Keiko Marchand, who had an appetite as big as the Ritz, which meant it was almost half the size of Valerie's.

There was a festive picnic on my bed one Saturday afternoon

in the middle of March. When the tube was removed, my affable, liberal friend Bob Towbin gave a small party in my hospital room to celebrate, with food and champagne from "21." (This time the champagne was good.) There was even a red-checkered tablecloth over the bed, which Valerie had borrowed for the occasion from Steve and Barbara DeClerque, very old friends of mine from my *Time* magazine days who lived in Tudor City, just six blocks away. All that was missing was a Dubonnet umbrella. Knowing Valerie's esteem for the artist Manet (along with the artists Monet, Renoir, Cézanne, Pissarro, and a bunch of others I could name), I suggested she undress and eat with us naked. She blushed a moment and declined. She was not so prudish when it came to undressing and showering me or to sticking a carbon dioxide suppository up my ass. With this last, I must advertise, she had an extremely delicate technique which I made known to other nurses filling in who were not so instinctively gifted as she was in this area.

So there I was, in a hospital in New York City with a physician, Dr. Kristjian Ragnarsson, who not only wasn't Jewish but was from Iceland. (Go figure.) I commented on this surprising irony to Dr. Mary Swajian, the young resident-in-training who, I believe, also was not Jewish but who, nevertheless, under his supervision, kept medical watch over me. Both are physiatrists; that is, they are specialists in physical medicine as contrasted with, I think, internal medicine, a distinction I won't try to explain here because I don't think I'm able to. Dr. Swajian found me in good health, though quadriparetic, and there was not much for her to do with me all the time I was there, for I remained in good health. The single interruption arose from spells of violent dizziness I suffered for two or three weeks upon moving my head quickly, even when turning it from one side to another while in bed. Everything in view would, in a fraction of a second, start moving uniformly, accelerate, and whirl about my head with a sickening, bewildering speed. Since I was lying down almost all of the time, I soon came to understand that I was not in real danger of the first terror to possess me, of falling. Once I absorbed that, I next perceived that invariably the spinning would cease and the nausea recede within a few seconds after I shut my eyes, and after that these episodes stopped being horrifying and were only intolerable. My activities went on through this period with no break in my schedule. After the first few days the incidents were more alarming to Valerie than to me. I would simply shut my eyes and say, "It's starting to spin." And she would shoot forward to hold me and prevent me from falling off the face of the earth, even though, more often than not, I would be lying in bed or sitting safely in my wheelchair while it was happening. My blood pressure was fine. No explanation was ever given for the cause or disappearance of this vertigo.

My physical therapist was a tall, blue-eyed, effervescent young woman in her twenties named Carol Recker Hughes, who was attractive and spirited and was married to a lawyer very much taller than even she and not much older. Like just about all of the physical therapists there, she was friendly and irrepressibly encouraging—everything she asked me to do she asked in a way suggesting it was possible, even though almost all at first was not. As with the nurses on the day shift in the intensive care unit at Mount Sinai, just about all the therapists were young, indicating to my speculative imagination that most here too do not choose to continue working where I saw them until they are even thirty. There is very much lifting to be done in a rehabilitation hospital. Almost all of the patients are at least partially immobilized, and many weigh more than I did.

My occupational therapist was another young married woman named Susan Miron Bernstein, who had red hair and brown eyes and also was good to look at. Susan was soft-spoken, pleasant, and reserved. She smiled and laughed quietly a great deal during my conversations with Speed when he chanced to show up on his rounds while I was working with her, and she possibly will be surprised and contrite to find out now of the very considerable anguish I experienced so often in my sessions with her or one of her coworkers.

My work on occupational therapy was both easier and harder than my physical therapy. (Occupational therapy is not vocational; it is therapy through exercise activities similar to those a person normally performs daily, mainly with the muscles of the shoulders, arms, and hands. A disproportionately larger area of the brain than anyone would imagine is devoted to the operation of the small muscles of the hand, as it is also to the small muscles of the face.) It was easier because the amount of raw strength demanded by each of the exercises there was so much less. (At the start I moved tiny objects with tweezers, stacked cones, moved small cubes, reached for checkers on a checkerboard.) It was harder because of the frustration I suffered straining to perform them and discovering myself unable to. It was harder too because the resistance against which I worked, whether friction or gravity, was systematically increased with my ability to overcome it. I felt, as a result, that what they intended was to keep me always at a standstill. On a mat in the physical therapy room, if I couldn't do something, I couldn't do it (move myself from side to side or up and down, support myself on my elbows, or lift my head), and that was that; and when I began by small degrees to be able to do all of these things, the improvement was conspicuous and cause for rejoicing. But in occupational therapy, as soon as I could sand a block of wood (with a need to rest both arms, it was written, after every seven repetitions), a change was made to a coarser grade of sandpaper, increasing the amount of force required, and it was just as punishing and demoralizing for me to have to execute then as it had been at the beginning. Similar adjustments were made in the supporting weights of an antigravitational device called a "counterbalance sling," which meant it was always as grueling for me to do things with my arms above lap and table height, and also with the different densities of the plastic "clays" I was given to squeeze and to flatten. Exercises like these were never allowed to feel easier. We can understand, I now am sure, why, in occupational therapy, I embraced the opportunity to lace a wallet, bake a cake, and beat an egg when I had advanced enough to be able to. I was pretty good on the keyboard of an electric typewriter, although they were hard put to find much to type that would hold my interest. My left elbow needed to be stabilized for everything.

The central problem against which we had to contend was described officially as severe muscle weakness in the trunk and neck and in all four extremities as a result of nerve deficits secondary to Guillain-Barré syndrome.

In the fingers the muscles are so very small. When I was asked by Susan to spread my hands, I could not move my fourth finger or open my pinky on either hand. When she spread these fingers for me, I could not move them back. An exercise I remember as especially torturing emotionally was to gather in, just by curling my fingers, a handkerchief or paper tissue (I forget which) laid flat beneath my stationary hand. Worse than that was Susan's then asking me to push it all away, which meant using those muscles of my fingers that worked in the opposite direction. I got nowhere. My inability to straighten my fingers against such immeasurably small resistance as that was a mental agony almost indescribable. With Carol at the start of my physical therapy I was mostly dead weight. (My legs felt so heavy that I truly could not picture myself ever able to walk again—I could not, and still cannot, picture how *anybody* is able to walk!) But the tiny exertions and failures I've described were infinitely more draining.

Much worse than both, much worse at the time than anything I could recall having experienced before, was the EMG test to which I was subjected at Rusk in my third week there, on February 10. With a clear recollection of the ten-minute abbreviated electromyography examination at Mount Sinai (and no inkling that it *had* been abbreviated), I allowed myself to be wheeled away for it in that mood of jaunty heroism and self-sacrifice people like me routinely affect when going to a dental office for an ordinary cleaning and scaling. I should have been tipped off to something more than I expected when Valerie was told to come back in an hour. In fact, it was almost two hours before they were finished with me.

None of the pain from the individual electric shocks or from the needle punctures was so intense as to make one wish to cry out. It was the repetitions of the electric shocks that rapidly wore me down, and which gradually proved more and more terrible as I began to understand I had no way to predict the number to be administered at each separate place. Some nerves were dull, others were not. Each stimulus was discrete. In one sensitive nerve in my right leg, I counted, as I have said, thirty-eight painful electrical impulses given me. Each was inflicted methodically after an interval of a second or two. I was in disbelief when the number passed *fifteen*! I wondered pathetically what the fuck they were looking for. The test was not dangerous, I had been assured at the start. The doctor was a stoic Oriental, and that was about all he had said to me. A young student-technician from Brooklyn sat protectively in a chair beside the narrow table on which I lay, which had no guardrail or restraining straps. He joined in cooperatively whenever I sought distraction through conversation. Many people cried before the test was finished, he told me while mine was still in progress, men sooner than women, and people from Brooklyn, he'd noticed, most rarely of all. Inasmuch as we both were from Brooklyn, I did not credit this last heavily.

My left arm was done first, then my left leg. Each took longer than the entire procedure at Mount Sinai. This was undoubtedly something new. My heart sank further when I realized he was going to do my right side too. As in the first test, a sickening instant of piercing pain came with the very forceful plunging of a needle into my palm at the base of the thumb. Again I had the illusion I heard loudly the splashing, crunching noise of human tissue ripping.

Put crudely, I suppose, the test measures the speed and the concentration with which sensations we know as pain are transmitted along the nerve fibers to the brain and brought back in an appropriate reaction, which probably includes the recognition that something hurts. I believe the transmission is supposed to be sharp, quick, and unified. With me, if you care, the electrodiagnostic examination revealed diffuse and delayed abnormal spontaneous activity in all muscles tested and other findings highly suggestive of polyradiculoneuropathy, which is a condition about which all of us by now know as much as we want to. My F-wave responses were not too good either. When the testing of all four of my limbs was completed and I thought we were finished, a needle was put into my right cheek near my mouth, and the doctor muttered to himself that there was definite facial involvement. I could have told him that.

I was exhausted when it was over, heartbroken too, and so very pale that Valerie sent for Dr. Swajian a little while after wheeling me back to the room. Dr. Swajian found nothing wrong. By nightfall my color was back and I was able to keep to my exercise schedule the next day.

Before that, though, there were some letters that had been delivered. Among them was one, on bright stationery, from Minna Towbin, Bob and Irene's daughter, who was then a student at Dartmouth. Minna had been sending me humorous cards and pep notes and amusing novelties: a water pistol with which I squirted good friends arriving empty-handed instead of with something I could eat, a bubble blower with which I could show off my arm movements and blowing power, a harmonica on which, to everyone's tolerant astonishment, I played "Swanee River," the one song I could. Arriving that day from Minna was another four-page letter filled with good wishes and good feeling, the different paragraphs in different colors of ink, the pages aglitter with different kinds of sparkling ornamentations, the text making reference to that month's St. Valentine's Day as the inspiration for writing it. It was a letter brimming with fun. In closing, she wrote that everybody there in Hanover, New Hampshire, was rooting for me. Just back from the EMG test, I read it aloud to Valerie while I was still in my wheelchair. When I came to that last line, my voice choked with tears and I began to cry.

I stopped in a minute. I telephoned Irene for Minna's address and told her I'd just received a letter from Minna that moved me so much I'd wanted to cry. I phoned a telegram to Minna saying much the same thing. When I woke up alone very early the next morning, I wanted to cry some more. That happens to people sometimes in a hospital when they wake up very early. It happens to some of us even when we're home.

Dr. Kristjian Ragnarsson was about twenty years younger than the fifty-eight-year-old, alert, well-oriented, well-developed but moderately thin, pleasant individual now in his care. He had the fair coloring and chiseled features of his Viking ancestors. Dr. Ragnarsson had something of the venturesomeness too: his idea of a vacation was to go on camping trips with his wife and two small children, driving at least one time as far as Florida for the pleasure of doing that. He related to me at our first meeting that his superior at the hospital, the medical director, was a neurologist named Goodgold, and this fact had endowed with a special amusement for him my novel *Good as Gold*, a work, I could not tell him then because I did not know, that was fated to be introduced in my divorce trial as "the Mein Kampf of matrimonial strife." (It doubtless is bad organization to give prominence now to an incident I will relate later that took place long after the time period covered by this book was over, but how many people do we know who have fathered a *Mein Kampf*? I can think of only one, and his was not about matrimonial strife.) A man living most of his life in New York City will normally not run into a large number of people from Iceland who are doctors. Nevertheless, most of the questions I found myself putting to Dr. Ragnarsson were about myself.

From the looks of me, he estimated hopefully I would be there no more than eight weeks, but emphasized he could guarantee nothing. He was not even positive I had Guillain-Barré. (The results of the EMG test were inconclusive, neither confirming nor eliminating Guillain-Barré.) In a case more typical, he illustrated, as I rested on my back with my arm bent comfortably and my hand idly holding the rail, I would have more strength in my shoulders and be unable to flex my biceps or close my fingers, as

I was doing right then. As it turned out, I was at Rusk more like fourteen weeks.

It was a day or two later that I remembered the question I had forgotten to ask, and I lost no time asking it as soon as he was free for another private discussion with me.

"What condition will I be in when I leave?"

Here the news was not as rosy. Probably, I would be able to walk short distances, although I might have to use canes or a walker. (That told me a lot more than he specified: I was going to need a wheelchair and a person to push it.) I would be able to dress and groom myself, probably, and even to prepare light meals, if the things I required were left in reach when I was alone. In all likelihood, I would be able to get out of bed unaided, if only to a wheelchair with the aid of a "transfer board" if I still could not stand up when released. I *would* be able to work, in longhand and at a typewriter. I was already putting in close to a full day's exercise schedule without fatigue or any other unwelcome effects. He could not promise I would ever be able to run in the New York marathon again if I had ever done that before. (I never had and had never wanted to.) The future he outlined held problems I would not be able to cope with alone.

On my first day of therapy in the pool, where the weight on my legs was lessened by buoyancy to a fraction of that on land, it was apparent that the latent ability to walk normally was intact. This was not so with the rest of the patients in the pool with me at the same hour. The other two functions I wanted most strongly to recover were to swallow and to get up on my feet, and there was nothing, not a blessed thing, that I or anyone else in the world could do to hasten or ensure the return of either one.

I was admonished more than once by Dr. Ragnarsson for trying too hard. Once when observing the effort I was making to propel my wheelchair, he directed me to stop trying and ordered an electric wheelchair put at my disposal. Given the weakness of my shoulders, it was too early to try. There were reasons for supposing, he explained, that with Guillain-Barré, strain produced changes in the nerve structures that diminished rather than enhanced the ability to innervate the muscles in which they were embedded. As to swallowing, my gag reflex was decreased to almost half the normal, and nobody but me saw a need to rush.

Following my first evaluations, I was given an exercise schedule that began with an hour in the pool each morning from nine to ten and called for an hour on the tilt table from eleven to noon. In the afternoon there were consecutive hours of occupational therapy and physical therapy, from two till four. After a while, as my legs and endurance grew stronger, the free hours I had in the morning and after lunch were filled in with ambulation sessions (it was necessary to learn how to walk again) and with exercises on different pieces of equipment to strengthen the muscles of my legs and buttocks still more. On Saturday and Sunday there was no activity, and the abrupt void left all of us patients looking stunned and stupefied at discovering ourselves with nothing to do until after lunchtime when the visiting hours began. I doubt there are depressives in mental institutions anywhere looking more forlorn than we did in our wheelchairs on weekend mornings as we waited for the hours to pass. I was lucky in having a nurse. I would not have wanted to be alone long in the room if no visitors came. And I had not the character for socializing easily with the strangers in wheelchairs in the hallways outside.

Just before nine each weekday morning I was taken from my room in bathing trunks supplied by Rusk and a plain bathrobe bought for me by Speed. The pool was on the second floor and I was on the fourth. In the deep part of the pool, I could not only walk normally but hop and jump and simulate trotting. Seats were suspended into the water from metal mounts along the sides of the pool. In one of these, I could pump my legs vigorously in a bicycle-riding action. I could raise my arms to the surface easily and move them back and forth and up and down against the resistance of the water. I would practice standing up from a sitting position, doing ten or twenty repetitions a set. I would do this in water of less depth, where it was harder, as my strength returned gradually.

But before any of these Herculean gambols could even begin, I had to be lifted from my wheelchair by a man named Ed Starkey and laid out on a white canvas stretcher that was hoisted mechanically at his control and carried out over the pool to the therapist waiting there. Valerie would remind both anxiously every day to be sure to support my head. The therapist would lift me off when the stretcher was lowered and, at the beginning, carry me over to one of the seats and steady me there. Later on, she would set me down on my feet, after she had ascertained from the days before that I was able to stand and that I had overcome that fear of the water whose presence was vivid on the face of everyone I saw coming there for the first time.

A human body weighs less in water—how much I have never found out. I asked and still don't know. But the deeper the water, naturally, the greater the decrease. (The measurements have something to do with Archimedes's discovery that the weight of a body in water is lessened by the weight of the amount of water it displaces. But no one was weighing the water I displaced.) In this pool the water was divided into different areas of depth by changes in the level of the floor, the landings delineated by a step the width of the pool with a rise of about four or five inches, the steps themselves being used for exercise. This difference in inches was a big one for most of us. It took weeks before I was able to work my way up from the deepest area at one end to the more shallow one in the center, and even longer to graduate to the next one, where the bottom then sloped up gradually to knee level and to a short staircase with a railing at that end for people better off than anyone I saw to use for coming and going.

The fears usually experienced starting pool therapy were groundless in my case. I'd forgotten that I knew how to swim and to hold my breath to remain afloat if I wanted to, and that I was only in a small pool. When a knee did buckle while I was going up or down one of the steps (it takes about as much to go down as it does to go up, and the three times I fell after I was out, I fell while stepping down), I did not crash to the bottom, flounder, and drown. I simply floated a second or two while I righted myself, laughing with joy at finding myself able to. Besides, with a physical therapist but a yard or two away, working individually with one of the three or four of us, with Ed Starkey and a female attendant at poolside, and with Valerie Humphries back from the cafeteria with her container of tea and on guard vigilantly while trying to read her *New York Times,* there was not much danger of anything happening to anyone that would not bring able-bodied help immediately.

It was known from experience that a person strong enough to move safely about in the shallow part of the pool probably was strong enough to stand and to begin walking between the parallel bars upstairs, and after nearly seven weeks I was doing both.

But at the end of each pool period even then, I still had to be hoisted out on the stretcher. Ed Starkey would put me into my wheelchair and Valerie would take over, wheeling me into a curtained dressing area to dry me and change me into gym clothes, into sweatpants and T-shirt, with socks and sneakers. Had she not been there, the attendant would have done that, and a different attendant would have come from the fourth floor to make sure I was delivered to where I was slated to be next.

I did not have any trouble on the tilt table, either. Those dizzy spells I suffered would be triggered there only when my head was being lowered as we made ready to begin. Mel Tucker was on duty at the tilt tables, and he too had been at Rusk a long time. Like Ed Starkey he was a black man, and the two were friends. Mel was very tall and skinny, a bit gangly, and incredibly strong for so thin and gentle a person. In his fifteen or so years there, he had never allowed an ambulating patient to fall to the ground while he was doing the contact guarding. He mentioned this disapprovingly after each of the two times I did drop and strike my knee while walking with someone other than him.

Mel and an aide would use a two-man lift at the beginning to raise me out of the wheelchair onto the horizontal tilt table, with my feet against the rest at the lower end. Restraining straps would be tightened around my knees and breast. Slowly, the head of the table would be raised toward a vertical position, locked in at 65 degrees at first, and gradually by days to the maximum 90 degrees by the second or third week, when it was clear I could tolerate it. The purpose was to condition for bearing weight again limbs that had not done so for some time and to effectuate the physiological changes facilitating that function. I suffered none of the undesirable results that I had been told sometimes assailed others: leg pain, often acute, faintness, nauseating fear, and sensations of imbalance so upsetting as to cause panic-stricken patients to beg to be excused.

Joseph Heller was not only a model patient but a model to other patients, like the woman named Betty Buccolo, who was emboldened to allow herself up to an angle nearly as steep as mine only when she saw me there a few inches above her.

Betty was probably slightly overweight when I met her, for she had not exercised in a while, and she told me she was one of those people with a passion for golf. She had a sense of humor and a ready chuckle, and the two of us talked in wisecracks for much of the short while we found ourselves upright on the tilt table beside each other.

"You're lucky," she said to me one day. "I know a woman who had what you have and now she does almost everything."

Not till then did I ask her about herself. When she finished talking I knew I was very much luckier than she was.

Returning from a visit to a son in college, she was wearing her seat belt while she did the driving and she traveled at moderate speed. Her husband in the seat beside her was wearing his harness too. In the back seat of the car were her two daughters. For an undetermined reason, the car simply went off the road into a ditch and turned over once slowly. Her husband's lip was cut. Nobody else in the car was scratched, not even she. But when the car turned over she heard a sharp noise, and she sensed she was in trouble. The noise was very near. It was the sound of her neck breaking. She seemed to be telling me now that she knew she would not play golf again.

She soon gave up on the tilt table, but our schedules coincided also in the occupational therapy room. The wheelchair she needed cost thousands. There was a supervised excursion outside the hospital one day to familiarize her with those public buses with special facilities affording access to people in wheelchairs. I met her husband and a couple of her children one weekend in one of the ground-floor reception rooms to which we patients sometimes went with visitors to be in roomier and more congenial surroundings. She offered me a taste of a cake they had brought her.

"Gimme all," was the way I refused. "I don't like to share."

She had a weekend at home that went well and she had already decided to check out a few weeks sooner than the hospital thought she should, to be back home for good in time for some family ceremony that meant much to her. The week of her discharge, I watched from the upright tilt table as her husband and her children were coached in the techniques of lifting her in the various ways that were going to be necessary. As I watched I was sad for myself also. I was reminded again that there are some disadvantages to living alone.

From my perch on the upright tilt table I faced out the windows toward the East River and could see the structures on the other bank. There is a busy heliport just outside the window, on sidewalk level. I would watch the whirlybirds coming down and going up or stare past them at the tugboats occasionally steaming by with their cargoes of garbage in tow. I could see almost all of the other twenty or thirty or forty more people in that physical therapy "gymnasium" the same period who were engaged in other kinds of activities at the mats or in the ambulation area or with the various units of exercise equipment and machines. I could look down from my upright position on some narrow padded tables just across an aisle from me to which a red-faced

Irishman whose name I never learned came regularly for some kind of electrical stimulation for the relief of pain and a woman recovering from a stroke whose name I did know, Mrs. Becker, was brought for heat pads and certain mild exercises performed while she lay there supine. The Irishman, it was said, was free to leave evenings and went by himself to spend them in one of the several cozy pubs an avenue away that were accustomed to serving food and drink to Rusk patients in wheelchairs. (My first meal out was in one of them, and I made sure my friends Steve DeClerque and Speed were there to eat too and to assist Valerie in assisting me if any kind of difficulty arose that she could not deal with alone.) The recumbent woman would smile back at me as I loomed over her on my tilt table but a few yards away (it is a picture of the past both comical and grotesque, and when I conjure it up and say it is comical, I get a glimmer of an idea of what other people mean when they speak of black humor); when she tried to return my greetings, however, her jaw would flap open and closed on the same soundless syllable. Often, the therapist, Anita Berger, I think, could find out through questions what Mrs. Becker wanted to tell me and relay the message.

When Mrs. Becker was sent home, her hour was taken by a spare, white-haired, smaller woman who also had suffered a stroke. She was older, well into her seventies, and frail, and judging from the constant flow of cajolery and prodding from the therapist attending her, was of a mournful and complaining nature. But when her time was up, she rose laboriously to a sitting position without help, moaning and grumbling to herself unintelligibly, stood up by herself, and swiveled herself down into her wheelchair.

"That skinny old lady is stronger than I am," is the way I gave dejected voice to some rueful discontent of my own.

I made this observation to Dr. Walter Sencer, who, though the location was inconvenient, was stopping in regularly at the beginning to see how I was progressing. He made certain to arrive with a stethoscope hanging well out of his jacket pocket, to ensure by this symbol of official status that his coming outside of visiting hours would not be barred. Dr. Peck came once to visit also.

And once, in Dr. Sencer's aggressive determination to see me completely well, he brought me a gift I did not expect. It was just by chance that I was on the tilt table when he showed up. Looking around with impatience and irritability as he waited for my hour there to end, he told me candidly that the place had always depressed him. About half the patients always in view while I was there were stroke victims, almost all the rest were there because of injuries or of other diseases to the brain or the spine, several from tumors. Most of the young male quadriplegics had been brought there by diving or motor accidents. The therapists were good-looking and strong, but that did not do much to brighten the overall impression. Dr. Sencer surprised me by saying he'd come with a present for me. From the other pocket of his jacket he produced a brown paper bag, and from inside that brown paper bag he pulled out a huge, overstuffed salami sandwich he had brought there for me to devour.

He remembered the improving state of my palate, tongue, and pharyngeal constrictors from the last time he had examined them, and he was doggedly insistent I would be able to eat the sandwich provided I did not allow my fears to get in the way of the effort. I marveled at his uncanny insight as he held it up before my eyes and nose: How in the world had this genius divined that throughout my life I have always preferred my salami sandwiches on a seeded roll? I promised to try as soon as we were back in my room. His eyeglasses glistened in anticipation.

I have seen the Sistine Chapel. That salami sandwich was more beautiful. But when I did try to eat it, we both saw at once that I could not open my mouth wide enough to bite. Even with the upper half of the roll removed, I could not do it. The tiny amount I could get by nibbling had not much taste for either of us. Dr. Sencer was downhearted. (I could have informed him a month later when I was able to swallow that even then I could not open my jaws wide enough to bite into an ordinary tuna fish sandwich on white bread unless the top slice was first taken off.

Now I am able to take large bites; when I do, though, it's still not possible for me to deal without visible clumsiness with the greater amount of food I find in my mouth.) At the time, I made the one suggestion to Dr. Sencer I could think of to cheer him up.

"Why don't you eat it?"

I don't remember if he did or not. I do remember that he told me gravely, to cheer me up, "Of all the people I saw in that room, I think you're the only one with a chance to recover enough to live a normal life."

A few days after I entered Rusk a woman appeared in my room, in the company of her husband, and identified herself as a former GBS patient who'd been discharged about fifteen months before. She did not have to tell me that she had dropped by as living witness that people could recover. We had both been spared a tracheostomy. Her swallowing and her face had not been affected, and if she was suffering any residual defects, I didn't see them.

About a week or two after that, a friend of Dr. Sencer's came by with the same humanitarian goal, arriving about noon when Valerie was with me and I was about to try eating my lunch from the tray. He was large and energetic, looked robust and strong. This was Stanley Rosenstock, and he was in the building that day as an outpatient for what he called "fine-tuning." His manner was hearty. He was astonished by what he saw in me, that I was sitting, even with the support of the back of the bed, and could hold up my hand and turn it, could bend my arms and close my fingers to grip a fork in one hand and a suction tube in the other, that I was trying and managing to eat, even a little. His surprising entrance and booming encouragement had the jovial quality of a good-natured rebuke.

"Look at you," he called out, after apologizing for intruding and asking permission to enter. (It was not until the second or third time we saw each other that I recognized a mild lumbering action in his gait and detected a recurring stiffness about the mouth when he formed certain words. His sibilants are thick, and his name is Stanley Rosenstock. My *l*'s are indistinct, and my name is Heller.) "You'll be out of here in three months if you do what they tell you. Do everything they tell you."

"They said eight weeks."

"Maybe less. Do you know what I looked like when I got here? You look like a million. Do you know how long it took before I could do all that? Before I could sit up or bend my arm? I had more tubes than you."

Here's what I found out about Stanley Rosenstock. Two weeks or so after an intestinal flu, he was in Raleigh, North Carolina, on a business trip and found when he got up on his last morning there that he had trouble raising his head off the pillow. At breakfast he could not swallow certain of the solid foods (with me it was hash brown potatoes, with him it was grits). His home is a few hours outside New York City. Leaving Raleigh, he had trouble lifting his briefcase at the airport and going up the steps of the plane. Arriving, he had trouble sitting up in the car on the way home from the airport. In his house, he started slurring his words and his wife joked that he'd probably had more to drink on the plane than he should have. (Both of us like to drink, if that is of help to a researcher.) Denying her charge while sitting on the bed to take off his shoes, he suddenly slumped over on his side, and he could not sit back up. There is a critical difference between feeling faint and feeling weak, and if you ever have Guillain-Barré, you will find out what that difference is.

Otherwise, he felt fine. He had a doctor in his family who was telephoned at ten-thirty at night and had him rushed to the emergency room of a hospital nearby. Twenty-four hours later Stanley Rosenstock was paralyzed everywhere, except for his breathing muscles. A day or so later, those went too, and he was on a respirator. He could not empty his bladder. For the next nine weeks he was in a Benedictine hospital in Kingston, New York. When his friend Dr. Sencer learned by telephone what he had, where he was, and that he was in a hospital administered by nuns, he advised: "Let him stay where he is until the danger's over. He'll do just as well there now as he will anywhere else."

When he came to Rusk he could move only his eyes and eyelids and his toes. He did have more tubes than I had—he had four: a catheter for urinating, and IV tube, a nasogastric tube, and a "trach" tube connecting him to the respirator. He was too weak for anything but bedside therapy. He began with respiratory therapy to save him from drowning in his own thoracic fluids, and with passive exercises, exercises in which the energy for movement is supplied by the therapist. He tells me his lungs were suctioned continuously; he would cough and gasp for breath while this was done and feel, he told me, like cashing in his chips right then. Had a gun been left on the table he would have wanted to shoot himself. (I can imagine him trying to use it!) When finally he was breathing well enough to be weaned from the respirator, he thought for a minute, after ten weeks of hearing the noise of the equipment every minute of every hour of every day and night, that he had gone deaf. He was totally inanimate at the start of his therapy when they lifted him on and off the tilt table. When he began in the pool, it was necessary to strap him into the seat on the side, for he was unable to maintain himself in a sitting position.

Now he looked like a professional football player, and it was only about a year later. He'd spent five months at Rusk. He had moved into the city for his program of outpatient therapy there that had already lasted five months and would continue five months longer. In the city, he explained, he now made it a point to carry a cane, but not because he needed it; he'd noticed that even in New York City hurrying pedestrians, with instinctive courtesy, would give a slightly wider berth to people they saw carrying one. His illness had cost about a quarter of a million dollars. Luckily, he'd been covered by a great deal of medical insurance.

"Do whatever they tell you to," he directed me again and again. "Put that up on the wall right in front of you so you won't forget. Just keep doing everything they tell you, and you'll get all better faster than I did. You don't even know how good you look, even now."

It would never have occurred to me then to do anything other than everything I was asked to do.

I was getting this from a cheerful man in good health. But when I spoke to Stanley Rosenstock in December of 1983, two years after I was stricken and almost three years after he was, he was curious to hear if, in going up steps, I was able to do so using one leg after the other. He could not. (In May 1985 he still couldn't—his left leg was too weak.) Neither of us could run, both of us sometimes have difficulty chewing and swallowing as easily as we formerly could. (With me, the running could be largely due to a failure in memory. I can run on a treadmill for more than five minutes at a clip, but I may have forgotten how to do it on real ground.) Yet both of us think of ourselves as "all better." I have an amiable pen pal in Canada named Bram Garber who reveals additional limitations in his recovery just about every time we correspond. When I told him I was riding a bicycle, he confided in reply that his grasp was not strong enough for him to be able to. ("As I lost the small muscles in both hands, bicycling is impracticable, but I still swim several times a week.") Yet he thinks of himself as fully recovered, too. There is something about this disease that makes a person who has gotten over the worst parts of it grateful enough to be willing to settle for that.

Only twice at Rusk did I not do something I was asked to. When a physician at the medical school of New York University asked to come with a group of students for a medical interview, I refused: the facts were in the records. And when the medical director, Dr. Goodgold, with whom I'd become friendly, suggested a second EMG test, free, shortly before I was to leave, I hesitated and demurred, abetted with a timely forensic assist from Speed, who happened to be there at the time.

Otherwise, I was perfect. In the pool there was never a minute of idleness; when seated to rest my legs, I would work my shoulders and arms. I applied myself to the utmost at everything suggested. "Braiding" was one walking exercise supposedly requiring a complicated blending of nerve actions, moving sideways along a rail in the water with each leg going first in front of and then in back of the other. On the tilt table, instead of just standing there strapped in while waiting for the hour to pass, I had the idea of bending each arm as many times as I could (my left was much the weaker) and flexing my shoulders, upward, backward, forward. After several weeks, weights were added to my wrists in increments of a pound, first on my right, then on my left. With food, Valerie and I had set our sights on my totaling six meals a day, three from the tray, followed by three through the tube.

I had discovered the banana. A piece of banana would remain in a mash in one place in my mouth when chewed and slide down smoothly when swallowed; it also would take down with it the many bits of bread, meat, vegetables, and other foods I felt accumulating on the back of my tongue, which grew mildly irritating and had me thinking I might gag. It was mainly for cleansing away these crumbs that I had been using the suction tube, and for the phlegm in the morning that I still could not down or expectorate. Now I had the banana for these sweeping operations. I employed it at all three meals. Later on, as my improvements continued, I used eggnog and my soup for the same thing. Thin liquids were the hardest, as I'd been warned they would be by my doctors and by Steve DeClerque, and they came last.

We discovered the shower chair. On Saturday of my initial week at Rusk, Valerie took her first day off in four weeks. On Sunday she found out about the shower chair, which was already familiar to us as the commode, that seat on wheels with a circular cutout in the center for the buttocks, onto which a person is lifted. The unit was then pushed like a wheelchair and rolled into position over the toilet bowl in the bathroom. As a shower chair, the unit, bearing the naked patient draped in a sheet, was rolled through the hallway into one of the large stalls in one of the special shower rooms with hand-held shower heads. Theoretically, at least, every patient was showered daily, most of them early each morning, others, like me, late in the evening before getting ready to call it a night.

On Saturdays and Sundays, the languid routine of an unhurried breakfast, nap, and shower into which I lapsed helped make the morbidly dull part of those weekend days infinitely more pleasurable. It was almost like being on luxurious vacation. Between Valerie and me, of course, there were soon suggestive wisecracks and verbal games in the shower room, none of them compromising—to either one of us. When soaping myself, I could not extend my hands far enough to reach my knees, let alone to squeeze hers. I could not exert enough pressure on the towel when drying my thighs to produce any result. When other people were on duty to give me my shower, there could be tremendous, embarrassing awkwardness, as there'd been at first with the urinals and the bedpans—it took a lot of adaptation to reality on weekdays to allow myself to be showered by a different man or woman, someone, perhaps, whom I had never seen, and often I would pass it up sooner than subject myself to a person new to me or to one of the people there with whom I'd already discovered I had no rapport. There were some I thought clumsy and a few who were favorites. Nurse Humphries was a favorite. But she, alas, had time to oblige me in the shower room only on Saturdays and Sundays, when all rehabilitation work was suspended and she had not much else to do. Valerie brought a shower cap from home on Saturdays and Sundays to protect her hair against splashes. She shampooed my hair and combed it, and did not seem to mind doing that. After the shower, she would give me my second breakfast, the rest of my 1000 cc of blenderized food. After my lunch she would go downstairs for her own. On her return, she would give me my second lunch, another whole liter of my blenderized diet. At dinner too we would try to pack both meals in before she took off, and we did this with my food every day.

We discovered the scale. My weight was of interest only to the two of us. Medically, as I've said, I was in the pink. The scale at Rusk was different from the bed scale at Mount Sinai. This one had tracks leading up to a balancing pedestal large enough for a wheelchair. Valerie first weighed the wheelchair empty, then transferred me into it and rolled the wheelchair and me back on together. We computed my weight by subtracting the first figure from the second.

At the end of February, I was up to 145, from a low, I would guess, somewhere under 140. On March 6 my weight is recorded as 149.6. On March 13, I was another five pounds heavier at 154.2. And before the week after that one had ended, Dr. Ragnarsson cautioned me seriously against putting on any more. My legs were like matchsticks, and I was growing a paunch. I needed new muscle cells, not useless blubber. And I was placing unnecessary strain on muscles that were weak and hampering the extent to which I could employ them in exercise. From that day on I gave common sense priority over vanity. I took blenderized food only when I could not eat a meal from the tray. By the middle of March I did not often have that trouble. If I did, most likely it was at lunch, and I deduced from this that my difficulty stemmed from tiredness from the exercise of the morning that had affected my whole system. If I waited a half hour, eating seemed to grow easier. If I ate in the bed rather than the wheelchair, it seemed easier still. I fancied as well I was helped if I talked less and rested my mouth.

By the middle of March I'd already been switched from my soft diet of pureed meats and vegetables and creamed soups to one that was closer to the food most of us are normally accustomed to eating. I was lucky in timing. By the grace of God, I was able to change to hardier fare just as I was growing altogether sick of the pureed meats and vegetables and creamed soups. Even the blenderized formula was beginning to seem more appetizing.

Pea soup and lentil soup, lifelong favorites of mine, were on the menu at least once a week, and with these I lost restraint. With these, as with the sauce on the Italian meatball my daughter showed up with one night, I was eating before I knew I was doing it, without even trying to remember how. Before the bowl of soup was half empty, I would seize it in both hands, and I would find myself doing what I'd often in somber privacy despaired of ever doing again, consuming liquids ravenously in gulps. When my swallowing ability came back, it came back as an instinct, whole. Earlier, when I had to try to *remember* how to chew and swallow, I could not even begin to eat normally. You would not be able to, either. (I've asked dozens and dozens of people this one—to tell me, without starting to accomplish it, what they must do to get up from a chair. And no one has got it right yet. You try it now if you're seated. Don't move! What would you have to do if you wanted to stand up?) I found the same thing true of walking. Only when I was able to walk without thinking about it was I able to look normal doing it.

And also by the middle of March there were tentative exchanges between Dr. Mary Swajian and me about removing the tube. When I proposed it earliest, halfheartedly, she thought it better that I wait. There were the occasional medicines I took, liquid or pulverized, that were administered through the tube. When she suggested trying it, I shrank back in reluctance with fears of dehydration. My doubts made no sense; there were eggnogs, soups, and fruit juices I could drink by the quart. The only risk was the discomfort of having a new tube reinserted.

Late in the morning of March 18, when Valerie was away somewhere on another day off and a temporary nurse was filling in, Mary Swajian and I said let's go. It was accomplished painlessly in a second or two. (At Mount Sinai, I had watched spellbound as a young patient was extubated from a respirator; it would be preposterous even to hint that the two are comparable.) The tube looked filthy when Dr. Swajian extracted it simply by pulling it out and dropped it into the wastebasket. There was never trouble afterward, with the meal, the fluids, the medicines. In fact, everything went down easier with the tube gone and my esophagus clear.

Sometime during that day either I called Valerie or she called me, and I surprised her with the momentous news: Guess what, the tube is out! She was an hour or two away, but it seemed no more than a second before she was flying into the room with a shriek of delight to see for herself and was hugging me gleefully. By then she had been with me almost every day for something like ten weeks. Julius Green, who had came there sooner to have a look, discreetly moved to my motorized wheelchair, an apparatus dear to his heart, and rode out of the room into the corridor. Three months and three days had elapsed since the tube had been put in. It wasn't a record, but I had not wanted to set one.

Without exception, every staff member at Rusk—in the corridors, gyms, and other work areas—with whom I'd been having any kind of regular contact noted joyfully at first sight of me afterward that the tube had come out. Not at Rusk or at Mount Sinai were the personnel oblivious to me as an individual and a patient.

There were changes ahead I had envisioned previously. Now I could be taken out evenings; soon I could be taken home weekends. I would not need a private nurse any longer. I would miss mine, I thought, but I would be saving close to a thousand bucks a week. I wanted one Saturdays and Sundays. I could not face that threat of loneliness for the first half of the day weekends and for much of the rest of the day if the visitors turned out to be few. There was no opposition from Dr. Ragnarsson to this request, and the nurse I did have almost always turned out to be Valerie. She was still stopping by there most days anyway, on her way home from the different cases she had now back at Mount Sinai, returning in the evenings to see who was around or for the dates I still was arranging for her with other people in my continuing unrelenting courtship. I could read the writing on the wall: the day was not far off when I would have to begin going out with her myself.

I had already taken her out once, on our very first date! Properly and promptly, like the perfect and perfectly trained damsel she was, she came to my door to call for me. She greeted me respectfully, showered me and dried me, combed my hair, dressed me neatly in trousers, socks, shoes, sports shirt, and V-neck sweater, lifted me from my bed and sat me in my wheelchair, rolled me out through the hall to the elevators, and took me downstairs to the St. Patrick's Day celebration already in progress.

That red-faced Irishman I've mentioned had excellent local Irish connections, and there were colorful varieties of dancers, singers, fiddlers. On a different floor of the hospital was a young policeman patient who'd been shot in the spine interrupting a holdup, and a contingent of bagpipers from the police department of New York City arrived to pay respects to him by entertaining the whole lot of us. The long, large room was crowded, the crowd was spirited, Valerie had made herself up and did not look bad. I had not wanted to go, she had urged insistently. I was out in polite society again for the first time in months and enjoying myself sheepishly, and I did nothing, I think, that entire evening to disgrace my companion. I believe, for the sophisticated grown-up, there was straight booze in addition to the whiskey in the Irish coffee. I believe I passed both up.

At the end of the party, she escorted me right back to my door, came into my bedroom, took off my clothes, and lay me down on my mattress dressed in only my filmy pajamas. I told her right out that I did not believe in kissing on the first date. She swept my protests aside and said good night with a peck on the forehead.

About ten days after the tube was out, with approval from the hospital, I went home on a weekend with her. Speed left things in order for us. I was frightened beforehand, felt strange at the thought. I was missing the boldness of character to plan for more than one night away. (I am not the kind of person you want to rely on in a crisis, the man I'm sure you've heard about who will keep his head while others about him are losing theirs.) I made scrupulously certain of an ambulette to come for me in the late afternoon of one day and to call for me early enough the next to have the two of us back at the hospital in time for lunch. I was filled with apprehension. At what? I could not say.

I had learned twice from experience in the hospital that two people were needed to raise me from the floor if I fell. I therefore arranged for that friend in the building, Bruce Addison, to be present when Valerie arrived with me and to remain at least until he saw I was safely installed. Finding myself there was eerie for a while. A good deal in the furnishing of the apartment had not been completed when last I saw it, and all of it felt unfamiliar. Frankly, I could not think of much to do until evening, other than to fumble listlessly through the stacks of papers arranged on my desk. For dinner we were joined by a different friend, Stanley Cohen. I knew he liked Thai cooking, and we ate downstairs a block away in a good Siamese restaurant I used to go to often. Our table was in front, and space had to be cleared for my wheelchair. Afterward, Stanley returned with us to the apartment and remained just long enough to make sure there had been no accident going back.

Then Valerie and I were in the apartment alone. She knew me intimately. The inevitable question was in the air immediately. She had brought a nightgown. In my room was a custom-built, queen-sized platform bed with eiderdown pillows and a Swedish down quilt in a smart Swedish quilt cover, all picked out by Speed from a good Swedish shop when he was doing my apartment with the taste of a Swedish connoisseur and the sky was the limit. In the small living room was an ordinary convertible couch, for which the folded sheets and pillowcases had been taken from the linen closet by Speed and left in view to be used as needed. In which did she sleep? In the words of Montaigne:

*C'est pour moi de savoir et pour vous à découvrir.**

---

* "That's for me to know and for you to find out."

IT WAS NOT LONG AFTER Joe's tube came out that I was invited to the south of France. Life was getting better for us.

Until that time, his move to Rusk had not relieved me of my duties as accountant, postman, and shopper, and there had been no change in my role as escort and stand-in swain.

On Valentine's Day, as part of his continuing courtship, Joe suggested I go to William Greenberg and Sons bakery to pick up a chocolate-chocolate cake for Valerie. She'd told him she loved chocolate and he presumed she hadn't tried a cake this rich before (we think it's the best in New York). I congratulated him on his choice. No woman could resist that kind of attention. This was before I became a "writer," so Heller created the inscription: "Dear Valerie, Will you be OUR concubine?" She was crazy about the cake. I have no idea what she thought of the message. I hope someone told her it was not my writing.

I figured this specialized kind of work would decrease as Joe's health continued to improve and soon I would have to resume romancing on my own behalf.

When Mario Puzo called and told me he and Carol Gino were

coming into town to visit Joe, he invited me to join them for supper afterward at Elaine's. Heller asked me to take Valerie along. So, after her shift, Valerie went home to change and returned dressed for an evening on the town. I had not seen her that dolled up and neither had Joe, who obviously enjoyed what he saw. When he asked her to bring him some ice cream from the nurses' station fridge, she was quick to remind him that she was a guest and not on duty. Carol, a former nurse, and a feisty one, asked where they kept it and fetched it for him. The last time Mario had visited Joe it was at Mount Sinai and Mario couldn't wait to leave. This time, at Rusk, he was so relieved to see Joe recovering instead of "croaking" (a favorite Puzo expression) that he happily hung around until Joe got bored trying to entertain us and kicked us all out.

The evening at Elaine's was typical: the place was crowded with writers, actors, producers, onlookers, and Woody Allen. Elaine loves Mario, but when she walked over to spend time with us, she did a surprising thing. Valerie's purse was on the floor next to her chair. As Elaine approached, she kicked it under the table. I must have looked startled because she leaned over to whisper in explanation: "I don't trust everybody that comes into my place. It's safer now."

As usual, we ordered too much, but strangely enough, this time nothing at all was left over. Mario never really eats very much. Carol eats like a bird. It's true that I enjoy good food, but I can't consume more than a normal portion. What we found out that night is that, when there's food on the table, Valerie never stops.

The next day I warned Joe as a friend what his tall, thin nurse could put away. His face lit up like a Christmas tree.

We were invited to a birthday party for Texan Richard West by our friend, Valerie Salembier, but Joe still had the tube and did not want to go, even though they lived only a block away from Rusk. Joe thought Nurse Humphries would enjoy it. He was making me feel like John Alden, the surrogate wooer. But I warned him that once he was well enough to court for himself, there was a good chance he'd mess it up. The party for Richard was definitely high-spirited with lots of good food, drink, real-live Texans, music, and dancing. Nurse Humphries heard singer and guitarist Joe "King" Carrasco for the first time and later asked Richard to tape the music for her. At some point in the evening we'd been handed unusual percussion instruments for beating time and doubling the decibels. I was surprised nobody called the cops. Valerie Humphries and I were the last to leave. Valerie had a marvelous evening, and the next day at the hospital she was filled with gratitude—to him. Joe said he was pleased she'd gone (which also meant he was glad that he'd stayed in bed).

After the tube was out and Valerie Salembier asked us over again, Joe accepted the invitation. I joined him there with a date of my own this time. On his first night out, at a small restaurant up the street from Rusk, he seemed nervous and uncomfortable sitting in a wheelchair and eating in public. At Salembier's dinner, however, he enjoyed himself. Our hostess, because she lived nearby and knew that Joe lacked the strength to hold a book for long, had volunteered to come in the evening and read to him from the works of George Eliot. I thought it was a lovely offer. Joe turned her down flat. Joe confessed that the idea of being read to was as terrifying to him as visiting intensive care units was to Mario. He said he would rather eat a broom.

Now that Joe was permitted to leave Rusk for dinners out, we, his gourmet friends, suggested he join us for a meeting in Chinatown. Only then would we be sure that everything humanly possible was being done to speed his recovery. Thus began his real rehabilitation. We had to relax our rule about girlfriends so that Nurse Humphries could come. We simply decided registered nurses were exempt, bending over backward (at that late date) to accept Valerie as a health professional instead of what she really was—Joe's girl. (It was a shrewd move. We figured that a couple of friendly nurses might come in handy to those of us who were not getting any younger!)

For Joe's first Chinatown excursion, we arrived at Rusk in

Julie Green's station wagon and sent George in to announce us. Julie Green, Joe Stein, and I waited outside. We were standing in front of the hospital driveway as Valerie approached, pushing Heller in his collapsible wheelchair. We were just about to help him into the wagon when Valerie turned to us and asked, "How is it out?" Stein put his arm up in the air in a gesture of simple eloquence and said, "Like this!" She seemed to accept that as a reasonable answer, but then asked, "Is it cold?" The rest of us stood open-mouthed and didn't know which way to look, but Stein, moving his fingers as if he were appraising the quality of cloth, said, brilliantly, "Feel it!" Valerie said, "Oh."

The fact that she was already outdoors when she asked was not a matter of consideration. Her patient's comfort was. She just wanted to know whether she had dressed Joe warmly enough.

Once past that hurdle, I tried to be gallant and lift Joe out of his wheelchair. I couldn't, even though I'm strong. Valerie took over, easily managing to stand him up and swing him into the front seat. I watched her do it but couldn't quite figure out the technique. When we arrived at the Rickshaw Garage, I tried once more to lift him. With difficulty, I managed to get him up, pushing my knees against his and gripping the belt of his pants to assist. I also managed to attract a crowd and make Valerie and the others roar with laughter at my clumsy efforts.

We pushed Joe from the garage down to our favorite restaurant, Wing Wah, where we were greeted warmly by Dick, one of the owners. He was very happy to see Joe again. Dick was particularly sympathetic because he had recently experienced a neurological disorder that had paralyzed the side of his face for a time. After a few polite words, Dick brought us a bottle of Johnnie Walker, Black Label (sometimes we bought whiskey and gave it to him to hold for us, but this bottle was his own), and then he hurried off to the kitchen to order for us. First, the waiters brought the "house soup." This is a special concoction that is not on the menu; it changes each day but is invariably delicious. The soup is made for the owners, the chef, waiters, busboys, and, when we showed up, us. Soon other dishes began appearing at the table. I saw Heller's mouth quiver as soon as he spied the soy sauce chicken. His eyes popped when the roast pork arrived. The oyster casserole had him gasping, and he was riveted by the sight of the panfried noodles with beef. We noticed that he couldn't extend his arms all the way to reach with his famous spoons, but we don't make allowances for the handicapped. He also chewed and swallowed his food very slowly and he could not always keep it from falling out of his mouth. He was starting to develop the habit of keeping a hand over his mouth while he ate, a habit he still has. We sympathized silently but did not change our pace. The bulk of the meal was gobbled up by his surrogate mouth, Nurse Humphries, with a little help from her friends, the Gourmets. Except for pre-GBS Heller, Valerie is the biggest eater I've ever met. At Elaine's when I saw her attack, I thought perhaps she was unusually hungry, but I was wrong. Now when I hear, "Mmmm, it's too good. I can't manage another bite. I'm too full," I know I'm about to witness some serious eating. We needn't have bothered to stretch the rules to include her. An eater like that is always welcome to join us.

Before he was discharged, Joe had numerous dinners away from the hospital. On one occasion, Cheryl McCall's birthday celebration, Joe arrived with Valerie at one of our favorite Italian restaurants in Greenwich Village. The driver of the taxi that delivered Joe to the restaurant not only helped Valerie with the wheelchair but refused to let Joe pay for the ride. Valerie wheeled him to our table, the owners, Michael and Ennio, greeted him warmly, and we had a fine meal reminiscing about the last time Cheryl had eaten with him—the night before he entered the hospital with Guillain-Barré. We drank to his health and complete recovery. After the meal we planned to continue the celebration elsewhere, but Joe and Valerie were heading back to Rusk. It had started to rain and taxis were scarce. We finally were able to flag one down in front of the restaurant, but when the driver saw Joe in the wheelchair, this one, in contrast to the man who had driven us there and would not take money, sped off. We were outraged and frantically sought another. When we found one and were again rebuffed, we felt awful. Joe had never seemed so helpless and vulnerable and we were damned ineffectual. It was heartbreaking to see him sitting there. As we searched once again, Valerie managed to find a taxi that stopped for her. Almost before the driver knew what was happening, she opened the front door, pushed the wheelchair to it, swiftly lifted Joe out of the chair, and swung him onto the seat. After he was safely inside, she collapsed his chair and stuck it in the trunk—a beautifully executed move.

Clearly it was only a matter of weeks or another month or two before Joe would be strong enough to leave Rusk. It was standard hospital procedure to send special teams to visit patients' domiciles well in advance of their discharge to evaluate safety and to recommend devices to accommodate particular needs. They assumed Joe would still be in his wheelchair when he was released. An appointment was made with me, and I admitted the two Rusk experts, young women who knew their business, and escorted them through the apartment.

Certain changes were deemed necessary. For one thing, they thought the bed was too low. It was. I had designed it lower than conventional height to make the ceiling appear higher (and me taller). When it was built, Joe was healthy as a horse. Who knew then what fate had in store for us? I could accept their recommendation but I hadn't gotten around to doing anything about it before the experts were proved right. Because it was low, on Joe's first sleepover date away from Rusk, Valerie found it close to impossible to lift him out of the bed to his feet. Once he was standing, he had no trouble moving to the wheelchair. Joe also found lying flat strange and he wondered if anything could be done to raise the back like a hospital bed. For several months he had been in that position and he had grown used to it.

I called my cabinetmaker, Barry Rosenberg, the craftsman I'd employed to execute my designs for Joe's apartment, and described thc problem. It was solved with a little ingenuity. The workmanship was first-rate. Basically, Barry constructed two strong wooden boxes that fit perfectly into the existing frame. He added a series of wedges to raise the back. When the mattress was placed on top, it was exactly at the height the hospital people wanted.

The team from Rusk had also suggested installing a hand-held shower, acquiring a waterproof aluminum chair for the tub, and removing the living room rug, which they saw as a potential hazard. They felt that the clothes closet rods should be lowered so that Joe could reach them from a sitting position.

Most of those jobs I took care of myself. Then it began to dawn on me that the "real" Joe Heller would someday soon be returning and the imposter who was living in his apartment, still signing his checks and autographs and receiving deferential greetings from doormen, would have to leave. Poor Speed had to face a return to his walk-up and forget about the high life in a high rise. It was good news . . . and bad news. I was glad he was coming home and yet reluctant to surrender my role as his alter ego and let him take over again. I thought I did a much better job of impersonating a successful author.

Even when Joe came to the apartment for weekends, I was not really discommoded because, since early March, I had been spending every weekend on Fire Island. For years I've had a seasonal job there selling real estate and, at that off-season time, I occupied my own oceanfront beach house, fixing and cleaning, to get it ready to rent it for the summer. Normally, my job was finished by Memorial Day weekend, and I vacated my house so that my tenants, for a hefty rental, could enjoy it. I would share a house with several people somewhere else. This year was going to be different, but I did not know that yet.

It was highly unusual and out of character, but somehow I began to reflect on my future. I had not thought much about my life while I was intimately involved with Joe's. I started to have some thoughts about what to do when Joe no longer needed me. I was not terribly concerned about keeping busy. I've never had that problem. I knew I could always depend on my need to make things. It didn't matter to me whether I was making paintings, sculpture, jewelry, or clothes, repairing objects, or creating meals. And it was spring, the most congenial time for me to return to my loft in the flower district. Besides, I had plenty of time to get used to a change. Joe was coming to the apartment only for weekends. I still was there during the week. But unexpectedly there were hints that other events might soon occur to continue my life's upward spiral: Joe asked if I could leave my weekend job earlier this year.

Before Joe was hit with GBS, Bob Towbin had invited him to Cannes for the film festival. When Towbin goes to Cannes, he avoids hotels. He had chartered a fully staffed yacht (which he later bought), and as he was attending in his official capacity as a member of the New York Film Society, he also planned to take his well-earned vacation. So when Joe suddenly asked, "How would you like to go to Cannes?" I thought he was kidding, and said so. He said, "I'm serious. If you want to go, I can arrange it."

Now I *was* excited! When I was in business, I spent a lot of time in Europe, traveling deluxe, but it hadn't looked to me as if I would ever get the chance to live that way again. After protesting lamely that he couldn't spare me, I let Joe assure me he could. He said he would be either in the hospital or out. Valerie would continue to take care of him, and his brother, Lee, had volunteered to come to New York any time Joe asked. Lee could sleep at his son's place or on the convertible couch in Joe's apartment, and take care of the mail, shop, run errands, and visit his famous brother, as well as his son, Paul, and his grandchild. In other words, I would be doing Lee a favor by leaving the country. Mario would be in Cannes, too. All of them had now made me an offer I could not refuse.

From that time on, I had to get busy, and the name "Speed" was no longer a sarcasm.

Joe was getting out of the hospital at the end of May, and all of us were taking it for granted that he would be able to use his house in East Hampton for the summer from the middle of June. Even with all of the changes to the apartment, the kitchen and the bathroom would still not be big enough for the wheelchair, and the commode wouldn't go through the doorway of the bathroom. I borrowed Julie's car one day, and Valerie and I drove out to East Hampton to examine the premises.

The house seemed ideal for him. I had seen it before the pool was installed. It was greatly improved by this addition, and the beauty of the grounds as I remembered them was intact. Even though there were neighbors fairly close by, the setting gave one a feeling of space and seclusion. Valerie thought the house was lovely, comfortable, and nicely situated.

On examining the house, we decided that we would rearrange the first-floor study/guest room as Joe's bedroom, but the convertible couch in that room would have to be raised. I called my cabinetmaker and again we came up with a simple and inexpensive solution. Barry cut some thick plywood to my measurements and I donated a spare foam-rubber mattress from my Fire Island house.

I was troubled by the small step from the bedroom to the patio but felt that I could construct a ramp. I made room for a desk in the living room and took measurements of the downstairs bathroom. I saw there was enough space for his special commode to be placed over the existing toilet and that his hand-held shower and bench would fit in his stall shower.

Next, I had Joe's car checked and tried to have telephone service restored. The phone company was about to sue, claiming there was a delinquent bill for a year. They would not restore service until everything was paid. I obtained a duplicate bill and sent them a check. When I told Joe about that, he said I'd better contact the local water and lighting companies as well. They, too, claimed unpaid balances from the previous year.

Joe had suggested that while Valerie and I were there, we visit old friends, the Gwathmeys, and take them out to dinner—Joe's treat. I had met Bob and Rosalie in the early forties. Bob is from Virginia and Rosalie is from North Carolina. In all but spirit, they are no longer very young. Bob is a fine artist and Rosalie is capable of everything. She has the best taste in decor, clothes, and people of anyone I know, including her son the architect, Charles. (And it gets Charlie crazy when I say so.) I had introduced the Gwathmeys to Heller many years ago, and now I was introducing Joe's nurse, Valerie. She was obviously charmed by them and by their Southern accents. Bob and Rosalie declined dinner but insisted we stay for drinks and a few choice homemade delicacies. If it was Joe's intention to have Nurse Humphries stick around, he was definitely making all the right moves. Old Bob was flirting for Heller like mad, while Rosalie was in the kitchen putting the finishing touches on some appetizers that would astound Valerie. (In addition to her accomplishments as an outstanding wife, mother, textile designer, photographer, and knitter, Rosalie Gwathmey is a Cordon Bleu cook.)

Joe felt he was not going to be able to move to East Hampton unless we could find a physical therapist who would be willing to come to his house. Rusk couldn't help. For months we had been trying everything we could think of, but with no success. While there that day I went to the offices of the *East Hampton Star* and placed an ad for a local physical therapist. There were no responses.

Finally, the solution to this serious problem came about serendipitously. Early that spring, I'd arranged to have my Fire Island beach house painted by a young man who asked if I would mind if his girlfriend came out for the weekend. I didn't. She turned out to be pretty, intelligent, and personable. My father, who'd always upbraided me for not asking enough questions, would have been proud of me as I engaged this young lady in conversation and inquired about her occupation. When she replied that she was a teacher of physical therapy at Columbia-Presbyterian hospital, I told her about Joe's problem. She thought she knew some people she could ask. I had a strong feeling that she would come through. And she did. While I was in France, she called Joe and referred him to a Riverhead therapist, who in turn found Don Shaw. And Don, a likable young guy with curly blond hair and a good therapist (he also gave me exercises to help my bad knee), later arrived on a motorcycle on the day he was supposed to and became an amiable and welcome addition to Heller's East Hampton "staff."

In New York, Joe had asked me to buy a tall chair with arms, to match the twenty-six-inch-high chair that he used for exercising. There was a stool that height in the kitchen of the occupational therapy section at Rusk. Because everything of that kind on the market was too ugly, I decided to invent one. I used one of the existing dining chairs and raised it in a way that would allow it to be lowered. It looked funny but it did the job. My mother would have been proud of me. She'd had one son who was a doctor and another who was a lawyer. Since I, the youngest, didn't want to be a dentist, she thought maybe I should invent something. At the time I thought she was foolish. Forgive me, Ma.

Because I was on a tight schedule—I planned to leave New York for East Hampton just two days after my return from France—I arranged for a local moving man Joe knew to pick up the plywood at Barry's, go to the Eighth Avenue apartment for my bicycle and Joe's belongings, including his special commode and the antique wheelchair I'd given him, as a joke (though it turned out to be useful), for his birthday. The moving man would then stop in Bay Shore for the mattress, and drop everything off at the East Hampton house. It all worked perfectly.

A few days before Joe was released from Rusk, I was in his room when Dr. Goodgold came by and suggested another EMG test be scheduled. Joe was reluctant, recalling how painful that last EMG had been. Normally I would not have said anything, but this time I had the impertinence to ask whether the test would benefit the patient. Dr. Goodgold replied, candidly, that it was not going to help Joe at all, but that it *might* help doctors doing research. I turned to Joe and said, "If I were you, I wouldn't do it." Joe declined.

By the time Joe was finally released on May 14, I'd had plenty of notice, so I'd changed the linen, cleared out my few personal possessions, and gone back to my studio on Twenty-eighth Street to begin packing for the trip to Cannes.

It was just before I vacated his apartment that I thought of an elaborate practical joke. I had recently posed for a photojournalist friend who was expanding into portraiture. I filled the large blank space above Joe's bed between two bookcases with an enormous photomural of his friend Speed.

I was not present when Joe got there to see my portrait, but Valerie told me that he laughed for at least five minutes, she for ten. I later told Heller that he could rip my picture down whenever he found himself strong enough to do so. His reply was, "No, I like it and I think it looks good there." I was touched. Now, however, he complains, "I have not been able to be rid of it since." (After he vacated his Eighth Avenue apartment, the huge photo was moved to East Hampton with the rest of his possessions, and it now dominates the bedroom of his guest cottage—where the most frequent guest is me.)

While Heller was getting used to coming home weekends, there were still a few more things to do for him before I left for Cannes. Joe was dissatisfied with his coffeemaker and wanted something better. I told him about an elegant glass and metal filter type, made in France. I said it was rather expensive but that it was supposed to make excellent coffee. He said, "Get it," so I did. He hated it. "This little thing costs that much? For what? It makes only four cups and the coffee is lousy. Throw it out. I want a twelve-cupper." I told him I would research it and consulted my friend, the maven, Saul Zabar. He told me the latest, state-of-the-art machine was a Japanese electronic model that did everything—ground the beans, added the boiled water, and made perfect coffee every time. It was foolproof but expensive. I gave Joe the information. He said, "Get it." I did. The next time I saw him, I asked how he was doing with the electronic beauty. "It makes terrible coffee, that's how, all twelve cups."

My friends Ken and Barbara Cooke threw me a bon voyage party at their Soho loft. Heller had just been discharged from Rusk and wanted to come but knew the building did not have an elevator and he could not make the stairs. We told him there would be at least four guys there who could easily carry him up. It was going down with the same men drunk that scared him.

The party was a nice send-off. Heller never gives presents. But this time he surprised me. He had arranged for his gift to be handed to me at the party. When I removed the wrapping, I was again touched. It was the elegant French coffeemaker that I loved and he hated.

The following day I was off to the airport, on my way to Cannes.

EARLY ONE MORNING at the beginning of March I was able to turn from my back to my side. My brother, Lee, sounded crestfallen when I gave him the good news. "Oh, no," he groaned. Once a week I would make a telephone call to Florida to either him or my sister. "You know, Joe," he explained somewhat humbly. "All this time I never realized you weren't able to do that." He could conceive I was paralyzed. He could not believe I was unable to move.

In May he saw much more that he could not believe, when I was out of the hospital and he came to New York to help Valerie take care of me after that heartless knave Speed Vogel had abandoned me to go off on his pleasure junket to the Mediterranean with which I had magnanimously provided him, at somebody else's expense. Lee could not bring himself to look squarely at me as I sat in my wheelchair and went feebly through my face and arm exercise routines. He got huge pleasure, however, watching Carol Recker Hughes put me through more animated paces on her home visits and seeing Valerie take charge of me and the apartment, even on days when she disappeared early to work at Mount Sinai on other cases and did not come back until late in the afternoon. He could not get over my luck in finding myself with such pleasant women. It was that talent I have, I told him facetiously, for bringing out the best in people.

Another refreshing person from Rusk who came to my apartment occasionally was a nurse named Anna Gorelik. She filled in those evenings Valerie deserted me callously to go about her own life as though it were as important to her as mine. I needed somebody professional for just two functions, each of which did not consume as much as five seconds: to lift me from the toilet seat, and to lift me from the shower bench Speed had fitted into the bathtub. By then I could do all of the rest, even to drying myself and to walking in and out. Neither the wheelchair nor the commode would fit through the doorway of the bathroom. I could enter the kitchen in the wheelchair, but the room wasn't wide enough for me to turn around in. Anna and Lee would set and clear the table for dinner for the three of us; more often than not it was a meal sent up already cooked from the Carnegie Delicatessen or another of the various eating places nearby. (The city of New York abounds in restaurants, and I cannot think of as many as five outside of Chinatown in which the food is much good.) If not for the matrimonial conflicts resuming immediately and inexorably, the interlude between my leaving the hospital and going to East Hampton would have been untroubled and, as so much else that was occurring, enriched with a kind of suspenseful novelty. None of this had ever happened before, to any of us, and I was not in pain or troubled by symptoms of any internal illness. Vogel wasn't missed. Yet his return was anticipated to the day, and his cooperation for the summer was an indispensable to the plans already made as Valerie's. Without this summer staff, as I more than once had conjectured aloud, I possibly would have had nowhere to go but a veterans' hospital. And I was not sure if my government had left even that avenue open to me.

Back in the month of March much was happening inside me. In the first week, my gross grasp, which had been "barely measurable" at my first OT (occupational therapy) evaluation a month earlier, was showing improvement. With my right hand, but not with my left, I could press open a clothespin, and before the end of the month, I was able to use scissors against such resistive materials as a newspaper. I was put to work cutting out discount coupons for the staff from the advertisements of supermarkets. At the end of the month I was able to work at tabletop heights "with activities that present minimal to moderate resistance, i.e. opening screwtop jars, stirring cake batter, operating an electric beater." I was able to play air hockey and "able to bend and reach from my wheelchair for objects near or on the floor using either hand," an activity contributing "to increased head, neck, and trunk control and to improvement in arm placement patterns." I did not tell Lee about my recovery of these skills because I did not want to risk depressing him again with the awareness they'd been lost. I was independent with the use of the urinal. This return came gradually but, once started, was soon all there. And this return restored a measure of privacy I coveted, for at night I would not have to ring: the urinal would be emptied by whichever person looked in on me every two hours.

At the beginning of April there was an increase in gross grasp over the previous month of two pounds in each hand, from four pounds to six in the right, from no pounds to two in the left. (There was still not enough strength in both thumbs combined for the on-and-off switch of the electric toothbrush.) And three weeks later, the effort I could make with each hand had just about tripled. And less than three weeks after that, when I left the hospital, there was a further gain to twenty pounds in the right hand and nine in the left. But don't let the numbers overwhelm you: I don't know what my gross grasp is now or what it should register, and I don't much care. But my hands are greatly stronger than they were back then, yet still too weak for tight shower faucets or small shirt buttons with smaller buttonholes. One day in March I was able to get my bathing suit on over my hips. This came about through the tireless persistence—one might say it was remorseless, and I am the one who will—of my regular day nurses, Margaret George and Meryl Farquharson.

Meryl started it first, handing me the swimming trunks one morning after breakfast, instead of putting them on me as usual, and saying, as she started to walk away, "Here, do it yourself today."

I was startled. "I can't," I said. These are words the members of the staff at Rusk hear often.

"Do as much as you can," she answered imperturbably with her placid and beautiful smile and left me temporarily while she went to help prepare the rest of the patients in her care for the day's activities. Meryl was a brown-skinned woman from Barbados who had trained as a nurse in England.

And at the end of March I succeeded in getting the bathing suit over my hips myself. After I could raise my hips while lying down, I could manage undershorts and trousers and was practically independent in dressing—lying down. (At the end of April, I was brought to the homemaking area of the occupational therapy section, where I prepared a tuna fish salad and manipulated the Oster electric can opener. It was reported that I handled the cutting of the onion well, which is something I scarcely excel at now. So I was practically independent in cooking too.)

Clearly, some process of nerve-cell repair was taking place, and the "return" of which I'd been told was occurring.

On the counterbalance sling I had started out needing four pounds of support to raise each arm above table level. By the middle of March I could reach with my right arm "for objects at or above 90 °" without any assistance from the unit. However, I still needed three pounds of support for my left, and when I was discharged from the hospital, a pound and a half. Lying on my back, I could bend my left arm; I could not lift my elbow. Mel Brooks was awed again by this deficiency of mine when he showed up at Rusk one night with a number of the other dwarfs in the Gourmet Club. He asked me again to demonstrate several times how I could not raise my left arm.

"Come on, come on, let me see how you can't do it," he was just about saying.

I threw in an extra treat by showing him also how I could not lift my head.

This visit from Mel, like his first, was a total surprise. All of the guys who showed up that evening were on their way to Chinatown. There were five—Speed, Julie Green, Mel, George Mandel, and Ngoot Lee. Valerie Humphries, as I've said, is tall, perhaps five ten or more. She was flabbergasted to see so many short males enter the room one in back of the other in what for a moment appeared to her to be an endless file, and she did not hesitate to say so. She had never, she exclaimed, seen so many short men in one place. To her merry outcry of astonishment, George Mandel had a benign response.

"If there were just two more of us," he told her, "you could be Snow White."

I had Valerie move me from the bed into my wheelchair after they trooped in. Mel was uncharacteristically quiet after I had given him a complete rundown of my physical weaknesses. He seemed pensive for a while. I still weighed very much less than when he had seen me last. Then, perhaps to repay me for the assurances I had given him when I was in the ICU and the demonstrations I had provided now, he decided to extend himself to help me in the best way he could think of, one that was unpredictable and inspired, albeit inefficacious. Without a clue to anyone of what he had in mind, he moved from the wall near the window, against which he had been leaning, crossed the room to where I was seated, placed his hand on my head, rolled his eyes toward the ceiling, and screamed:

"For Jesus! Stand! Walk!"

I tried my best but failed.

Outside as they were leaving, I later learned from George, Mel explained with a dejected shrug, "I thought I'd give it a shot."

To which Julius Green suggested, "Maybe we just ought to all chip in and send him away to Lourdes."

By the middle of May I could lift my head. I could struggle up to a sitting position without help by the time I left the hospital, but I could not stand from a sitting position unless the seat I was occupying was twenty-six inches high or more. Standard chairs are between sixteen and nineteen inches. However, I was requiring less assistance standing up. That was a difference I could not feel but one which the various people lifting me could.

Comprehensive PT and OT evaluations are conducted monthly, and it is from the written reports of Carol Hughes and Susan Bernstein that I am obtaining these specifics. Between my first PT evaluation in February and my second one in March, Carol reported gains of a half to one grade in my trunk, neck, and upper and lower extremities, a general gain in grades from P– to P+ (where P stands for poor). There was improvement in bed mobility and transfer activity. I was able now to roll from side to side on the mat and to move myself up and down. I was walking between the parallel bars in the beginning of March and soon could ambulate short distances with contact guarding for safety and verbal cueing for technique in gait. Lateral trunk flexion was noted during ambulation, along with fatigue. There is a tendency of the body when impaired to recruit stronger muscles for the work of the weak ones, and it was easier for me and Frankenstein's monster to raise our legs by moving the trunk from side to side than by employing the small hip flexors supplied by nature to *Homo sapiens* to do that job of walking erect with fluid grace and dignity. Here was one of the deviations of gait the verbal cueing was intended to correct.

One month later, by the end of the first week in April, I had been without a private-duty nurse for over three weeks and was moving from appointment to appointment on my own in a manual wheelchair, using both upper extremities to propel it, in conjunction with my lower left extremity, my left leg, which I now was able to lift from the floor and extend and contract. I was astounded to find that I had grown strong enough to employ the transfer board and astonished by the beneficial change the transfer board brought in the quality of my life. I could go from bed to wheelchair and back without standing, with no necessity, therefore, to rely on anyone. I had graduated from the parallel bars and could ambulate short distances using a rolling walker with bilateral upright arm supports to which my wrists were secured by Velcro straps. (My shoulder muscles—now to tell you the truth, I don't think I'd ever *heard* of shoulder muscles before—were too weak for canes or crutches or for a conventional walker used by invalids who are more robust.) At the end of her examination of me in the first week in April, Carol was impressed by the gradual gains in my clinical status and disclosed she was going to recommend that, because I was continuing to improve, I be kept there another four weeks. And that was the first I realized I was in danger of being sent home!

In May I was able to ascend and descend small steps with contact guarding, outside the pool now as well as in, and Carol recommended again that I be kept for further rehabilitation. But in May I had been outside to a large birthday party for me, and I no longer wanted to stay.

By then, I had been to Coney Island, on a sunny spring day with Sergeant Jerry McQueen, a friend on the police force, and with Mary Kay Fisch, another cheerful therapist at Rusk, who was new to the city and did not know many people yet. I had been to a Sunday brunch at Murray and Reene Schisgal's with Valerie and Jeffrey Cohen, in Jeffrey's car. Jeffrey would continue to exclaim in entranced wonderment that he had never in all his life met so many entertaining and good-natured people as he was meeting through me, but Jeffrey is a lawyer so that doesn't mean much. But Valerie was saying the same and continuing to enjoy herself. These days when I came back to the hospital at the close of a weekend, it was not always with eagerness as formerly but often with irritability and resentment. The more I recovered, the unhappier and more impatient I was growing with my condition and my confinement, and Susan Bernstein already had written that this patient "was at times frustrated and depressed at the slow rate of recovery." By the beginning of May it was already obviously only a matter of one month or another before I left; and I would still be crippled when I did.

So I spoke to Dr. Goodgold in my room and asked him, "Will it make any difference with me if I left in the middle of this month instead of waiting until the end?"

Although he and the rest in administration were suggesting I stay till the end, he answered candidly that it would not. He told me also that the cost of outpatient care was going to be greater than you or I would have guessed.

"Will it make any difference with me if I came to the hospital only two afternoons a week instead of three?" I asked. I had contracted with Carol for her to come to the apartment for home care on the days I did not go to the hospital.

He told me candidly that it would not. Then Dr. Goodgold inquired if I would be good enough to submit to another EMG test before I left. Remember my EMG test? This one too, like the second one proposed at Mount Sinai, was offered on the house.

There is a Yiddish verb "*phumpher.*" It describes a kind of evasive stammering and mumbling that is affected with the goal of procrastination in giving a straightforward reply. I found myself doing a lot of *phumphering* with him right then, until Speed chirped up to the rescue, asking:

"Is there any way in which it will help him?"

Dr. Goodgold was the author of a technical medical book on electromyographic testing and research. "It won't help him," he told us candidly, "but it might help me."

I told him candidly that I would not.

Downstairs in a corner area of the first floor of the Rusk Institute is a fully furnished apartment, staffed by busy personnel, which consists of a living room, a kitchen (with either a dining area or a small adjacent dining room—I forget which), a bedroom, and a bathroom with a hand-held shower attachment and a Lumex bench inside the bathtub on which one sits for a shower. Metal handgrips are embedded in the walls in several strategic spots near the bathtub and the toilet seat. Both the bathroom and the kitchen are very much larger than the corresponding rooms in many of the newer luxury high-rise apartment buildings in New York City, and, except for the location and the constant stream of people moving in and out to test themselves with the facilities of everyday living, the apartment could, by current Manhattan standards, be considered not a bad one to have.

In an open space outside the approach to the apartment is a mock-up of a conventional automobile. It was to this that Carol led Valerie and me one day to teach her to transfer me from a wheelchair to a car, in anticipation of the freedom to go out I would wish to make use of now that the nasograstric tube was gone and I could eat at a table in homes and restaurants and stay out overnight. (Here I enjoyed a big pecuniary advantage over people whose costs at the hospital were paid by medical insurance: they lost coverage for nights they spent out. I was luckier. I lost no insurance benefits because I did not have any.) This procedure of transferring me to a car wasn't difficult but it had to be learned and then practiced a few times. For example, if I were moved by one person, it could only be to the front seat of a car, and there had to be enough room between the vehicle and the curb for the wheelchair to fit parallel to the seat, on the same level as the car rather than on the sidewalk. Only Valerie was able to perform this maneuver for me nimbly in the few months it was necessary, although one or two others, to my peril, did have a try.

Both the apartment and this replica of an automobile helped comprise an aspect of rehabilitation work that is as much social in objective as medical. In the parlance of Rusk, this training is called "activities for daily living," or ADL in abbreviated form.

On an afternoon in March, in the period usually devoted to physical therapy on the mat and, toward the end of that hour now, on a compact leg machine with pedals that is called a restorator, Carol and an assistant conducted me downstairs to the apartment for some work in ADL. In the living room there was very little for us to do: the upholstered furniture was plainly much too low. The kitchen was busy with other teams of patients and tutors; besides, I had not been able to cook for myself before, and I certainly was not going to be able to start doing it now. It was in the bedroom and bathroom in the rear of the apartment that our challenges lay, where my morale was first boosted and next shattered by my experience with the transfer board. I was elated to discover I had regained enough strength in my arms and shoulders to at last be able to make use of a transfer board. I was distressed by the obvious message implied in the lesson that I was going to *have* to make use of one when I left.

A transfer board is a manufactured piece of lacquered wood, beveled at both ends and about twelve inches wide and twenty-four inches long. It is employed by people who cannot stand but have use of their arms, to slide themselves from one surface on which they are seated to another of approximate height. Assisted by Carol now in lifting and positioning the board properly, with one of the beveled ends wedged under my buttock and the other set firmly on the seat of the wheelchair, I slid along the smoothed surface of the wood from the bed to the wheelchair and back. Then I practiced moving myself from the bed to the commode, which is an inch or two higher than the bed and the wheelchair. It is imperative for safety that the wheels of both chairs be locked. I was doing very much better than I had supposed I could. Earlier attempts had been futile. Next, I went back into the wheelchair, released the brakes, rolled to the bathtub, and transferred to the shower bench. My feelings as I proceeded successfully grew more and more conflicted, and finally I balked when told to go onto the commode again to wheel it into the bathroom and back it into place above the toilet bowl. I did not want to try. It was a waste of our time. When was I ever going to have to know how to do that? I demanded unhappily in a restrained tantrum. (They'd told me I'd recover, hadn't they, and it took no effort on my part to believe them.) I told Carol angrily that I was never going to live alone and have to take care of myself until I knew I could. It was then that I uttered my empty, histrionic threat to put myself into a veterans' hospital if I had to. But by the end of the hour I was docile again, and I submissively placed a purchase order for a wheelchair, a commode chair, a

Lumex bench, and a shower attachment, to be delivered when I was discharged.

And a day or so later I canceled it, after trading notes as customary each evening with Mrs. Belle Simon, who did me a thousand-dollar favor by asking:

"Why are you buying them? If you're going to get better, why do you have to own them? Lou's going to rent his."

So I did rent the wheelchair and the commode instead, an alternative that had not occurred to me.

Belle and Lou Simon are the parents of Paul Simon, whose music most of us have listened to, and with whom I was acquainted only casually through several meetings at the gym of the West Side YMCA a few years earlier. Lou Simon came into the hospital a few weeks after I did and was installed in a semiprivate room a few doors down from where I was. They have another son, Eddie, to whom I was soon introduced, and a daughter-in-law, Rosemary, Eddie's wife, who stubbornly refused to believe that Valerie was there with me as my nurse. She insisted instead on believing her own eyes. What she saw in my room the afternoon we met was me in my wheelchair and Valerie stretched out comfortably on my hospital bed, like Madame Récamier in her boudoir recuperating from a heavy lunch but chatting away as usual with everyone present.

Belle would show up at the hospital to see her husband every day at about four o'clock, at the end of the work schedule there, and it did not take long after we met for her to begin hanging around in my room—or should I say our room?—almost as much as in Lou's, for the atmosphere in his was not always as agreeable. Soon people were coming to visit me weekends on the chance of catching Paul Simon and his family. On weekday evenings Belle helped me with my dinner when Valerie was not there anymore and I was eating alone. I was frightened the first week I had to do that, and I pinned down one person or another well in advance to come there as early as the dinner did and stay until I had consumed it without choking to death. Probably this fear of choking was no more rational than had been my fear of drowning in the pool. But there it was. I soon saw that the biggest danger I faced was having the salt or the mustard out of my reach.

Belle confided to me one evening when we were sitting in my room alone that Lou complained he sometimes felt very sad in the morning, and I think I reassured her a bit when I told her I suffered these spells too. The means I'd found for terminating my low emotions were grounded in my knowledge that Valerie disconnected the ring on her telephone every night. Shortly after awakening, I would begin placing all kinds of calls to her answering machine, weather and traffic reports from the radio, salacious invitations, commands to be on time, obscene accusations, any music from the radio featuring the baroque trumpet, and everything performed by Neville Marriner and the Academy of St. Martin-in-the-Fields, an orchestral combination for which I knew her to possess a special partiality.

There was a favor I owed Belle Simon that I could not perform, though I tried my best, a promise I'd given to Dr. Ragnarsson even before I had met her and her husband that proved to be outside my power to keep: to cheer Lou Simon up and see he was in good spirits. Keeping Lou Simon laughing then was just not possible. Once I found out the details of his being there I did not even try.

Heart trouble was the start of his neuromuscular adventures that had brought him to Rusk as a fellow patient. Coronary bypass surgery in another hospital in New York City had been performed successfully. But in consequence or coincidence (no one could say which), an embolism had entered the tissues of his spine and he found when recovering from the surgery that one leg and one foot were almost completely paralyzed. It was impossible for anyone to tell how long the paralysis would last. This was not a foreseeable danger of heart surgery against which one about to undergo it normally braces himself. In Rusk a series of demoralizing medical afflictions assailed him almost from the day he entered and interfered with his starting and continuing therapy. A day without therapy at Rusk is a long one. He and Belle had judged beforehand that he probably would be better off sharing a semi-private room with somebody he could talk to. His roommate turned out to be an aphasic stroke victim who could utter only the one sound "achma" whenever he tried to speak.

No wonder Lou Simon was a tough audience then. He could get out of bed but would not come to my room often, and I could not go to his. I went to Paul's wedding in 1983 and not long ago, in May 1985, I addressed a meeting which Lou attended, and our conversation both times was more convivial. He walks with a cane, I climb steps slowly, but we reminisced triumphantly with wonder and incredulity, and the laughter came easily to both of us.

I did give him small tips now and then when we met in the hospital corridor in our wheelchairs. I predicted he would feel good in the pool once he started, and I turned out to be right. I advised him to start getting used to sleeping with the head of his bed lowered to a normal horizontal position, as I now conscientiously made sure to do every night. Lying in a flat bed that first time in the apartment was like lying in a sheer, deep hole, a grave. He thanked me for that too. By then both of us were tentatively scheduled to leave at the end of May.

There were other patients there I was equally ineffective at drawing out when asked to try, a couple of young quadriplegics who did not know who I was and were not impressed when told. Good humor may be one of the few things in a hospital that is not contagious. (My old friend and former supervisor at Time, Inc., Steve DeClerque, had not long before contracted a virus in a hospital following surgery to remove a vocal cord and was kept, because of a persistent high fever, on a nasogastric tube for thirty-five days. Steve knew before I did the specific fantasies that would haunt me about never being able to swallow food or drink again. Steve also knew, from his globe-trotting days as one of the heads of Time-Life International, of an Australian fellow employee who'd come down with Guillain-Barré syndrome while on a business trip to New Zealand more than thirty years earlier and has not been able to walk without metal canes since, but

Steve was thoughtful enough to conceal this last from me, until recently.) One of these two young men at Rusk was a good-looking, clean-cut, rusty-haired twenty-year-old with a neck broken in a diving accident who left a couple of weeks after I came there. I did not attend the going-away party given him by a few of the therapists at a pizza parlor down the block the night before he was to leave. I still couldn't eat then, and I really don't relate well to people that young, nor do they relate well to me. His two sisters found me a novelty for a short while; but I sensed gloomily and awfully that he and I had not much in common. I could not be jolly and I dreaded being patronizing.

Nor could I find much to talk about in occupational therapy with the teenager with a neck broken in a freak motor accident. He came in after I did and was there when I left. Picture a high school student waiting for the bus to take him to the classroom one morning, who is hailed and given a ride by some schoolmates in a car that soon afterward crashes into the undercarriage of a trailer truck coming onto the highway from the wrong access road. He was talking to Susan Bernstein in the occupational therapy room the last time I saw him, and what I overheard him saying was this: "Last night I had a dream again that I was able to move my fingers, and this time the dream was so real that when I woke up I was sure I would be able to and tried. The dream was so real I just know I'm going to be able to."

Poor Susan.

You should be glad you didn't have to watch her trying to find something to say. My recurring dream back then had me sitting in a chair when I heard my name called from another room, and I simply stood up and went to answer.

I had a much brighter influence on a woman named Brenda Halper, merely by walking by her in the exercise room during one of my ambulation sessions while she was turned up on the tilt table. Brenda Halper was a forty-year-old woman with Guillain-Barré. She had come into Rusk a few months after I did, following six harrowing months in a medical hospital with urinary, cardiac, and respiratory complications. At least once she had been given up for dead. A housewife with three children, she had taken a bath one day when alone at home and found that it was all but impossible for her to get out of the tub. Almost an hour passed and both knees were bloody by the time she succeeded and dragged herself to the telephone. A half a year later she was watching me walk, admiring my style from the tilt table at Rusk.

By April and May I was no longer depending on the rolling walker, although I still had a self-protective tendency to lock my knees. I would push my wheelchair instead, once or twice with Mel Tucker sitting in it for increased resistance, using the handles to steady my balance. Or I would walk with nothing but Mel Tucker contact-guarding me with his hands at my waistband should my right knee buckle once more. There were long mirrors on some of the walls, in which I could spy my deviations in gait and attempt to control them. Brenda would tell me how much better I looked each day she watched me walk past her. I believe I was the same embodiment of hope for her that Stanley Rosenstock, drawing to the end of his ten-month outpatient program, still represented for me. I would meet Stanley some mornings as I wheeled my way back from the pool and I would ask him to tell me of the day he had first stood up again and the day he had first lifted his head. His memory was hazy, for there was no "one day" for either, as I know now from my own story. Keep trying, he would tell me, just keep trying everything, do everything they tell you and it will all come back. One day I told him of Brenda Halper and asked him to go see her when he had the time. He found the time that same day and did. A different day when I was on an exercise machine called a Kinetron I heard a sudden joyful cheer go up near the mats. Brenda Halper was on her feet for the first time. And the therapists were applauding her in a spontaneous outburst of enthusiasm.

The Kinetron is a machine basically used to exercise the muscles of the legs and the pelvic girdle. The seat is of adjustable height, and when my normal exercises were over, I improvised the additional routine of standing up from it twenty times in two sets of ten, lowering the seat by inch or half-inch gradations as I continued to improve. (After coming to my feet at the end, when I was due next at the tilt table, I would walk the ten or so yards there without holding on to anything, showing off.) The problem with the Kinetron seat arose when I worked down to twenty-six inches, for the seat would not go below that. Speed Vogel pondered the problem, staring at the unit awhile in silence as though his mind were on something else, and devised a contraption for me that did the trick at home, using a chair of my own with each leg mounted on one-inch blocks of plywood that could be removed individually without much effort as I resumed at twenty-six inches and continued to go lower. An additional feature of this chair, as I soon discovered, was to provide me with a second place in the apartment to sit, offsetting the monotony of the wheelchair with a seat I could rise from without help.

It was at the beginning of April that the two-person team from Rusk made an appointment with Speed to inspect the apartment and reported that much of it was inaccessible by wheelchair. Even without these negative findings, the thought of spending my first months out of the hospital in a small city apartment I could not go out of at will was one I almost could not bear.

With what I now knew of my prospects—I would be able to work, I would continue to exercise, I would be in a wheelchair much of the time, I would need people around to help me—I made plans rapidly to spend the summer in East Hampton. I spoke to some friends, to have them speak to my wife, then I spoke to my wife about my having the house.

I spoke to Valerie: She agreed to come there and work for me five days out of seven—but only through Labor Day, she stressed—and she agreed to do so only at a weekly salary lower by much than the one I offered. She was taking into consideration that she would be spared expenses for food and transportation and would have the use of a car and swimming pool and a beach and an ocean. There are some people who don't always get to spend all of every summer in a comfortable house at a popular seaside resort. ("I'm so glad I met you!" she exclaimed to me recently at a dinner Speed put together for the three of us in a break between rewriting. "Otherwise I never would have known how good borscht is, and I wouldn't be eating so much of it!" I have heard her in an ode to joy of commensurate ardor to an electric dishwasher when viewing the pile of plates and pans to be done after a simple meal.)

I spoke to Speed—I must have spoken to Speed, although I have no recollection of doing so. But I think he had no other plans for the summer and consented to giving East Hampton a try, at least for the week or two I might need him. (Three winters have come and gone since—four by the time this page is published—and he is still giving East Hampton a try, and Valerie has not spent much time in other places, either.)

Then I spoke to Bob Towbin—I don't know where that whim of mine came from, to send Speed Vogel away on vacation to the Cannes Film Festival. But I relished the notion from the instant I imagined doing so, and, knowing Bob Towbin, I did not shrink from asking if he could find a place for Speed to sleep on the boat I knew he was chartering again for the period he himself would be there. I also knew that Mario was planning to be in Cannes that year.

Mr. A. Robert Towbin probably is not the only one of fifty partners who is responsible for the growth of the brokerage and investment banking firm of L. F. Rothschild, Unterberg, and Towbin. But he is the only attractive feature of Wall Street I know about and the only virtue of finance capitalism of which I have ever heard. He didn't just say yes: he said that he and Irene were sailing to Venice afterward and would treasure Speed's company if he would be kind enough to join them. A good man like Speed, who can talk to anybody about anything and listen too, and who can put together a good Chinese meal out of thin air, ginger, and a clove of garlic, is hard to find, even on boats with a hundred times the passenger capacity of Bob's.

Then I spoke about it to Speed, who thought it over a second and decided he *would* be kind enough to join them. He would not let me treat him to the plane fare.

For the rest of April and much of the month of May he was occupied getting ready for his trip, getting the house open and ready for the three of us to move to after his return, getting the apartment ready for me to live in and be cared for by my nurse and my brother, who would come up from Florida as soon as he was sent for, and getting his own studio ready for him to move back to. Speed was going to need a vacation by the time he left for this one.

I, meanwhile, was leading an active social life, going home weekends and going out weekday evenings more often than I normally want to. I felt a vague urgency and some kind of haste to show myself in public, as though to vindicate my hope that what was wrong with me was only temporary. And I was starting to enjoy myself too as I shed the concerns besetting me at first, that I would not be allowed into a restaurant, for instance, or would find myself in desperate need of a bathroom I could not get to.

There was a funny dinner with my daughter, Valerie, and Belle Simon at a restaurant up the block with an entrance too small for a wheelchair. The three ladies had to lift me and pass me through and stand guard nervously while the wheelchair was folded and passed in after me. As Belle and Valerie were taking me back to Rusk, a heavy downpour began. Valerie is tall and Belle is small and both had umbrellas that they frantically used to protect solely me from the rain as they waved back cars and pushed me through traffic when we crossed the broad and busy avenue. Much the same happened one evening when Valerie and I went to the Russian Tea Room with my friends police sergeant Jerry McQueen and Artie and Barbara Gelb. It was through the Gelbs that I had met Jerry. I was dry as a bone and neat as a pin when I was finally inside in my wheelchair; Valerie and the three others were drenched and disheveled, almost an embarrassment, I insinuated, for a person of my station to be seen with in a place so fine. I discerned while kidding them that there is a limit to the biting wisecracks a person in my dependent condition can make, and I shrewdly decided that I did not want to find out what that limit was.

I was learning a lot that surprised me. I found, to my enormous astonishment, that, with the exception Speed mentioned, taxi drivers did not mind stopping for people in wheelchairs and waiting the few minutes it took for me to be placed in the front seat and for the wheelchair to be folded and stowed in the trunk. I soon stopped giving immense tips in apology. Restaurants did not seem to mind having me. I noticed as I was taken around from one place to another that there were many more people in wheelchairs in the city than I had been aware of. I went to the birthday dinner for Cheryl McCall in an Italian restaurant in Greenwich Village, at which I joked to her that my drink had a metallic taste again, and a dinner at a different Italian restaurant with Sydney and Marit Gruson. And I learned from both these Italian dinners that I would have to cut spaghetti into fairly small sections if I did not want to be repulsive to anyone seeing me eat it. I saw that both Sydney and Marit knew how to help with the wheelchair and remembered that each had learned how to do that through separate unpleasant personal experiences greatly exceeding my own in severity.

Steve and Barbara DeClerque lived six blocks away from Rusk in an apartment with a terrace on a very high floor, to which they invited us for dinner. Valerie and I took a lovely walk together, there and back, on a crisp, clear evening, with Valerie doing the pushing. I sat on their sofa beside the fireplace and soon grew very warm. I remembered reading of a Spanish king far back who allowed himself to be roasted to death before his fire sooner than stand up unaided or stoop to summoning his retainers. I was not that Spanish king and I asked to be moved. Richard West and Valerie Salembier invited us down the block for another Texas evening of Pakistani cooking, and this time I did go, because this time I could go.

On Easter Sunday weekend I did not go to my apartment.

Valerie invited some people to hers and cooked a dinner, with a turkey and a ham and other things. (In a kitchen she is fearless. She made dinner for Craig Claiborne the first time she met him, with a cooked capon bought for her by Barbara Gelb from a barbecue chicken place.) At about noon, as arranged, she left her kitchen and came to the hospital by bus to dress me and take me to her apartment. At the end of the day, when all of her other guests had departed, she brought me back in a taxicab and waited until she saw me placed in the capable hands of a tall attendant there named John, who knew how to shower me and put me to bed. I knew I was in danger when she would not let me pay her for that day.

On the first of May in 1982 I was fifty-nine years old, and I went to a birthday party for me organized by Irene Towbin and Barbara Gelb, and I was more deeply affected than I wanted anyone to know. I could not cut the second of the two pieces of chicken on my plate—my arm was too much weakened from cutting the first—but I said nothing about it because I am a good sport. That was a Saturday. On Sunday when I was back in the hospital, I was overcome by a wave of terrible melancholy. I did not want to be there any longer, and on Monday I had the conversation with Dr. Goodgold. Except for the tilt table, on which I was now doing sit-ups at angles steadily made harder, I was not excited by any of the procedures and was finding the various routines pleasureless and boring.

We agreed I would leave in the middle of the month rather than wait until the end. Then, having won my point, I timorously changed my mind, pleading a need for more time to get used to the idea of separating. It was pointed out to me delicately by Goodgold, Ragnarsson, and Swajian that postponing the separation was not really a beneficial way of preparing for it. So I changed my mind back and spoke to Julius Green about picking me up. "Don't worry, I'll be there. And if not, you can stay in the hospital a few months longer. What could be so bad?"

On May 14 he was there with his station wagon at the hour

we picked, and I left the hospital with him, Speed, and Valerie. At the apartment, he gave me back the wallet and the wristwatch he had taken away with the clothes I was wearing the day I checked in at Mount Sinai. (I have let him know that the watch has not worked perfectly since.) The rug in the apartment had been removed, as the people from Rusk had recommended, and the chair had been mounted on blocks of plywood to a height of twenty-six inches. Speed moved the last of his things out of the apartment and I moved in. I was used to the place because of my weekends there, and the transition was effected with little drama and no trauma. The biggest shock was the photomural of Speed's face on the wall of the bedroom, overlooking the bed with a beard and a smile. It did not look like Dorian Gray. It looked like Speed with a beard and a smile. A couple of days later there was the going-away party for him I did not attend, and before I knew it he was gone for Paris on his way to Cannes and the ninety-four-foot ketch *Erna* (now renamed *Sumurun*). I do not think he suffered much trauma either.

Somewhere along the way I read the three hundred and twenty-five typed pages of *God Knows,* agreed that they were pretty good, and had them sent to Bob Gottlieb, my editor at Knopf, who said he thought they were very good and advised me to go full speed ahead.

Bob Gottlieb, I must tell you, is not a person who says things to me that he does not mean. He was twenty-five years old when he read the first two hundred and fifty pages of *Catch-22* back about 1956 and offered a contract to publish the book. He did not ask for an oral or written outline of the rest. I probably am the first novelist he signed, although others with completed manuscripts were published by him before I could finish mine. We have been good friends since, and we talk and see each other almost never. There is an anomalous reticence we share in speaking to each other of personal matters. Yet nothing one of us wishes to know from the other will be concealed, and much can be understood between us in very few words. Bob had heard of my disease before, he told me, through a friend in Canada.

"It's not a good thing to have," was the only comment he made about it.

This time too he did not ask for a description of the rest of the book.

The contract we agreed to for the publication of *God Knows* was drawn up by him and Alan Altman while I was still a patient at Rusk. It guaranteed me an adequate income for two years, whether I completed the manuscript or not, and I did not have to turn in any pages to receive it. I'd been told by the doctor I would be physically capable of going ahead. I believed my doctor and Bob believed me.

Following Speed's departure to Europe, just about everything that happened was oriented to the day of his return and the move to East Hampton, which is around two and a half hours away by car.

I spoke on the telephone to Don Shaw, the physical therapist I'd finally managed to locate through the good offices of Speed, the only qualified practitioner that far out on Long Island anyone knew about who would come to the house. Under New York law, a licensed physical therapist can practice only under a program devised and supervised by a physician, and Don worked that out in consultation with Dr. Ragnarsson.

I spoke to Mario Puzo, who was back from France earlier, at the beginning of June, and borrowed twenty-three thousand dollars from him. My finances were in chaos. Mount Sinai wanted forty-five hundred from me, Rusk wanted fifteen thousand more. I still owed money to Dr. Sencer and Dr. Peck, and there were ancillary bills from other doctors at both places. The only reason I asked for twenty-three thousand from Mario was that I could not make my voice say, "Twenty-five."

Two afternoons a week Valerie took me to Rusk as an outpatient and made certain to reappear at the hospital in time to take me home. On the other days she worked at Mount Sinai, and my brother came to keep an eye on me and perform what errands I wanted. Lee stayed in Paul's apartment, which was not far away, and, at my request, came later and later each day as my confidence in being alone increased. I gradually found I enjoyed being by myself for a few hours at a time. It was with a sense of complacent adventure that I put together my breakfast out of the things that had been left for me, made the coffee in that automatic coffeemaker that ground the beans and did everything else except make a good cup of coffee. Valerie knew enough to place below shoulder level everything I would want. It was noted on my discharge report that I would have trouble lifting and carrying things. If a container of milk or juice was full, half glasses would be poured out and put at the front of the low shelves in the refrigerator that were below my shoulder level when I was seated. Using the transfer board, I could move from my bed to the wheelchair. With a wooden wedge and a foam-rubber cushion on the wheelchair, I now could get to my feet and walk to the chair mounted on plywood. From this third stage I could rise without trouble, and I sometimes surprised visitors by greeting them at the door on my feet. I could walk into the bathroom to urinate standing up or into the small pullman kitchen for things from the refrigerator or cupboard. I was afraid of falling and I performed none of these feats unless someone was with me.

Lee was absolutely thrilled at meeting Joe Stein, the author of *Fiddler on the Roof,* and praised him so highly that Joe, thrilled by the accolade, came back often to hear him some more, bringing his wife, Elisa, a few time to witness. With Joe and Elisa, Valerie, I, and my wheelchair went to the theater one night and for a snack in a coffee shop afterward. The evening was perfect but for the quality of the show. (Julius Green kept telling people slanderously that he could see I was getting better by the return of the irascible temperament that he thought of as characteristically mine.)

At least once a week Lee pried off another level of plywood from that elevated chair that stood near the wall above all others like a throne, and soon we were down to twenty-four inches, then twenty-three. One evening I watched George Mandel rise from my sofa as he made ready to go and I thought with dismay that I would never be able to get up from a sofa again—so vast seemed the difference between sofas and the standard chairs I was working down toward. (Arms and shoulders are more necessary for a sofa than they are for chairs. If you watch what you do the next time you get up from one, you probably will find that you're helping with your hands.)

The novelist Noel Behn had an apartment just across the avenue from mine and was available for aid and for company. He was there helping Valerie push me in my wheelchair on the long trips we took into Central Park on days Valerie decided the weather was too nice for me to be holed up indoors.

Friends named Chet and Blanche Ross reminded me they had a house in Saint Croix and said I could have it for a while that winter if I'd just give them some notice. I told them I expected to be jogging by August and would not need it. When December rolled in and I still wasn't jogging, I asked if we could have it for the month of January. (They held it vacant and I went to Saint Croix with Valerie and Speed.)

A friend from Houston named Jerry Argovitz showed up one weekend, bringing gigantic corned beef and pastrami sandwiches. Like western prospectors of old, Jerry seldom ventures anywhere without food. Dr. Jerry Argovitz from Houston, Texas, was born and raised in the Texas panhandle. He had begun his working life in Houston as a dentist, moved into real estate, and then was the managing owner of a professional football team, the Houston Gamblers. He and I have nothing at all in common except a tremendous affection for each other. With Jerry I have a pact like the one with Dustin: he won't read a book and I won't watch a football game. He'd had some experience with injured athletes. Jerry was another who lauded me for my courage, and I did not know what he was talking about. What else is a person with GBS supposed to do?

On those days of the week I did not go to Rusk, Carol came to the apartment in the late afternoon to continue the physical therapy. We used the bed in place of the mat for those exercises in which I lay down. As always, I hated the most those hardest for me to do, the ones in which progress was too gradual to detect. I loved the long walks in the hallway from the door to the elevator. A day I remember was sunny and warm, and I went downstairs with her, pushing my wheelchair as I walked with her around a whole city block, stopping only to look in windows.

There were no picture postcards from France from Speed.

There was a weekend at Fire Island, where Valerie had never been, and Julie Green and his son Jason did all of the kitchen work in their house. Edie stayed home to finish another novel. Acting on impulse the first night there, as though in receipt of some occult sensory message, I bent myself forward and stood up from a chair of standard height. It was more than intuition that told me I could do it. I could not succeed when I tried it a second time. I was able to repeat the action the next day, but just one time.

I was communicating with my wife now mainly through Edie Green, who confirmed the bad omens. The divorce lawyers weren't getting along. My wife's was a man named Sheresky. Mine was Jeffrey Cohen. The two seemed incompatible and were accusing each other of acts of mental cruelty.

Instead of postcards from Speed, there came a beautiful woman with the alluring name of Wendy McTavish, an Australian living in Hong Kong who, with her husband, had spent a few days on the boat while it was still anchored in Cannes. She brought color photographs and handwritten messages of good wishes. She was lively and witty and we took her out to dinner. She had been to one of the film banquets with Speed and she showed us pictures of him in formal dress.

There are people one meets now and then who are not as completely taken with Speed as his friends expect them to be, and I began to suspect that she was one. A businesswoman herself, she sounded more perplexed by him than charmed. And inevitably there arose from her that question with which all of the people who know him long and well are frequently confronted and which grows harder to explain the longer we know him.

"What does he *do*?" Wendy McTavish wanted to know.

This time the reply was easy. "He helps me out," I answered.

Speed Vogel proved a much better cook that summer than Valerie and I could have hoped for. He irons too and makes minor house repairs.

I'VE DISCOVERED THAT it isn't hard to enjoy a vacation on a ninety-four-foot yacht without spending much money—provided you have a couple of friends, one sick and the other rich. It helps if the rich one is generous and the sick one riddled with guilt. Providence gave me the perfect pair: Towbin and Heller.

I managed to spend six days in Cannes, twenty-four hours in Capri, seven days sailing the Mediterranean, four days in Venice, a week in Paris, and another day in Amsterdam, with one small suitcase—all for five dollars.

My first sight of *Erna,* the blue-hulled sailing yacht that was to be my home for the next three weeks, surprised me. I'd assumed she was a motor yacht. No one had mentioned a sailboat, which, as it happens, is more to my taste. I was welcomed aboard with a big friendly smile by Bob Towbin and immediately offered a glass of champagne by Susan, a very pretty stewardess with a smile no less cordial than my host's. Not a bad start. I was formally introduced to Julian, our handsome captain, first mate Freddy, engineer Gary, and buxom cook Moira. All proved genial companions as well as able seapersons.

The yacht Towbin chartered that year and now owns was built in Fife, Scotland, in 1914 for Lord Sackville-West (Vita's dad). It has three well-fitted staterooms with toilet facilities, a saloon, galley, and crew's quarters. The master stateroom is exceptionally luxurious. Most of the original appointments and fine woodwork have been meticulously maintained. The hand-rubbed antique mahogany main saloon is splendidly proportioned, containing two built-in couches, a writing desk, bar, library, dining table, and captain's chairs that swivel. It has the unmistakable feeling of a venerable London club room. The large skylight, directly above the saloon dining table, provides very agreeable daytime lighting and opens to admit cool evening breezes.

The crew of five, in addition to making certain no guest on board ever experienced hunger or thirst, took care of personal laundry and cleaning, brought newspapers, ran errands of every sort, and still had time to see that fresh flowers adorned every cabin and dining table. The top deck has ample room for sunbathing, aerobic exercises, and dining on a beautiful mahogany table, flanked by comfortable banquettes and side chairs. When the weather permits, this is where one has breakfast, lunch, and aperitifs at sunset. Another advantage of a yacht in Cannes is that the port is within easy walking distance of the main and secondary festival theaters on the Croisette (the main drag). If I may borrow a phrase from my friend Mel Brooks, "What's the sense talking!" Obviously, this ninety-four-foot sailship is fit for a king, lord, investment banker, or even Heller's friend Speed. As compared to a noisy, garish, almost-impossible-to-get suite in any of the better hotels, this lovely yacht, at merely a thousand dollars a day, is a downright bargain.

I like to travel light, but before I had left New York, I'd been reliably informed that black tie was *de rigueur* at film festival screenings. I supplemented the black loafers and blue blazer and slacks that I wore on the plane with a tuxedo and dress shirt and nothing but the following: 1 pr. swim trunks, 2 pr. undershorts, running shoes, 1 pr. walking shorts, 8 T-shirts, a "Journey World Tour" windbreaker, comb, toothbrush, 1 bottle cologne, a Walkman, and 15 cassettes. The 8 T-shirts might seem excessive, but they were not ordinary. Each one was a rock-and-roll rarity that I intuited would be the envy of the natives and might come in handy as barter.

The excitement in Cannes at film festival time can be overwhelming for some people. Frankly, I thought it was like Market Week in New York's garment center. But that did not diminish my enjoyment. My first evening on the Riviera turned out to be special. Mario Puzo was there and I called him from the boat when I arrived that afternoon. He wanted the news about Joe and a rundown on who else was on Towbin's yacht besides me. Mario, displaying his legendary largess, invited me, Bob Towbin, and anyone else we wanted to bring along to join him and Carol Gino for drinks at the Carlton and dinner at Felix's on the Croisette. We ended up with an intimate table for eleven.

Puzo was intrigued by Bob's business associate, an attractive French lady banker named Claude Noat, who was not only a very smart banker but also smoked better cigars than he did. Her Gallic charm, wit, vivacity, and good looks were not exactly lost on him either. Pretending he was a neophyte in the gambling world and his chances of winning were good, he asked, naively, "Madame Noat, perhaps you can help me. I know nothing about the tax laws here. What if I win a hundred thousand francs at the gaming tables? Do I have to report it? How do I leave the country with it? What should I do?"

"Simple," Claude replied with a mischievous smile. "You put it in your pocket and go."

Mario chuckled and invited the entire table to join him at the casino. Everyone declined but Carol and me. I don't gamble but enjoy hanging out with Mario. At the roulette table, he turned to me and said, "Now watch this, my boy." And, stacking mountains of chips on what looked like most of the table, he proceeded to hit big. At this point I tried to persuade him that it was time to go, and I recruited Carol as an ally. We finally got Mario to agree that if he lost on three consecutive plays, signifying that his lucky streak was over, he would leave. He kept his word and quit a winner, exuberantly dispensing lavish tips with both hands to croupiers and others, including, after cashing in his chips and over my loud protests, me. (He actually looked stricken when I declined his gift, and swore it was bad luck not to accept a commission for bringing him good luck.) I apologized for my stupidity and, without another word, stuck his offering in my pocket.

I was feeling very good about my interference with Mario and his gambling habits, but as we were walking out of the casino, I nearly had a heart attack. Carol, who I thought was on my side, discovered that she still had some chips and wanted to go back and put them on her favorite numbers. Figuring that was all Puzo needed as his opportunity to give all his winnings back—and more—I uttered a horrified "Nothing doing!" as I grabbed her chips, ran to the cashier's window, and redeemed them for francs. Mario enjoyed my frantic moves to keep him and Carol away from the casino as much as he did his big win.

It was now three o'clock in the morning and I wasn't the least bit tired. As we walked to the taxi stand, Puzo told me that he'd changed plans and was leaving for London the following morning. He said he'd only stuck around to spend an evening with me and get me started right. I was disappointed he wouldn't be there and flattered that he had waited. Mario hailed a cab, and he and Carol had themselves dropped off at their hotel before I continued on to the port. After I got there, the taxi driver would not let me pay him. Mario had paid him and, judging from the extraordinary vehemence of his refusal to take any money from me, paid him so well that I was now convinced that Mario must be the world's most lavish tipper.

I'm not gauche, so I didn't look at the bundle Mario gave me until I was back in my cabin. I'm not at liberty, at this time, to divulge how much it was, but a kidnapped king, if he knew, wouldn't mind having me as his friend.

Each day in Cannes brought new surprises. Business aside, Towbin loves to sail, and he loves having guests. Among the various people who joined us were American television stars like Robert (*Lou Grant*) Walden, European movie producers like

Albina du Boisvouvray, and world-famous novelists like Gabriel (*One Hundred Years of Solitude*) García Márquez. And then there were many others, most of them interesting, some with no better credentials than mine.

We would weigh anchor at about noon or as soon as all the invitees were aboard and sail somewhere along the Riviera. Anchored once more, we enjoyed a swim before aperitifs and lunch, then conversation and sunbathing until it was time to return to port, drop off the afternoon guests, and shower and dress for the evening's activities. To break the monotony of this routine, we sailed twice to Cap d'Antibes, frolicked in the Hôtel du Cap's salt-water pool, and lunched at Eden Roc. I smiled with smug satisfaction when I overheard a prominent Hollywood actor say, "That's the most beautiful boat I've ever seen!" as he pointed to our yacht riding at anchor. Once we sailed to Cap-Ferrat for a bouillabaisse lunch at Roquebrune, between Monte Carlo and Menton. Go there when you are in the vicinity. And if you can possibly arrange it, have someone else pick up the check.

I had to miss a day of sailing when friends from New York unexpectedly arrived in Cannes and insisted I join them for lunch at a small country restaurant. I was not aware of it at the time, and would not have been perplexed if I had been, but they had made reservations a month before arriving in Europe. The place seemed almost empty, though every table was occupied. The service, food, and wine were excellent. At the end of this fine meal, a handsome, gray-haired chef appeared and asked if everything was all right. His question was polite but superfluous. He acted as if he knew he was not about to hear complaints. The restaurant is Le Moulin, near a town called Mougins. I understand it's considered the best in France. Try this one, too, the next time you're in the neighborhood with well-heeled friends.

It wasn't all roses, though. Certain hardships had to be endured. Because Towbin's hospitality knows no bounds, I was sometimes politely asked to give up my stateroom and share the saloon with the Towbins' older son, Bram, a student in Paris for a year, and his school chum, who had also given up theirs. Once a young fellow named Pigozzi came aboard. I overheard him tell some lady guest he was a plumber. He also joined us in our makeshift dormitory. I'm no snob. I liked the guy, but his snoring made me wish he had slept elsewhere. (As Mel had done with me, I wanted to let him know in big letters: "Pigozzi, you snore! Snore, snore, snore!") I found out later he was not a plumber but a photographer, and incidentally, the scion of a prominent automobile-manufacturing family. I liked him better when I realized he had told his innocent lie to the overbearing matron who asked, "And what do YOU do, young man?" Sometimes we were as many as four sharing the same washbasin, and I began to think I was back in summer camp with my bunk-mates.

After the lunch at Roquebrune that Claude arranged for us, we were able to sail back only as far as Antibes before having to dock for the night because of choppy seas. The following morning Claude left for Paris to meet her daughter, Alexandra, who was returning from a holiday in England. Claude and I had become good friends in the short time we'd been together. Bob, always hospitable, suggested that, since there was room on board, she bring her daughter back and sail with us to Venice.

On the last of our nights in Cannes, we attended a charity gala. Bob's wife, Irene, had arrived just in time to join us. My date for the evening was Wendy McTavish, from Hong Kong, a recent fellow guest on the *Erna,* who had just missed her plane to New York. She and Heller had met in Hong Kong, she told me, and she planned to call him when she got to New York. Spotting our "22" table card, she suggested we each write a few words of greeting which she would deliver in person. I must confess that from the time I left New York until that moment when Wendy mentioned him, I had not given Heller much thought. Suddenly, I felt a bit guilty. I tried to write something nice: I hoped he was doing okay.

The next afternoon, we set sail for Capri, the first stop on our voyage to Venice. Now we were nicely outnumbered by our crew of five, as we were reduced to a very comfortable gang of four: Bob, Irene, Bram, and me. We had sunshine and good wind. Perfect weather. We arrived in Capri the following evening, passing a few famous islands along the way. As we glided past Corsica, I remembered that Heller's squadron had been stationed there during the war, and I began to think about him, his life as a bombardier, and the experiences that had resulted in *Catch-22*. I'd been reading a book Joe had recommended, Richard Ellmann's biography of James Joyce, and once again I thought of Joe. The book reminded me of what he faced with Valerie, who seemed to be no more in awe of Joe as a celebrated man of letters than Nora was of Joyce. Both Heller and Joyce, to their credit, are apparently amused rather than affronted by these unsophisticated attitudes.

Abreast of Anzio, the famous World War II beachhead, our compass was no longer reliable as a result of the large amount of metal sunk in those particular waters, but we stayed to course without getting lost and approached our first port of call on schedule. After docking in Capri, we ate supper at a waterfront trattoria and exercised our sea legs with a stroll along the quay before turning in for the night.

Remembering the Chinese dinner I'd prepared for the Towbins in New York, I had volunteered to prepare another, and spent the morning shopping with our cook. This done, I rushed to meet Claude, who, to my delight, had decided to accept Towbin's offer and rejoin us with her young daughter. They had just arrived from Paris.

After a good lunch atop Capri, we rode the funicular back to the port and set sail for Brindisi, on the heel of Italy's boot. That was to be our next scheduled stop for fuel, food, and water. We never made it. Just out of Capri, the *Erna* developed a serious engine problem that could not be repaired without new parts. We were becalmed, the engine conked out, and I was not at all perturbed. The boat's owner might have felt otherwise. We, however, accepted our fate like good sports. We swam, read, ate, drank, sunbathed, and slept soundly. Captain Julian even rigged a rope swing for us to take turns dunking ourselves into the sea. I really did feel like Huck Finn.

After our water sports and early evening drinks, I began cooking the Chinese meal. In the midst of preparing barbecued shrimp in the shell and beef in oyster sauce with spinach, I realized I lacked several ingredients. Two lessons from the master, Ngoot Lee, came to my rescue. The first, "If you don't have it, you don't need it," and the second, even more important, "Never cook without whiskey!" I was helped considerably by this dictum, perhaps too well.

Although we sailed only seven miles in the next two days, we remained cheerful. On the third day the wind freshened and we sailed past Stromboli and around the toe through the Messina Strait. As we approached the port of Reggio di Calabria, our immediate destination, the wind suddenly picked up to twenty knots and docking without the engine became hazardous. The captain, using a reefed staysail, sea anchor, and the Zodiac (a rubber craft with an outboard motor that we carried for a tender) as a sort of tugboat, managed to secure us to the pier without mishap.

Reggio has a rather large shipyard and the captain hoped the engine could be repaired quickly. It could not. It was time for a change in plans. Irene was anxious to get to Venice in time for an artist friend's birthday party. The crew had to stay behind in Reggio with the *Erna* to supervise the extensive repairs. Our sea voyage was over. We would continue by air. While waiting, we checked out the town. We discovered an interesting local museum, shopped the market stalls, had dinner, walked back to the boat, and slept soundly until 7 a.m., when workmen started dismantling the town pier with the noisiest jackhammers in the whole Mediterranean.

After breakfast, we said adieu to the *Erna* and crew and left for the local airstrip. Our flight to Venice was short and uneventful. Just the way I like it. The pilot helped us unload and we pushed our baggage cart to the *motoscafo* (Venetian limo), ordered for us by the concierge at our hotel, the Gritti Palace, maybe the best hotel in Europe. (I am learning to take the sweet with the bitter.)

We were right on time for Geoffrey Humphries's costume party. The theme was "Sailors and Mermaids," which seemed apt. We improvised getups that passed for costumes and had a splendid first night on the town.

Four days in Venice in early June is not hard to take. With the help of artist friends who were year-round residents, we found the best eateries.

Our reservations at the Gritti had been made on very short notice. (We had expected to use the *Erna* as our home.) And there was a slight misunderstanding about departure dates, so after two nights we were obliged to vacate two of our rooms. Bram moved in with his parents, and I shared a room with Claude and her daughter. It was a slumber party. The next morning, the manager, apologizing for a new inconvenience, asked Claude, Alexandra, and me to vacate our room, too. We were now six sharing Irene and Bob's room until we left that evening. We'd already learned how to rough it on a luxury yacht, therefore queueing up for the WC and shower, banging shins on furniture, and stumbling over suitcases in the posh Gritti added up to just one more educational experience.

Bob and Claude were flying to a business meeting in Zurich. Bram, Alexandra, and I were traveling by overnight train to Paris, and Irene was staying on in her room at the Gritti to attend the Biennale. Our happy bunch was splitting up, but only briefly.

Toughened by our experience in Venice, Bram, Alexandra, and I shared a triple-decker compartment to Paris. Very little sleep, but lots of giggles. We kids go for that. It was my second slumber party in two days. We were met at the Gare de Lyon by Bernard Vidal, Claude's friend, who drove us to Bram's rented flat on rue St. Guillaume and then whisked off with Alexandra. This lovely Left Bank apartment overlooking the architecturally famous Maison de Verre was to be my home in Paris for the rest of the week. Bram, finished with his year of school in Paris, was leaving for New York the next day, and invited me to stay on. (The rent had been paid through the end of the month.) When

Towbin rejoined us in Paris, Claude, who had returned from Zurich earlier, called to suggest a reunion dinner, and I volunteered again to prepare barbecued shrimp and beef with asparagus, both Chinese style. This time we were able to get all the ingredients and the meal was superb. My new Parisian friends and I saw a great deal of one another. The object of a generosity that was touching and continual here too, I was simply not allowed to put my hand in my pocket for anything but a handkerchief.

By the oddest stroke of luck, I was able to repay them in an unexpected way. Claude and Alexandra expressed a wish to attend the sold-out Simon and Garfunkel concert.

At breakfast with Bob at the Crillon, I found out by chance that Paul Simon was staying there, too. I was bold enough to leave a note, he was gracious enough to call and arrange special VIP tickets for all my friends. Using Paul Simon to repay my French hosts was a technique of social legerdemain I had picked up from Joe.

I'd met one of Bram's school friends in Cannes, a fellow with the imposing name of Phillip Beauregard, and when I was in Paris, Phillip invited me to lunch at his flat. I met the young man's friends, whom I liked, and after lunch, Phillip and I decided to visit Amsterdam. I drove a small rental car, leisurely enjoying the French, Belgian, and Dutch countryside. On the way to Amsterdam, I remembered that once Heller had raved about a placed called Otterloo and the Kröller-Müller Museum. I checked the map and found it was on our way, so we stopped off. It was a fine idea for me, but Phillip would have preferred to keep going to check out Amsterdam's famous red-light district. I assured him there was time to do both.

The Kröller-Müller is in a large wooded park and boasts a collection of first-class paintings, many by Van Gogh. An interesting feature of the place is that white painted bicycles are parked at stations on the grounds and visitors are invited to use them whenever they want. I missed my bike riding and was delighted when Phillip forgot his hurry and suggested we take a long ride before continuing on.

This excursion was my treat (with Mario's money) and we booked a bed and breakfast in a small town close to Amsterdam. The home was immaculate, the beds comfortable, and the breakfast delicious. We rented bicycles at the train station and had a good *rijsttafel* dinner. After dawdling as long as young men can stand, we rushed to stroll through the red-light district—just looking. Safely home, we turned in for the night. After a hearty breakfast the next morning, we went to the Van Gogh Museum and I was stunned by the number of famous paintings that I had seen only in reproduction before. We left Amsterdam and drove back to Paris in time to meet Claude for dinner.

Claude also arranged a small farewell party for me the following day. I love food markets everywhere, especially in Paris, and was happy that she had asked me to join her in shopping for the meal she planned to cook. That afternoon she got to work on a *gigot d'agneau* that proved to be superb, and special *pommes frites* by Dominique, another male friend of Claude's, that were astonishing. (I tried to make them for Joe and Valerie later, substituting chicken fat for goose fat. They were not nearly as stupendous as they had been in Paris, but still the best they'd ever eaten.) Every dinner with Claude included champagne as well as other fine wines, but this one was a record-breaker. There was more champagne poured at this dinner for six than at my sister's first wedding—and my father was a sport! At the airport I said au revoir to Claude and my new friends with last-minute embraces and assurances that we would see each other again.

Flying over the Atlantic, I reflected on my vacation and my benefactors. I'd already thanked Mario in Cannes. When I thanked Bob in Paris, I'd mentioned a bit of advice I'd once received from a smart woman, my mother, who said, "When you give, give a luxury, not a necessity. *That's* a gift." Towbin did exactly that for me. I also thought about Joe's role in all this and the best way to thank him. I speculated on getting sick and letting him take care of me, but knew that was not my best idea. I felt he had too much to thank me for as it was.

I was completely unaware of what was actually going on in New York. I did not know that while I was having the time of my life in France, Heller was having trouble in court.

On the flight I also found time to figure how much my trip had cost and discovered that the commission Puzo gave me for bringing him luck took care of the air fare, car rental, restaurants, presents, and everything else.

To my complete surprise, my good friend Barbara Cooke, who had thrown my going-away party, was there to greet me as I cleared customs at JFK. She was picking me up to escort me to an intimate welcome-home dinner being prepared by my friend Paula at Joe's apartment. When the limousine pulled up to the building and the driver let us out, I slipped him a fiver. That's all the trip cost me.

I think people are crazy to stay home.

MR. NORMAN M. SHERESKY was born in Detroit, Michigan, in 1928, attended Syracuse University, and went to Harvard University for his law degree. Mr. Sheresky is listed in the Martindale-Hubbell Law Directory as the author of *Uncoupling—A Guide to Sane Divorce.* In 1978 and 1979, he was president of the New York Chapter of the American Academy of Matrimonial Lawyers, and on October 27, 1981, in the Family Court of the State of New York, to which I had been summoned for purposes I still find obscure, he accused me of raping a house.

Now this is not a laughing matter.

The allegation was made orally about six weeks before I went into the hospital. Among those present when he leveled this charge were the Honorable Jack Turret, presiding, and Mr. Salvator M. Lavanco, the official court reporter, who certified that the transcript from which I excerpt is a true one. Said Mr. Sheresky:

> . . . he announced . . . any time whether you like it or not . . . I will be coming around. I won't tell you when I am

> coming to remove whatever it is that I want to. And he already did it out in Long Island. He already raped that place.

Mr. Sheresky charged me additionally with intending to repeat the action, asserting I was "talking about raping" the apartment in which I had dwelt for almost twenty years.

Jeffrey Cohen was inclined to view the matter in a somewhat different light.

> Most respectfully, your Honor . . . Prior to the time Mr. Heller went to the East Hampton home [which was unoccupied] . . . he wrote a letter. . . . Instead of a rape, a mischaracterization, your Honor, out of 100 pieces of furniture in the East Hampton home Mr. Heller takes 2 pieces. He didn't come unannounced . . . and not because there is anything wrong . . . , but because he is a decent man, and a sensitive man who wants to approach this in a civilized way.

From Judge Turret earlier had come a trenchant rebuke to the lot of us that went to the heart of the matter.

> THE COURT: . . . If you two gentlemen, who have considerable experience in the field representing clients who know their obligations can work out an agreement with respect to temporary support until all of this is decided, I will be very happy to recall the case, and take your stipulation. This is an Intake Part of the Family Court, and you are not going to delay 45 or 50 indigent people waiting outside by having this argument before me. Go before the hearing examiner.

In the lobby outside, one could pick out interpreters assisting people unable to understand English and even, perhaps, to afford attorneys as expensive as ours.

We learned there would be an indeterminate wait for a hearing examiner. At the start of the day, Jeffrey, with that tactical clairvoyance he was to exercise to my advantage over the next three years, had directed me to write out a maintenance check for the approaching month; with a touch almost of grandeur he had presented this to Mr. Sheresky before Judge Turret, along with assurances that the rent for the apartment would be paid by me, and certain medical expenses too. (In the Family Court of the State of New York, a person is not likely to be deemed a blackguard if he has just committed himself to forking over more than three thousand tax-free dollars for the support of just one person for just one month.) After whispered discussion between the two attorneys, a payment of five hundred dollars more for only one month brought agreement by the four of us to adjourn for the day rather than wait longer.

Before we could return to Family Court, I had trouble swallowing that sweet potato, and my life in court was interrupted for almost seven months, until about two weeks after I was out of the hospital.

In a letter to Jeffrey Cohen written before I was summoned to Family Court, which was later made part of the record under the auspices of Mr. Sheresky, he had stated:

> . . . you might just as well know that I don't negotiate with guns to my head, particularly when they are loaded with hot air.

In this regard, Mr. Sheresky is a much better man than I am. I *would* negotiate with guns to my head, without procrastinating a moment to wonder if they were loaded with hot air or bullets, and so, I fear, would all of my friends whose minds I think I know.

On May 28, 1982, two weeks after I was discharged from the hospital, Mr. Sheresky wrote in another letter to Jeffrey Cohen that my statement of need for the East Hampton home was "out-and-out bull." For a couple of months I had lived with the clear impression that I would make some financial provision to my wife for the summer and that my move to the house would be unobstructed.

Because this letter too was made part of the court record under the aegis of Mr. Sheresky, I am permitted to reproduce it in its entirety. But don't worry, I won't. Some of his passages, however, do not invite synopsis or compression, and I would sooner present these in the whole rather than risk adulterating the flavor I assume he intended.

Mr. Sheresky opens by saying that "once again" he sees Jeffrey Cohen in a "self-serving letter writing mood." Taking umbrage at an imputation in one of Jeffrey's letters that he might be experiencing difficulty controlling his client, he goes on as follows:

> The disastrous history of this case would prove to a cretin that it is . . . you and your predecessor who cannot or choose not to control Mr. Heller. Your theory that Mr. Heller requires the East Hampton home is out-and-out bull and you know it. I willingly admit that he is fortunate enough and more than rich enough to this summer, as in past summers, rent a place in Long Island (which he has never liked), New Jersey, Santa Fe or any other place he chooses. It is fortunate, indeed, in view of the tragedy that he has recently suffered that he is not "poor" as you are accustomed to picturing him in the past and that he is not like the tens of thousands of other human beings recovering from serious illnesses who cannot have the luxuries that Mr. Heller can.

Mr. Sheresky was advancing the proposition that I should rent a different house for the summer rather that be moved to the one I had.

Mr. Sheresky's letter criticizes Jeffrey Cohen's "letter writing attacks" as "two-faced, insincere, [and] misdirected." He moves on to such other matters as the deposition, emphasizing how cooperative he's been and will continue to be.

> When you wanted Mrs. Heller's deposition, you got it. When you wanted documents, we provided them. When I went over to your office to review documents, they weren't there. I have repeatedly asked you for the documents relating to the present arbitration—I have sought them for months and months and months and have gotten zero from you. When I spoke to you last week about the deposition, I made it very clear to you that I had no desire to inconve-

> nience Mr. Heller, that I would be happy to take the deposition of Mr. Tucker [a man at my accounting firm] or Mr. Altman or anybody else who has the necessary financial backup information and who would serve my purposes at this time just as well as Joe Heller. Instead, you wish to parade Mr. Heller in front of me with nurses and wheelchairs when, believe me, I do not need those props to feel sorry for Mr. Heller and to regret deeply his present physical suffering.

Shortly before I came to the writing of this page, which was on March 10, 1985, I heard inadvertently that Mr. Sheresky had suffered a serious heart attack and had survived. And I would like the world to know (in the matchless turn of phrase I plagiarize from Gore Vidal, who was writing of Truman Capote in a context wholly dissimilar) that I feel no less sympathetic to Mr. Sheresky in his illness than he did to me in mine.

Mr. Sheresky is critical of Mr. Cohen for what he terms his "out-and-out outrageous arrogance" and appears, in commenting on it, to grow, perhaps, even a bit less temperate than he has been. Says Mr. Sheresky:

> Finally, I deal now with your out-and-out outrageous arrogance in suggesting that once your accountant prepares what he believes to be the answer to Mr. Eichler's [their accountant's] and my year old question: "What did Joseph Heller do with the millions upon millions of dollars that he has earned?" - that constitutes a waiver . . . of any further discovery. If you read the letter that you wrote to me two days before you cooked up that limitation, you will notice that you never suggested that my client should agree to such a waiver and I doubt that a first year law student or, indeed, a first year medical student would agree to it. Do you mean I can't question your accountant's figures? Do you mean I can't ask for proof? Do you mean I am still not allowed to find out the details of Mr. Heller's arbitration or inquire concerning other sources of income? Do you mean I am not allowed to inquire about how much money he spends on himself and his friends?

In Mr. Sheresky's penultimate paragraph he indicts my lawyers for turning the "pathetic history of this common garden variety matrimonial litigation" into "World War IV, V and VI" and questions "whether any of you out there are paying any attention." He concludes with a peroration of one paragraph containing one sentence:

> Will you stop writing me letters!!!

I had the opinion that it would not be possible to deal expeditiously with a man who expressed himself in such perfervid fashion. And I did not feel I should be kept waiting. On June 3, because I did want to obtain exclusive occupancy of the East Hampton house, I filed suit for divorce and made that request. Although my wife and I had been separated now a year and a half, no action for divorce had been instituted by either party till then, and the only counterclaim for divorce ever filed against me was stipulated in an arbitration agreement to which we both consented almost two years later, in 1984.

The legal action that I'm describing now was only over my request for the house. The paper requiring my signature was prepared by Jeffrey and perused and slightly emended by me before I signed it, and I imagine that this procedure between attorney and client is just about universal, that the attorney masterminds the plans and the prose in the papers submitted by the client. My affidavit was six pages, and almost all of it dealt with my plea for the use of the house. It was accompanied by an affidavit of two pages from Dr. Ragnarsson attesting to my illness, my debilitated condition, and my needs, and by an affidavit from Don Shaw, who stated that I had arranged with him for a program of physical therapy to commence when I moved (or *was* moved—take your pick) to East Hampton. (Jeffrey managed to put all this together in just about five days. Jeffrey somehow succeeds in the implausible feat of handling two dozen cases at a time and simultaneously giving exclusive attention to each of them twenty-four hours a day. There was not a free interval in all of my days in the courtroom in which he did not at once go hurtling into the nearest vacant telephone booth, and he was invariably a few minutes late getting back after the clerk announced that the judge was ready to resume. I spent as much time justifying his behavior as I did my own. Such dynamic vigor will not last him through his middle years, but it lasted long enough for me.) The pages we submitted totaled fifteen, and these included a four-page "affirmation" by Jeffrey in which he deplored that a court action even had been necessary to obtain the use of the house for me in the circumstances we described.

My motion was contested, of course. Although the argument here was only over the house, the opposing affidavit was itself eighteen pages long and was divided into sections titled HISTORY OF THE MARRIAGE, THE ECONOMIC SQUEEZE AND THE EAST HAMPTON HOUSE, ENTER MR. COHEN, and THE MOVING PAPERS. This was accompanied by a STATEMENT OF CERTAIN ASSETS AND LIABILITIES of mine as of January 1, 1981, which consisted of nine pages, the two letters by Mr. Sheresky from which I have quoted, two letters by Jeffrey Cohen, and a note from me, all of these comprising twelve more pages, and by a four-and-a-half-page opposing affirmation from Mr. Sheresky, bringing the whole past forty pages.

Mr. Sheresky affirmed in writing, "under the penalties of perjury," that he was respectfully submitting his affirmation in opposition to my motion for exclusive use and possession of the East Hampton property, "and in particular opposition to the gratuitous, unprincipled, feline, and unrestrained remarks of Mr. Cohen."

Mr. Sheresky stated that to Mr. Cohen I was "a very important client." He said, "I do not represent the famous Joseph Heller," but maintained he did know how much money I had, and added, "All of Mr. Heller's and Mr. Cohen's dirty tricks and legal maneuverings are not erased and they cannot be erased by Mr. Heller's illness."

In the affidavit itself I read that I was "in fact, worth several million dollars" and that there were "hundreds and, indeed, thousands of better facilities" which I could afford to use.

Mr. Sheresky truly believed (and was desperately sorry that his personal beliefs in this matter had become relevant) that the instant application was "without rhyme or reason," that to grant my request would be "to simply ignore the whole history of this case which preceded the request," and that to "award Mr. Heller exclusive possession of a house . . . in Easthampton [*sic*], New York when he can enjoy such facilities this summer, as he did last summer, with a virtual limitless amount of money will accomplish nothing for Joseph Heller" but a "senseless 'win' " over his client.

Mr. Sheresky respectfully suggested in ending that the affidavits of Dr. Ragnarsson and the physical therapist, Don Shaw, were "uncorroborated" and that there was nothing in them leading to the conclusion that I would be in any danger whatsoever if the exclusive use I was asking for was denied.

The issue was argued on June 10 in the Supreme Court of the State of New York. I was not there. (Had my presence been required in court that soon, I would indeed have been paraded into the courtroom with a nurse and a wheelchair.) Presiding was Justice Hortense W. Gable. The transcript is entertaining to me still for a number of reasons, not least among them the favorable outcome which Jeffrey was confident must surely result. (Jeffrey had predicted I would be awarded the use of the house, had vowed to take the courthouse building apart stone by stone with his bare hands if he was mistaken and to find and pay for the most luxurious home in Long Island with the downstairs facilities I needed.) Augmenting this pleasure is my amusement at the repeated urging by Mr. Sheresky for the court to read his papers and the obdurate distinction drawn by Judge Gable that she has "looked" or "glanced" at them. Finally, there is the propensity displayed by both lawyers to interrupt and for each to resent the other's doing so. I am told that the tenor of the hearing was more strident than the printed words indicate: Given the fervor manifested by Mr. Sheresky in his correspondence and the quickness of Jeffrey Cohen to react, I see no reason to doubt it.

Not until page 7 does Judge Gable announce she has learned enough and is ready to make her ruling.

THE COURT: I have read the papers, or glanced at the papers, and I can understand the terrible trauma. . . . But I think I have got a reasonably good idea that should at least take care of these summer months, no more and no less. What he is suffering from isn't funny, this condition.

MR. SHERESKY: No, it isn't, Judge.

THE COURT: It is serious. He does need help, and from the little I know of it he certainly needs not only the physical therapy that is required, but perhaps some kind of cushioning to cope with what has happened to him and, hopefully, his recovery. I suggest—it also was clear to me that Mrs. Heller has suffered a great deal. . . . What I think would make sense would be for Mr. Heller to have exclusive—listen; don't get excited.

MR. SHERESKY: I don't get excited. I have been at this too long, Judge.

THE COURT: He ought to have exclusive possession of that house for June, July and August and part of September, and at the same time it seems to me that Mrs. Heller also ought to have some funds so that if she wanted to rent a place somewhere on the South Shore, she would be able to. . . . I am only talking about a period of time, there would be less tension and less fighting. . . .

MR. COHEN: May I be heard?

THE COURT: Yes, surely. You didn't interrupt, so you may be heard.

MR. COHEN: I candidly admit that I have strong feelings about this application—a limited application by the plaintiff husband for exclusive occupancy. I think that I understand the countervailing forces at work. Nonetheless I will not tell you about the talks Mr. Sheresky and I have had and I will not tell your Honor that I think it's tragic that I have had to make the application, because we have been willing to talk about some way to rectify this situation that would give Mr. Heller the therapy he so desperately needs and use of that home he so desperately needs, your Honor. I know him well.

MR. SHERESKY: Well, Judge, you know, if he is going to testify—

MR. COHEN: Does it sound like he is interrupting me?

THE COURT: Yes, he is interrupting. Mr. Sheresky, I was counting on you.

MR. SHERESKY: I wasn't going to do it, Judge, but every time . . .

MR. COHEN: He is doing it again.

MR. SHERESKY: (cont'g) He is the client.

THE COURT: All right. In any event it makes sense to me.

MR. COHEN: Your Honor, the problem is—and it's a very serious one—could we go off the record for a minute?

I don't know what the problem was. Possibly they went off the record to fix a date and even to argue the sum of money. Certainly when they went back on the record Judge Gable knew her mind. And it seems from the way the dialogue unfolded that Mr. Cohen had been the more persuasive.

THE COURT: Right here and now I am going to rule and that will be the end of it.

MR. COHEN: Thank you, your Honor.

MR. SHERESKY: Judge, why don't you read the papers?

THE COURT: I have looked at them.

MR. SHERESKY: Oh.

THE COURT: I am going to rule the following. I am going to rule that for the months of—

MR. COHEN: June.

THE COURT: —June, July, August and up through September 15th, Mr. Heller will have exclusive occupancy conditioned upon his payment . . . of the sum of $7,500 to Mrs. Heller so that she may, if she so desires, use that $7,500 towards the payment of a summer rental, period. And that's my ruling.

Speed's plans for the summer had been preserved. I might seem to be gloating when I reveal here that $10,000 and the cost of a car rental for those months was the amount Jeffrey had persuaded me to offer if peaceful discussions had ever seemed possible.

Shortly after this day in court, Mr. Sheresky was replaced as attorney by the law firm of Gordon & Shechtman. I do not know the reasons for the change.

I HAD TWO HECTIC DAYS in the city to check my mail, make some calls, pay bills, see friends, and unpack and repack with summer things before meeting Joe and Valerie at the Eighth Avenue apartment. We were about to be driven to the Hamptons in a hired station wagon.

Everything Joe needed from the city had been delivered to the house before I left for Cannes except a few things which we were bringing with us now: his collapsible wheelchair, shower bench, hand-held shower, and transfer board. The convertible couch had been set up in the guest room for him, with the bed at a good height. Joe was able to raise himself from a sitting position to standing with no assistance from this height. The transfer board we'd brought with us was never used again. I installed the hand-held shower and shower bench and put the commode in place. Upstairs, Valerie occupied the master bedroom and I had the bedroom opposite. There were no closets in my room, but there was an armoire big enough for the few things I'd brought.

I took command of the kitchen. I hadn't done much cooking since I'd met Paula, who was a better cook than I, and now I was looking forward to renewing my skills. I saw what was needed,

Valerie wrote out the shopping list, and we all went to the supermarket. This was the beginning of what was to become standard procedure. Valerie or I drove to the supermarket and Joe came along to help. He couldn't walk far without someone assisting for balance. He used to walk behind his wheelchair, using it as a stroller for ambulatory practice, but now he had graduated to the shopping cart. The heavy cart helped him keep steady as he pushed it up and down the aisles. Valerie and I selected groceries and piled them in. It was the beginning of what was to be a fine though unconventional ménage à trois.

We acclimated ourselves easily to our new living arrangement and surroundings. Valerie and I had an advantage. We had both spent summers as "groupers"—we were experienced in getting along with roomies. Joe had to learn from us and he was a quick study. Heller knew he needed us.

We decided to eat out the first night and Joe picked The Laundry. Formerly a commercial laundry now cleverly redesigned as a restaurant, the place is owned by a combine of show business locals who wanted to have their own hangout. The food is not outstanding, but the bar is always lively and the place attracts a friendly crowd. We brought Joe's collapsible wheelchair and pushed him in. The hostess showed us to our table and quickly removed a chair. She handed us menus and summoned a waiter to take our order. After finishing our first round of drinks, Joe and I were about to order another when the hostess returned and insisted she knew me. She was very good-looking and I was sure I would have remembered if it were true. Regretfully, I said she was mistaken. She left to seat some others and returned with a huge smile, asking, "Isn't your name Spike? Slick? Swifty? . . . Wait, it's Speed!" She reminded me of where and when we had met. (Of course it had been at a Fire Island party. She also remembered that the guy who had thrown it was Diane Von Furstenberg's partner, but I can't remember his name. And at the time of this writing, I can no longer remember the hostess's name.) After an embrace, I introduced Joe and Valerie, who both teased me for my forgetfulness. Still, it was only my first night out in East Hampton and I had already run into a prospective date. Not so bad. The summer looked promising.

We didn't eat out much after that first night. In addition to the supermarkets, we discovered a wonderful poultry farm with fresh eggs and freshly killed chickens, a couple of good fish markets, the best road stands, an excellent Italian pork store, and the East Hampton branch of Dean & DeLuca, the trendy New York food purveyor. I enjoyed cooking and Joe enjoyed being able to get exercise while we shopped.

Valerie offered to share the cooking. However, I discovered that she is the kind of person who will buy canned peaches when fresh peaches are in season and use garlic salt when fresh garlic is at hand.

The effort of cutting his meat and bringing food to his mouth was tiring for Joe and sometimes he complained of cramps in his neck. When that happened, one of us would cut his meat for him. After meals, he helped with the washing up. Bending from the waist, grasping dishes and cutlery, sticking them into the dishwasher, and stacking them after they were clean and dry amounted to more therapy for Joe and a help to us. Since Valerie is an economical sort and Joe likes to keep an eye on the budget, we put her in charge of food maintenance and preservation. She is unable to throw out anything edible—sometimes I felt like notifying the garbage collector to go straight to our refrigerator. On the other hand, I forget to throw out things that are inedible, and some of my oversights could have crawled right out of the refrigerator to meet the garbage collector halfway. Joe and Valerie (and especially I) loved the meals I prepared, and it was much cheaper than restaurant food. So why eat dinner out?

One day a few weeks into our stay, we drove to Montauk and had lunch at The Lobster Roll, a popular roadside restaurant. We had Joe's collapsible wheelchair with us, but when Joe saw the high stools at the counter, he thought he'd try to manage without it. That was the last time we brought the wheelchair along. Joe wished to feel less conspicuous and so decided that, with our help when he wanted to get up, he could also manage chairs of normal height.

Don Shaw had agreed to come to the house three times a week. From the first day he came blasting down the driveway on his Harley-Davidson until the day Heller could manage without him, Don and Joe got on very well together. Valerie and I liked him too. We got a kick out of watching them do their resistance exercises with one pushing and the other pulling. Many were simple tasks, such as walking on uneven surfaces like the lawn or mounting the stairs. (I suspect Heller worked extra hard on that one; I'm sure he wanted to be able to get to that master bedroom.) I heard plenty of grunts and groans as Joe and Don worked out in the living room. I think it was strenuous for Joe, but the two of them were also having a good time, although Heller might have been throwing in extra groans just for show.

In the first few weeks, Joe was particularly fearful of falling, and Valerie and I were constantly at his side to prevent accidents. Joe did not have the ability to catch or control himself if off balance, and he could have been badly injured if he fell. On two occasions we were not quick enough and he did fall. Both times his knee buckled as he stepped down. Fortunately, he was not hurt either time. Thereafter, when we were guiding him, Valerie and I tried to remain even more alert. Joe was able to walk by himself on level ground; however, a slight incline up or down made him nervous and he was afraid to negotiate a small step unless we were right by his side.

Joe's pool was ready and Valerie and I were making daily use of it. Joe was unable to use the vertical ladder, even with our help, so he decided to order a rather expensive staircase. The pool company did not have any in stock but was expecting a shipment from the factory. In the meantime, Joe used Stanley and Toby Cohen's and Bob and Rosalie Gwathmey's pools, which had staircases instead of ladders. Joe enjoyed being in the water so much after he discovered that he could swim and keep afloat that he began pestering me to get the pool people to hurry his order. We tried to convince him that with the help of Don Shaw, Valerie, and me, he could get up and down his ladder. And once he tried, he discovered it was easier than he thought. Before the end of July Joe needed assistance from no one. It was my pleasure to cancel the costly staircase.

Joe was also making progress out of the water. He practiced getting out of chairs without help by pressing on the armrests and bending forward at the waist in a highly exaggerated way. As his strength increased, he was able to accomplish the task more easily. Now back at work on his book, Joe liked to sit outside in the antique wheelchair I had given him and to sunbathe as he wrote. Because it was high, it was easy for him to get in and out of it. He used his collapsible wheelchair to take himself from the dining table to his desk when he was too tired to raise himself and change chairs. And in the kitchen he sat on a step stool.

At first when Joe had suggested I have the movers take my bicycle to the Hamptons, I foolishly resisted the idea. I am grateful Heller persuaded me. My preference for Fire Island was based mainly upon the fact that no cars are permitted—you must walk or bike. In the Hamptons, one is normally committed to the automobile, and I felt that, though it was a beautiful area, I did not want to spend my vacation in a car. The bicycle made an enormous difference in my attitude. I particularly enjoyed bicycling the back roads during the week, when traffic was light. It was my daily practice to rise early and bicycle for an hour. When I returned in a happy sweat, I'd have breakfast with Joe. Valerie usually elected to sleep a little longer.

Joe had arranged for his newspaper to be delivered to the doorstep because of his condition, and one morning, while I was rolling out, I damn near collided with a car that was tearing into Joe's driveway at top speed. The driver and I were both shaken by the near miss. With a puzzled look, he asked, "Is this the Heller place?" When I told him it was, he handed me *The New York Times* and backed out. I turned to drop the paper off at the house when the same car and driver whipped back in. With an even more puzzled look on his face, the driver stuck his head out the window, stared at me on my bicycle, and said, "They told me you were an invalid!"

"Not in the morning," I said with a grin. (I did not have the heart to leave the man thoroughly perplexed and confessed that it was a case of mistaken identity.)

Paula called one day to tell us that a CBS colleague, Cynthia Kayan, was in Southampton Hospital with Guillain-Barré. She wondered if Joe could manage a visit to encourage her. Heller was glad to help, and Valerie and I went with him.

In Cynthia's hospital room, Valerie and I remained in the background as Joe listened carefully to Ms. Kayan's experiences: She was in the Hamptons for Memorial Day weekend, sitting in the sun at a friend's house, and when she tried to get up from the chaise, she couldn't. Friends helped her stand. After driving back to the house she was staying in, she felt weak and decided to go to Southampton Hospital. The doctors brought in a psychiatrist. (It is not unusual for GBS to be misdiagnosed as possible hysteria.) A neurologist, however, was also brought in, and he identified GBS at once and put her on a respirator.

Joe then described what had happened to him, emphasizing the positive aspects. He spoke reassuringly to Cynthia for a long time, told her about Rusk, where she was soon to be moved, and advised her to decline the EMG test unless she was convinced it was for her benefit, not theirs.

In the early fall of 1984, at the Russian Tea Room party for Joe's novel *God Knows,* a pleasant woman with a huge smile and a slight limp came over to shake my hand. The last time we met, she said, she could not stand, walk, or even move her hand to greet me or anyone else. I recognized the smile. It was Cynthia. She told me she was there to cover the party in her official capacity as a producer. She was now with the television show *Entertainment Tonight.*

On our way to the hospital I had spied my old friend Dr. Norman Pleshette in Bridgehampton, and we stopped briefly to greet him. Valerie knew him from Mount Sinai. Norman had also been a friend of Zero Mostel, who starred in Mel Brooks's first movie, *The Producers.* Mel and Zero met during an off-Broadway production of *The World of Sholom Aleichem,* directed by Stanley Prager. And it was Stanley who introduced me to both Brooks and Mostel. Dr. Pleshette, in fact, had been Mel's first wife's obstetrician, and he was now the houseguest of other good friends, Lillian and Miles Cahn, who would soon be kind enough to bring pelmeni Siberian (dumplings in broth) from the Russian Tea Room to Joe Heller. Lillian attended a dance class with Kate Mostel (Mrs. Zero), mother of artist Tobias, my neighbor on Twenty-eighth Street. I would soon run into Toby at the home of Adelaide de Menil, whose brother, François, had his house designed by Charles Gwathmey. I know it's a small world . . . but in the Hamptons, it's ridiculous.

On our drive back to East Hampton, we stopped once again in Bridgehampton to pick up some homemade ice cream at the Candy Kitchen, where we ran into Bruce Jay Friedman, an old friend of Heller's who used to be Puzo's boss in their editing days at Magazine Management. Mario had told Bruce about Joe's ailment, and Bruce was glad to see Joe on his feet again. After a bit of conversation, Bruce shyly said, "You guys gotta come over to dinner sometime." I noticed the look of surprise on Bruce's face when Joe immediately asked, "When?" (The old Heller would surely have turned him down.)

In retrospect, I am amazed at the number of social invitations Joe accepted those first few weeks. Normally he avoids them, preferring to stay home alone or have a few people over. Now he not only accepted but sometimes went out of his way to arrange invitations—all because he felt Valerie and I would enjoy going out. Surprisingly, he seemed to have as good a time as we did. He even went to cocktail parties. In the old (pre-GBS) days, that was unheard of. I remember once when a friend called and asked Heller to come over for a drink, Joe's reply was: "Why?" The friend, somewhat stunned by Joe's question, asked, "What do you mean why?" Heller's response was, "Why should I go to your house for a drink? I have my own here." The friend explained that he was asking Joe for his company as well. What Joe told him was, "Look, if it was for dinner, I might consider it. For a drink, it's out of the question."

After GBS, and in this period of recovery, Joe was an entirely different social being. It was an extraordinary contrast. That he was extending himself for others (Valerie and me) was remarkable. I remember years back when I needed help hauling a refrigerator up the stairs to my studio, Julie Green and George Mandel immediately volunteered. Heller wouldn't lift a finger, despite my pleading. Without him we managed to get the damned thing halfway up but no farther. Finally, he came toward us and offered advice: "Why don't you hire someone to do this?" We just yelled obscenities at him until he said, "Okay, I'll help." What he did next was infuriating and comical—he stood there doing nothing until we yelled at him to get out of the way. We completed the job in spite of him. Later, while we were eating and our anger was gone, I asked Joe how come he behaved so uncooperatively. Predictably, his answer had the ring of a line out of a novel: "I would not do for others what I would not do for myself." (This sounded reasonable, but there was a catch: Joe had the ability to get others to do everything for him, therefore he NEVER had to do anything for himself and he could justify refusing aid to others forever.)

So our social activity in the summer of 1982 was truly remarkable. Within three weeks we had gone to lunch at the home of Gloria Jones, wife of the late James Jones, and at the Gwathmeys', and also had dinner at Bruce Jay Friedman's, Irwin Shaw's, Craig Claiborne's (twice), and Pierre Franey's. In the same period we managed to entertain friends for dinner two times and hosted Carol and Mario for an overnight visit. They arrived with a bottle of Château Latour 1976 and a bottle of Dom Pérignon. Joe, of course, refused to serve either of these fine potables since diet soda and plain water are better for Mario's health. The next day, touched by our hospitality, Puzo magnanimously invited us to purchase whatever we wanted at Dean & DeLuca's. I cautioned him that the store was not inexpensive. "Take anything and everything you want," he repeated. "It's only a food place, not a jewelry store."

With merely the leftovers from Mario's generosity, we served a sumptuous lunch to two friends, which brought invitations to four dinners and three lunches in return.

I had actually met most of Joe's friends before, but I now perceived a slight difference in the way I was being treated. Either Joe said something or they assumed it without being told, but almost without exception they beamed at me as though I were some kind of saint, which I'm not. Denials did nothing but further that image.

The Fourth of July weekend Barbara and Arthur Gelb, good friends of Joe's, were houseguests. Arthur woke early and walked over to Heller's poolside, where I was relaxing after my morning bicycle ride and a quick swim. He introduced himself to me (I had been out the night before when he arrived) and mentioned that he had heard a lot about me from Joe, including the story of my recent voyage with Towbin. We chatted amiably and I told him about how I had toured Europe on five dollars a month and how the good life in East Hampton wasn't costing me much either. Arthur, deputy managing editor of *The New York Times,* was a responsive listener and a good laugher. Suddenly he stopped me in the middle of a sentence and suggested that I write something for the *Times.* I was stunned. I didn't know whether he meant it or not. I thought he knew from Joe that I was everything but a writer and I told him so. Gelb waved impatiently and said he was sure I could handle an assignment.

Later I told Joe about my conversation and asked his advice. Heller smiled and said, "What are you worried about? Do it!"

I said, "Seriously, do you really think I can?"

Lying again, Joe said, "It's easy. Of course you can."

I went along with him, adding, "I thought so and I already have an idea for my first piece. It's 'How to Beat the High Cost of Living in the Hamptons . . . All You Need Is a Sick Friend with a House.' "

Joe said he liked the idea (I was simply fooling around), and he insisted I tell Arthur, who also thought it was funny. "I think it should go in the 'Living Section.' Do a thousand to fifteen hundred words. How about a two-week deadline? Do you think you can live with that?" For the first time I began to believe he was serious. "Sure," I said.

When we all had dinner that evening with Craig Claiborne and Pierre Franey, I refrained from revealing myself as a fellow *Times* writer. I let my illustrious colleagues believe I was merely a friend of Heller's.

This new challenge was timely. I was, in truth, beginning to get bored with nothing to do but bike, swim, shop, cook, plant, weed, barber, invent, socialize, entertain and be entertained, stay healthy, and have a wonderful time. I dropped none of my usual activities and set to work writing freelance for the *Times.* Heller was absolutely right. Writing is easy. Doing it good is another story.

A few days after I began, I had a draft that satisfied me and I asked Heller to read it. Since he needed a haircut, he could hardly refuse. His only comment, gently put (he really needed that haircut), was that he thought the piece was to be about the high cost of living in the Hamptons, not the "Speed Vogel Story." I got the message and went back to work. I wrote and rewrote, and when I was finished—though not quite satisfied with what I had done (nor would I ever be again)—I gave it back to Joe. He read it through, chuckled this time, and said it was fine. Naturally, I did not believe him and said, "Stop fooling around. Tell me." He repeated himself, told me to stop bothering him and to turn it in.

I arrived at the *Times,* passed security, and Arthur ushered me into his office. I handed over my typescript and was about to say good-bye. But I was not getting off the hook that easily. Arthur proceeded to read what I'd given him. I pretended to study the photographs on the wall, but I was really watching him read. His face was expressionless and he took forever to finish. I knew him as an easy laugher, and he didn't even crack a smile. I was sure he hated it. Finally, he looked up. "It's funny," he said. "Needs some editing . . . Thanks. . . . We'll get back to you . . . Regards to Joe." I heard "Don't hold your breath."

As I walked out of the *Times* building, I told myself it didn't matter, I wasn't hurt. I then remembered my favorite story about Joe Louis, the great heavyweight boxer. Before Louis was world champ, one of his opponents tagged him with a good right and he went down. Joe was up before the referee began his count and won the fight by a knockout. In the dressing room, Blackburn, Louis's manager, removing his bandages, looked up and said, "Joe, if you should ever happen to get knocked down again, stay down till the referee counts to nine. It scores against you the same and the time might help clear your head. Besides," he added, "you can't spring up to your feet so fast they didn't see you were down." What Gelb handed me was not a heavy blow, but I saw I was "down" and there was no sense lying to myself.

I told Heller that my brilliant career as a writer was over. Joe told me not to be so pessimistic.

And the next day the "Living Section" editor called, said he had made some changes, and would mail the edited draft for my approval. The edited draft was practically intact, but a few of my jokes were missing. Cocky again, I had the nerve to try to negotiate them back in. I settled for two out of three and was told the piece would probably appear in the paper the following week or the week after.

The morning of July 28 I went for my usual bike ride, not even bothering to pick up the paper in the drive. When I returned, Joe, giggling like a kid, shoved the paper at me, saying, "There, see for yourself!"

Sure enough, I was in print: "Helping a Convalescent Friend (in Style)."

Joe warned me not to expect the Pulitzer Prize. I told him not to be so pessimistic.

DON SHAW WAS PAID fifty dollars an hour and came three afternoons a week, riding his motorcycle almost another hour to get to me from his full-time job at a day-care institution, where he worked often with children suffering motor disabilities from such diseases as cerebral palsy and spina bifida, and riding a third hour when finished with me to go to his home in Riverhead, Long Island, some forty miles away. A former marine somewhere in his thirties, he had a young child by a first marriage and an infant by a second marriage. He was gentle, strong, and wiry, and he had a long lateral scar on one side of his chest, a consequence of open heart surgery to correct a defect resulting in some way from a serious automobile accident in which he had been involved not too many years before.

Valerie Humphries was paid three hundred dollars every week for the rest of the year. This includes the week she and I quarreled (in a farcical misunderstanding over an impromptu picnic on the grass Speed gave one afternoon in the course of his multiple newfound duties as an attorney, a writer, and a popular East Hampton host and socialite). I suggested to Valerie that she go away on vacation for seven or nine days and decide if she wanted to come back. (She decided, of course, that she did and was back in five.)

I had been talking about money in the course of the interview I was giving to Cheryl McCall for *People* magazine. Cheryl and I sat outside, and, as was true of almost all days that gregarious summer, other people were about. "You see my nurse and my therapist there," I am recorded as saying in a long-winded answer to Cheryl, who was already acquainted with Valerie and Don. "I mean, they both get paid. It's expensive to be sick and a luxury to recuperate."

The bill from Mount Sinai Hospital lists two hundred and sixty-five medical items for my forty-four days there, excluding the daily cost of the bed in the intensive care unit and then in the private room, and the total for all of the hospital charges amounted to $32,585.02. Of this, $27,102.99 was paid by my medical insurance and $5,482.03 was paid by me. I find in examining the bill now for the first time that my Blue Cross policy was one providing full coverage for only twenty-one days, and I tell you from experience that this is not enough.

My hospital bill from the New York University Medical Center, of which the Rusk Institute is a part, came to $43,073.10 for the hundred and eight days I was a patient there. Of this, $4,982.75 was paid by Blue Cross for thirty days of discounted coverage. And the remainder of $38,090.35 was paid by me. In both places my costs would have been lowered considerably if I had gone to something other than a private room, and probably that's what I will do next time. But I won't have much fun.

Neither of these hospital bills includes charges for personal physicians or private-duty nurses. I did not have Blue Shield or anything equivalent to help pay for these. In metropolitan New York, the amounts allotted normally for doctors' care under policies of this kind represent so small a fraction of what is usually charged that I had decided a decade or two back that maintaining one was not worth the bother. Supplementing what Blue Cross coverage I did have was only that archaic major medical policy, obtained in 1966, with a maximum benefit payment of $10,000, and I tell you categorically that this too is not enough. The $10,-000 was gone in the twinkling of an eye. That second major medical policy, which would have paid eighty percent of all costs above $10,000, had carelessly been allowed to lapse in February of that year through a failure to pay an annual premium of $132, and I did not know it had lapsed until Julie Green made those telephone calls for me and found that out.

My costs for my two Dr. Baders, Dr. Sencer, Dr. Peck, and Dr. Ragnarsson, as compiled from my check stubs on a six-dollar pocket calculator, totaled $8,480. There were charges from other physicians for special examinations at both places, but none was huge. My costs for nurses for the entire year amounted to $23,402, of which about $6,000 went to my around-the-clock nurses at Mount Sinai in the twenty-two days I was in a private room and $10,000 more went to Valerie from the time I got out of Rusk in the middle of May until we returned from Saint Croix in February of 1983 and I felt I no longer needed her as a nurse. Don Shaw, working with me in one-hour sessions from the middle of June until the end of the year, with occasional days off at his request for personal reasons, cost another $2,700.

Working with the stubs in my checkbook for all of 1982, I arrive at the following total medical costs of my illness: hospitals—$75,658.12; physicians (all)—$9,425; nurses—$23,402; therapy (Don Shaw, Carol Hughes, outpatient)—$3,887. There were other charges related to the illness too numerous to itemize and not impressive in the aggregate. The figures I have given total $112,372.12 (on my six-dollar calculator, which produces different subtotals each time I try to tabulate them; the error is mine rather than the instrument's, and the differences I get are never very different). Of the $112,372.12 I've mentioned, $39,-189.64 was paid by my two medical insurance policies and $73,-182.48 was the cost to me of my case of Guillain-Barré in 1982.

This was something of a bargain compared to a few of the cases I heard about after the interview in *People* appeared and the letters rolled in. Stanley Rosenstock estimates a quarter of a million for his. I have a retired military man in Phoenix, Arizona, who paid $142,000 for his, for everything from aspirin to codeine. And in Cheney, Washington, there was a man named Emery Babb who had been in ICU at Deaconess Hospital for almost eight months, with his bills for just the hospital already at $199,000. Bob Samuels, about whom I will tell you more shortly, is by now close to a million. There is a cruel paradox in the high cost of Guillain-Barré; it is expensive because most people do survive, and because they survive, they're hospitalized longer than they would be for most other diseases and require longer periods of recuperation. (There was a letter from a man in New York named Jerry Basille who did not talk about the cost but wrote: "It felt so good when I was able to reach around and wipe my ass." His statement lacks poetry but is eloquent in feeling.)

In addition to the high cost of illness, there is the high cost of living and the high cost of litigation. A frugal person might avoid all three.

I was supporting my wife.

On top of that, in 1982 I paid out $35,248.04 in nonmedical professional fees, to lawyers and to accountants, and most of that was in connection with my matrimonial litigation. Jeffrey works hard and he works well, but he does not work for nothing. The $15,000 I paid to him between May and December of that year was only the beginning.

And then there was the cost of my own maintenance, for once the medical necessities were over, I wanted to go on living too. My nonmedical expenses were negligible in the six months I was in hospitals: I did no traveling and very little entertaining. But my normal everyday costs of living started up again once I was out and I found, to my surprise, an active social life beginning and increasing enjoyably with my move to East Hampton and even more with the publication of Speed's article in the *Times.* (Who would have thought there was so much power is *his* printed word!)

Summarizing, in that year, when my adjusted gross income was $36,565.00, my check stubs show outlays for unreimbursed personal expenses of $278,673.81. You may not believe it, but $278,673.81 was a lot of money to me then, and it is a lot of money to me now. Some people don't earn that much in a whole month.

For most of that summer of 1982 I was living on the last of my liquid savings and the loan from Mario. At the end of July I enjoyed a windfall of some magnitude from Simon & Schuster, an unexpected royalty check of $21,890.07 from a special hardcover edition of *Catch-22* published by that firm a year or so before. I am only a saint, and my powers of benediction are questionable, but I nevertheless blessed passionately everyone at Simon & Schuster who'd subscribed to the idea that the time might be ripe for another new printing and a national distribution of that first novel of mine. It was not until the end of the year that I received any money from Knopf, and I devoted much of that new advance to paying off to friends most of the loans I had taken—on the chance I might someday have to return to these same people for larger ones.

The article by Speed produced a couple of letters from strangers to me and a delightful ripple of fame and attention for the three of us as a group. There were people who had not known I was in the hospital until reading I was out. There were a number of jocular invitations to Speed and Valerie to come work as a couple—one of them from a member of a presidential family during Speed's incredible "Presidential Week," about which I know him to be already eager to tell you. There were letters and phone calls for each of us from people we had not heard from for long times, and there were a couple of mash notes for Speed from old flames from his young years, or young flames in those old years.

The two letters forwarded to me soonest after Speed's article was published were from persons with much more experience with Guillain-Barré than I had then. The first was from a man in Greenville, New York, named Anthony Lobb, who wrote that he was seventy-three and had come down with Guillain-Barré at sixty-four. To cheer me up in my recovery, he was letting me know that at age sixty-eight he'd become a Peace Corps volunteer in El Salvador, where he'd worked for close to two years, and now, retired, he worked as a hobby on a small farm owned by his son, a practicing attorney who maintained the farm as a diversion for himself. Mr. Lobb was writing just to urge me to keep my spirits up and to say that "this has been one hell of an experience! Unless you have it—you will never know." That letter was a good one.

The second one made very short shrift of Speed Vogel, beginning, "Dear Mr. Heller: I read Mr. Vogel's article in the *N. Y. Times.* I am more interested in your illness than his food." The writer was a woman, who went on to say:

> My husband had GB 19 years ago. . . . He is in a wheel chair due to nerve damage. He has lost his balance and some areas of sensation. He also has no reflexes.

She had been interested ever since in keeping up with any new discoveries in the cure of such residual effects. All I could do was refer her to Rusk, and I felt useless doing so, because Rusk was the place her husband had gone to nineteen years earlier.

I received a phone call from a woman in Pennsylvania named Estelle Benson who, because her husband had fallen ill with Guillain-Barré a few years earlier, had started a GBS Support Group (P.O. Box 262, Wynnewood, PA 19096), which, among other services, collects and distributes information about the ailment. I refer people to her who are desperate to know more about it than they are able to find out anyplace else.

And that's pretty much the way the letters went once the interview appeared in *People* and they began to arrive in volume. Some were encouraging, others daunting, and others were a perplexing mixture.

> My wife, Ann, was stricken by GBS in 1967 and we thought you would like to know that she has recovered from this terrible disease with the exception of the following:

> Some partial paralysis in the right hip and right leg. This causes her to limp slightly. Her right calf is almost two inches smaller than the left.
>
> Difficulty in swallowing, due to some paralysis of the throat.
>
> Most of all, she occasionally experiences violent spasms in her leg and sometimes in the back of her neck which continue up into her head.

As I've said, there is something about this disease inducing people who've overcome the gross defects to think of themselves as recovered.

Cheryl McCall is my friend, and I told her truthfully in our interview that I really thought I was having the best summer of my life. She believed me, even though I'd been grudging in consenting to the article and displayed at times a weary moodiness that emerged in places in the printed piece as a dour bitterness I did not genuinely feel or intend and for which I was quickly repentant. I tired quickly, and that could have been part of the cause. Cheryl and Michael Abramson, the *People* photographer, along with Valerie and Speed, were socializing with me a good deal of the time when we weren't working, and often I would have preferred resting alone. I found it simpler to be morose and caustic than to be uncivil and withdrawn. Certainly, these months were much more interesting than any I could recall, and I did not hesitate to rejoice in that aspect of them.

"This is the happiest summer of my life," I did exclaim sincerely to Cheryl on her tape recorder, and I told her of a conversation I'd had a week before with friends who had driven out from the city to see how I was doing. It was exactly the conclusion I had come to with them.

"A lot of people wouldn't believe you," Steve DeClerque had agreed with a nod, gazing at me and smiling and talking hoarsely with his one vocal cord, "seeing the condition you're in. But I think I know what you mean."

I could not remember a time in my life, in childhood, adolescence, or adulthood, when my vision of what I wanted to accomplish was so uncluttered. I knew where I was and I knew why I was there. My conscience was clear. My children were self-supporting. I felt under no obligation to anyone other than the people who were helping me and those I felt friendly toward. Never in my past had my emotions and my moral life seemed so uncomplicated. My problems were few and I knew what they were. I needed to make money, I wanted to finish my novel, I wanted to get better.

"I have the feeling now that I'll never be able to jog again or jump up again with both feet," I said to Cheryl, and she reported much of this in her piece. "I can see myself walking normally, normally enough to walk out without fear of falling down. I think that will come by the end of September. Driving a car will take a couple of more months than that. I don't think I'll ever be able to run again. I long to do that."

I was more pessimistic on all counts than the outcome warranted. By September I could stand up to get out of a car without help and by October I was beginning to drive one. In November, Don Shaw would hold my extended hands, and I *was* able to jump up and down "with both feet" off the ground. And I noticed something that piqued my interest in the operation of the brain, nerves, and muscles. I could not perform these jumping actions slowly, had no power to regulate the pace.

There was a different quirk in another exercise which I found equally intriguing. Don would hold a wooden rod in both fists and, in the living room or in the pool, have me push against it to force him backward while I moved forward, as he opposed me with just the right amount of resistance to compel me to exert to the utmost what strength I possessed. He changed his direction as he faded back to force me to alter the angles of the various parts of my body as I heaved against him. Then he would direct me to go backward, to pull against him as we reversed the action. Each time he told me to change the direction, I was stunned for a second and did not know how to comply. I could understand the words. I could not comprehend the instruction. I had to reason it through, recall how to do what was expected of me. Don explained to me that we think with one part of the brain, the cortex, and execute our intentions without thinking through a different part, the brain stem, and that with me, the swift neurological connection between intention and instinctual performance had not yet been reconstituted.

Just consider the multitude of coordinated neural signals flying back and forth inside me with the speed of lightning as I sit here simply writing these few words—inside you as you read them—and you have to concede there are miracles involved, and mysteries, too. Who can number the infinities of neuromuscular activities going on within either one of us at just this moment alone? Nerve impulses are electrical in nature and fly along pathways of fibers in minute charges transmitted from one microscopic node of the fiber to the next. Billions of bursts of invisible biochemical synchronizations are completed in a half a minute of Ping-Pong! Biological processes are phenomenal, you know, and a biological process like this one is almost enough to make you want to stop believing in Darwin's theory of evolution and in any of the creationist theories with which we are most familiar. There is a third explanation, of course, for so much life on this world, and no one has any idea what it is.

(Contrary to what I've written earlier, I've discovered about two weeks before today—June 2, 1985—that I am starting to learn how to run with my brain stem instead of my cortex, and I can go about a hundred short steps at a time while thinking about writing sentences like these instead of thinking about how to run. And also, a few days before this one, I found myself reaching for the morning newspaper on the ground by bending both legs instead of stooping forward at the waist rigidly as though built of wood. Without realizing it, I had regained, after three and a half years, the strength and the unconscious know-how almost to do deep-knee bends again.)

At the beginning of December, Don Shaw told me he could not in good conscience keep taking money from me for what was now conditioning rather than physical therapy. There were no exercises we were doing that I could not do alone. But I also knew I was more energetic and conscientious doing them with him, and I asked him to continue coming through the end of the month, when Valerie, Speed, and I were planning to leave for five weeks in Saint Croix anyway.

Don taught me at least one more thing of value before we parted at Christmas, how to get up from a sofa by moving to the armrest and utilizing my elbows and shoulders upon it. He did not think my knee would buckle again in the walks I was taking alone outside the house, and he turned out to be right. I might fall when off balance if budged or tripped, but that would not be from a weak knee but from my inability to replace my legs under my new center of gravity quickly enough, which is what almost all of us are doing unconsciously almost all the time. (The following year I fell several times dismounting from a bicycle, but neither of us was looking that far ahead then.)

There was a striking photograph of Don Shaw and me in the *People* article with a misleading caption giving the impression I was in pain when I was not. There was another photograph in *People* showing me descending a small outdoor staircase backward, protected by Valerie and Speed, and that is the way it had to be for much of that summer. I had to be escorted everywhere we went, helped on each side going up steps, protected going down. And there was another photograph of me working hard to close the snaps of a shirt I was donning, and that is the way it had to be too.

Once that issue of the magazine appeared it proved too much for any one of the three of us to answer all the phone calls that began coming in from every part of the country, so we took turns. I remember the first, from a builder in Arizona who'd checked himself out of the hospital upon learning nothing could be done there to accelerate his recovery and went on his own initiative to very high doses of vitamin C crystals, but still suffered occasionally from numbness in his feet. (Immediately, I put myself on very high doses of vitamin C crystals too.)

After several weeks I gave up trying to reply to all of the letters. A surprising number were from people in small communities who had not once heard of anyone but themselves having

Guillain-Barré and were relieved, in reading of me, they said, by the reassurance that they had not merely imagined the harrowing experience they truly had gone through. Many of them were sent by their doctors for a consultation with a psychiatrist to rule out conversion hysteria as the cause. A letter affording me immense solace arrived from a man in Canada named Bram Garber. I will present my abridgment of his graceful sentiments without marring the appearance of his text with the suspension points that usually signify deletions.

Dear Mr. Heller:

It appears every year or two I find myself writing a letter similar to this one.

On Sunday morning in September 1960 I awoke with tingling in my arms and legs, rapidly losing muscle strength. By the following evening, I was in the Montreal Neurological Institute, in a lung, my legs and arms, hands, feet, neck, mouth fully paralyzed.

For a month I was unconscious or semi-conscious, virtually on my back for six months. During this period I started with water therapy, ligament stretching, and into various stages of physio. After a total of eleven months, I left the hospital in a wheelchair and then virtually lived with a therapist for two years doing exercises thru the day until we finally got so fed up with one another's company, we parted, albeit friends.

You were right about the EMGs, they are torture. I tried it once and refused thereafter. The same with the puncture into the spine; took that once but never again. It's true, medicine has no cure for Guillain-Barré; however, I was very fortunate in having a fine man, and thorough doctor, who was genuinely concerned, and, incidentally, not a money gouger. We are friends today. I was fortunate, having the same three nurses around the clock for the eleven months in the hospital.

During my hospital period and two postrecovery years, I constantly kept in touch with my business and at no time did I ever doubt full recovery. Today, I lead a very normal life (after 90% recovery) and in addition to my work, I travel, booze it up, party, chase chicks, and have no regrets.

Things like ligament pains, muscular aches, a restricted range long stopped bothering me. Look for the nicer things in life. I never did become bitter, although I admit to some unrestricted cursing at times, and I did develop some new values, like collecting paintings and antiques.

What can I say to you? If you live in the Hamptons, sand-walk barefooted. Excellent for foot and leg muscles. Knees, that's a tough one. For the buckling knees, try sand-walking with bended knees, even if it is only a few steps. In my case, it helped. Swimming contributed greatly to my general recovery, particularly the gross muscles.

It was on the eve of my forty-second birthday when I was struck.

Well, this letter may be just a lot of verbosity to you; I write it in the chance and hope it might do you some good.

This letter was dated August 30, 1982, twenty-two years after he was stricken, and his memory is clear and his sympathy and compassion, to my mind, saintly and majestic. Leg cramps are his worst aftereffect discomfort, he wrote me in another letter, although he is the one spoken of previously who lost the small muscles in both hands, making bicycle riding impracticable.

And soon after hearing from him, along with my megadoses of vitamin C crystals, I began sand-walking at the beach and sand-walking with bended knees. Had somebody suggested séances, I would have tried those too.

A month after Bram Garber's, there arrived a letter from a woman named Rikki Samuels about her husband, Robert, who had come down with Guillain-Barré about two weeks before I had.

Dear Mr. Heller:

I hope your progress with G.B.S. is continuing and your recovery will be complete. My husband was also stricken in December and just last month was taken off a respirator. [Stricken before I was and "just" taken off a respirator, two months after I was already finished with hospitals!]

> We have started arrangements at I.R.M. [Rusk] for an evaluation. I want so much for him to be accepted. He's been at the Neurology Institute of Columbia since Dec.'81. (He had 4 EMGs! Then refused to have any more.) Can you help us?

By the time I telephoned to say I doubted I could help him gain admittance to Rusk, he had already been accepted there.

Now here's what's happened to Bob Samuels. He was a writer with an international oil company who had aspirations of someday writing books on subjects of his own choosing. About six weeks after a series of immunization shots and a business trip around the world, he awoke one night and noticed weakness in one leg. When the weakness persisted through the day and seemed to be worse the following morning, he telephoned his doctor, who told him to go at once to the emergency room of the nearest hospital, which was in Nyack, New York, not far from his home. A spinal tap disclosed a high protein level, and he was put into the intensive care unit for close watching, with a diagnosis of Guillain-Barré. That night he was put on a respirator and could move very little. The next day he was totally paralyzed and was able to move only his eyes. ("I moved them left to say 'No,' right to say 'Yes.' I could not close my eyelids.")

From that small hospital, he was transferred to Columbia-Presbyterian Hospital in the city, where he remained with private-duty nurses around the clock for the next nine months. (My total time in both hospitals was less than six.) He was on a respirator for these nine months and could not talk! (It is my guess that the company he worked for paid these expenses and that it pays for his medical expenses still.) He was fed by nasogastric tube for two or three months and then by stomach tube for six months. He was younger than I and had fallen sick two weeks sooner; but he entered Rusk at the end of October 1982, whereas I had been able to go in nine months before him, at the end of January, and he stayed there six months, compared to my three and a half. He went home in a wheelchair in April 1983, after *fifteen* months of hospitalization. And two years after our first symptoms, in December of 1983, when I was riding a bicycle and driving a car and using a gym and swimming pool in Guerney's Inn in Montauk, Long Island, and starting to walk and trot a little on a treadmill in a fitness center in East Hampton, Bob Samuels was still in a wheelchair at home and still using a transfer board.

He still had private nurses. Because of a weak cough reflex, he needed suctioning daily. Much of the time in his first two hospitals his wife was afraid he was going to die. They'd had to move from the house they'd lived in to one that could be renovated to accommodate a man in a wheelchair, with ramps and widened doorways. He was an outpatient at Rusk, going three times a week by ambulette; he was able to stand up at the parallel bars but he could not walk. (And only in the summer of 1985, after nearly four years, was he at last able to move with a walker, but he still could not rise to his feet by himself!) Because his fingers were too weak to be used in feeding himself, he had splints on both hands with attachments for a knife and fork. He needed a "sleeve" over each of his index fingers to be able to type with just those two fingers. He was using a word processor to work on a book.

I remember again that Dr. Walter Sencer had predicted on the day he saw me that my case of Guillain-Barré probably would be a mild one, and it is only when I deal with the accounts of others I know of who've had the same disease that I am willing to concede that Dr. Sencer was right and that my case was indeed mild. In the words of Julius Green, I "could have done much worse." In the words of Bob Gottlieb, "It's not a good thing to have."

By no means were all of the well-wishing letters I received a pleasure to read ("I was nineteen years old at the time. . . . I, like you, was terrified of closing my eyes. . . ." or "My daughter's name is Dana, she is 14 and in the 9th grade. The weakness in her legs started . . ."). One of the most depressing came from an exuberant woman named Peggy Manion, who described herself as all the way back to normal and included a sentence so startling

I almost could not get by it: "I was struck with Guillain-Barré twice."

I did not want to think of the horrifying possibility of having to go through that same thing again. But I could not escape the idea for long.

At the end of the summer there was a large outdoor feast celebrating Craig Claiborne's new birthday and new book. Valerie and Speed took me there and sat me down, and someone brought me a plate of food with a grilled Cajun catfish, something I had never eaten before and wanted at once to eat more of. As I sat there enjoying myself, I watched suspiciously as a stranger approached slowly, walking with a cane. He told me his name was Mike Alexander (we have met each other socially since) and that he was a friend of Speed's. He was coming to wish me the best, and added that he also had been hit by Guillain-Barré. I answered him warily, for I had witnessed his limp. I had seen him using his cane.

"How long ago?"

"I had it twice," he answered. "The first time—"

"I don't want to talk about it now," I cut him off, and then attempted to affect what I hoped would impress him as a jocular laugh. "Really, I don't, not at a party."

I don't want to dwell even now on the unimaginable tragedy of going through all that a second time. So I'll return to Bob Samuels and his word processor and to an irony I've saved. When we talk on the telephone, he wisecracks as much with me as they tell me I used to wisecrack with others. He has been using his word processor to write a book about his experiences with Guillain-Barré. When he finished a hundred pages, he sent them to a well-known literary agency, which received it with enthusiasm, optimism, and delight—and which subsequently notified him that publishers thus far were reluctant to contract with him that year for a book about his case of Guillain-Barré, as good a book as it promised to be, because it was known that this book about *my* Guillain-Barré was already on the way.

Along with everything else that had happened to him, one

of us remarked ruefully to the other, he now had to have me.

I have saved this bit for the end of the chapter because I know the sentence with which Speed begins the next one, and I feel Bob might find amusement in the juxtaposition. No one else might find it funny, but I think Bob Samuels will.

I HAVE NEVER, as an author, known rejection. Getting into the writing profession is easy and I don't know why it doesn't attract more people. (All you really need is a friend who is an established writer and who comes down with a rare and nonfatal disease, and who also has a friend who is an important editor of a prestigious newspaper.) Being a writer also brings great rewards: social, if not monetary. (The newspaper game doesn't pay all that well.)

It appears to me that everyone reads *The New York Times* on Wednesdays and that they carefully scrutinize the "Living Section." Joe's phone in East Hampton was ringing off the wall for days, and the tape on my answering machine in the city ran out.

Comments ranged from the effusively complimentary to the simply congratulatory. Mario told me that I wrote funny stuff and thanked me for creating the wittiest remarks for him. When I confessed that I did nothing but report his words verbatim, he didn't believe me. But as an afterthought, he said, "Hey, if you're telling me the truth, I'm a very funny guy." A couple of people thought Heller wrote the piece for me (an insult to both of us). And a few people didn't seem to get it. One friend thought I presented myself as an awful moocher. She was worried that people might get the wrong impression. I thanked her for her solicitude.

Before I was a published writer, Joe, Valerie, and I were invited to a lunch at Lauren Bacall's. I was happy to go, and though I was welcomed graciously, I was a bit uncomfortable. I felt more like Heller's lackey than his friend and might have been more at home in the kitchen with the rest of the help. Trying to make conversation with literary lions like George Plimpton, Wilfrid Sheed, William Gaddis, and Charles Addams was intimidating. I should include the hostess, as well, but I warmed to her immediately and was able to forget that she is a writer because when she greeted Joe she was so touched seeing him back on his feet again that tears came to her eyes.

After my piece in the *Times,* however, my feelings of inferiority changed dramatically. I now began to act more like the cock o' the walk than a wallflower. At social gatherings I was approached by those who had either read or heard about the article, and I ate up flattery. I was no longer simply Joe Heller's noble and altruistic friend. (My halo was getting a bit tight anyway.) I was the Speed Vogel who wrote the story for the *Times.* I loved the new image! And like Scarlett, I vowed never to go hungry (for attention) again!

I had plenty of dates. Sometimes two ladies at once, and inadvertently I developed a kind of game that kept Heller laughing. Each time I had a date, I made it a point to visit Bob and Rosalie Gwathmey. My motive, at least in the beginning, was simple. I always felt welcome and I could depend on the Gwathmeys to charm the pants off anyone I brought around. Bob is a marvelous raconteur and Rosalie has a keen wit and fine memory and she prompts Bob with admirable subtlety when necessary. If my dates were less than enthusiastic about the Gwathmeys, it indicated they had no taste and I lost interest in them. It was a timesaver. Both Joe and I thought it was funny that I was parading such a large number of attractive women before them. Hearing Rosalie call out from her deck as I drove into their driveway with a fresh companion, "Bob, get out here and take a look—Speed's got himself a new one!" was gratifying. I was glad the image I presented as a bon vivant was still intact.

But the question of who really deserved the title was a matter of debate. The New York *Post*'s gossipy "Page Six," still interested in Heller, cited a reference to Mario from the *Heller* v. *Heller* court record, in which he is portrayed as a bad influence on Joe and described as " 'the famous writer, and unfortunately, the equally famous bon vivant and womanizer.' " To which Joe had responded, " 'Anybody with good vision and good sense cannot with a straight face describe Mr. Puzo as a bon vivant or womanizer.' " I asked Mario how he felt about his new reputation. He said, "I like it. And I intend to sue them both for libel."

Rosalie Gwathmey may have considered me a man-about-town, but when I began house hunting in the Hamptons, she helped me face a grim reality. "Find a house with a bedroom on the ground floor," Rosalie advised me, adding with a smile, "You're not *always* going to be riding around on that bicycle, you know." It's not my nature to think in terms of age. I never realized I was hanging out with "young" people because I never felt "old." Take Cheryl McCall, for example. I am at least twice her age, but we are simply buddies.

When Cheryl had phoned with the idea of doing a story on Joe, I told her I didn't think he'd want it but naturally I would intercede for her. Joe surprised me—he was cooperative. "Of course," he said. "Tell her 'sure.' " However, later, when I asked Heller when to schedule Cheryl's interview, Joe responded, "What interview? What are you talking about?" Gently I reminded him of our previous conversation, but he brushed me aside with a flip of the hand. "Not a chance," he said. "Forget it." I was about to tell Cheryl to abandon the project, when I decided to try one last time. "Okay," Heller grumbled. "I'm doing it only for you and Cheryl."

In the interview, much to my surprise, Joe was unusually open about his feelings toward his family, his career, and his friends. Once again he made me and Valerie appear selfless, noble, and saintly. The way Heller expressed it: "There's nothing that Speed or Valerie can ask me that I'd deny them, ever. I owe them more than I can possibly repay—so I won't even try. And that's what I'll tell them when they come to collect."

After the *People* story hit the stands, there was an avalanche of letters. And again, the phone did not stop ringing. Most inquiries were about GBS. But some people just wanted Valerie and me to know we were nice to stand by our sick friend. There were hours we hardly had time to do anything else but field telephone calls. One time when it was my turn to pick up, I was greeted by the voice of my friend LuAnn Walther, who knows something about publishing. "Speed," she said, "I read your *Times* piece and the *People* story on Joe. Why don't you think about writing a book about it all?" I was flabbergasted. When I told Joe her suggestion, his response flabbergasted me further: "Yes, do it," he said.

A couple of days later, when I was in the city, Joe called and said something like this, I believe: "I've been thinking about your book, and I would like to be the co-author if you don't mind. Is that okay?" I asked Joe to hold on as I contemplated his question. And I debated his proposal just as long as it had taken me to say yes to the invitation to Cannes.

The first thing I did was, of course, tell my friends. So I called Mario and told him I was writing. Mario said, "Speed, don't begin before you have a signed contract and an advance." I thought that sounded wise. I then called George Mandel, told him what Mario said, and he said, "Mario's got it wrong. Don't listen to him. You don't write a word until you've *spent* the advance. Why should anybody write when he's got money?"

So I still had time on my hands. Joe, always willing to educate, told me that anyone could be an attorney without ever passing the bar, graduating from law school, or even getting a high school diploma. To my astonishment, the dictionary confirms this incredible fact. All you need is to act on someone's behalf and you are an attorney—literally, one who is "turned to."

Shortly after I learned this, Mario said he wanted to buy a tennis club in the Hamptons. To amuse Joe, I called a prominent local real estate office and, announcing myself as Mr. Puzo's attorney, arranged to see some prospective properties. And so I began another new career.

My next dinner date became a client when she accidentally learned that Joe and I shared the same lawyer, Jeffrey Cohen. Jeffrey was not only her legal adversary, he was also her soon-to-be-ex-husband's best friend. I asked a few questions and was soon convinced that I could settle her divorce case easily. She said, "I trust you, go do it."

I called Jeffrey, told him whom I was representing (telling him to look it up in the dictionary if he didn't believe I was a bona fide attorney), and gave him the amount my client would be willing to accept (I had to hold the line while he actually opened up his Webster's). "This is crazy," he said, "but if what you say is true, I think we can wind it up!" I decided to quit this game while I was ahead, and Jeffrey's best friend's wife became my bicycle companion instead of my client.

She had introduced me to splendid back roads in the Hamptons, and one day, after a long ride, we decided to pick up a photographer friend, a few dozen chilled clams on the half-shell with oysterettes, and a couple of bottles of wine. I suggested we head for Heller's lawn and sit under the trees for our picnic. We spread a blanket, and I went inside to ask Joe and Valerie to join us. Joe said he was still exhausted from the *People* interview and all the picture taking and asked me to please stay outside and not invite anyone in. I told him I understood, which I did, and went back to my guests. I heard Valerie's voice from upstairs. Then I heard Joe yell something back, but I could not make out what either of them said. And the next thing I knew about them was that Valerie was angry as hell and leaving for good.

It took me a while to put the pieces together. Just as I had finished promising to keep my guests outside, Valerie, who has a hospitable nature, was calling from the window upstairs and asking them to come in. Joe, from the ground floor, shouted up to interrupt her. And what Valerie understood was that he was telling her to shut up.

Valerie left East Hampton the next day on what they called a vacation. When Joe asked me if I thought we could manage without her, I realized that he thought she might not return. But when she phoned to remind me to remind Joe not to go into the pool unless someone was watching, I would have wagered anything that Valerie would come back. And, of course, I would have won.

One thing I would never have bet on was that within the space of ten days I would meet six members of three presidential families.

Pat Lawford, JFK's sister, was having a small party in Southampton. Joe, Valerie, and I arrived at the specified time, and naturally we were too early and had no one but ourselves to talk to until a few houseguests appeared. Joe introduced us to Jean Smith and Pat Lawford, who remarked that she had heard about my piece in the *Times* and asked for a reprint. I was flattered.

I seldom listen when introductions are made, but the nice woman I spoke to with the soothing Southern drawl told me she was born in Georgia and lived in Texas. A little while later, Gloria Jones asked, "Speed, how do you like being at a party with three sisters of presidents?" I was puzzled and said, "I only count two, Pat and her sister Jean Smith." Gloria laughed and said, "And that lady you were coming on to, Ruth Stapleton Carter, that's three!"

A couple of days later we were having lunch at Bob Towbin's. Three attractive women arrived as we were leaving, and I stayed to be introduced by Irene. As usual, I didn't catch the names of the first two, but my ears sharpened at the sound of "Ruth Roosevelt, I would like you to meet Speed Vogel." Ruth Roosevelt shook my hand and said, "Speed. What a marvelous name!" I countered by suggesting that her name was also not bad. I offered to fetch her some champagne and we chatted a bit. Ruth told me she used to be married to a grandson of Franklin Delano

Roosevelt. Then she invited me to a gathering at her house later on. Bob had already asked me to drive him to a Ted Kennedy fund-raiser in Southampton, so I asked her how late her party would last. Her reply was stunning: "It won't start until you get there."

At the fund-raiser, Towbin introduced me to Teddy Kennedy, who shook my hand and said, "Oh, yes, Speed Vogel. I've seen your pictures!" I figured he mistook me for somebody else, or else I didn't hear him right. His sister Pat thanked me for sending the reprint, said she'd loved it, and hoped I would be available for her if she found herself in Heller's spot. Then she asked if I had met her brother, who overheard her and again said, "Yes, I know Speed. I've seen his pictures!"

Towbin later explained that he had flown out to East Hampton with Ted and had shown him the snapshots we'd taken on the yacht. He *had* seen my pictures!

Afterward I called Ruth Roosevelt to find out if her party was still going on. "Just about everyone's gone," she said, "but why don't you come over anyway?" I was on my way. I, Speed Vogel, formerly a nobody, now had himself a late date with an ex-granddaughter-in-law of FDR.

And guess what . . . a week later I was at the Bridgehampton home of James Salter, the author. He had a few people to dinner and I arrived late. I was introduced to Jim's guests and was startled once again when I heard, "I would like you to meet Carol Roosevelt." Amazingly, she turned out to be another granddaughter-in-law. "Are you related to Ruth?" I asked. And, to add to my list of Hamptons coincidences, she replied, "Maybe I am. She married my former husband!"

By late August, Joe was much improved and expected that Valerie and I would be leaving by the middle of September. He started making plans to live without us. We all felt certain now that he could survive. He even was trying to learn how to cook, and he thought he should find someone to stay through the winter with him in the guest house—someone he did not know socially whom he could call on in an emergency. We were all still there weekends, and the weekends for Valerie and me usually lasted four or five days.

Fall in the Hamptons is nice, and Joe hadn't thrown us out yet. The summer crowding vanishes. The parties are different. They move indoors and the food is more substantial. I was surprised to find that the social activities hardly declined. The three of us continued to enjoy our popularity, and we gave and accepted invitations. Among the invitations we received was one to a New Year's party, which we accepted, and another to the house in Saint Croix offered by Joe's friends for a month after that, which we also accepted. Almost before we knew it, the winter seemed just about over. Could spring be far behind?

WHEN MR. SHERESKY was replaced by the law firm of Gordon & Shechtman, an attorney named Diane Serafin Blank took over the responsibilities he had shouldered. It was not my luck ever to meet Ms. Blank, but I did have access to her legal writings about me. You can imagine my feelings when I came across her statement of belief, submitted under penalty of perjury, that I was "milking" my condition for all it was worth.

Naturally I was upset by this denigrating assessment. Anyone better acquainted with me than she was could have told her that I probably was milking my illness then for only a *fraction* of what it was worth. I have since been able to milk it for very much more, and the publication of this book is additional testimony to that effect.*

My life in court with Ms. Blank commences near the end of the summer of 1982, when I realized that a lot more time would

* There has also been a contract for an original motion picture script about a brash, young American novelist who is brought to bed suddenly by an ailment of mysterious origin known as Guillain-Barré syndrome.

be needed for my recovery. Only toward the end of August did I return my rented wheelchair and commode. I could get up from a toilet but not from a sofa. In August I was still living on the first floor of a house with a staircase I could not mount alone. I was working again on *God Knows,* in longhand for my first draft, as has been my method. I could use my typewriter for short spells, but with no more proficiency than I had ever possessed. We have gross muscles and we have fine muscles, and the fine muscles of my fingers would shake when I was inserting the paper. (They still do.) At the East Hampton house there is at least one shallow step outside each of the four entranceways, and simply using them produced improvement of my muscles and my coordination (and of what is called my "proprioception," the subtle sensory neuromuscular facility that lets each muscle group know at all moments what the others are up to and which of them need reinforcement or counterbalance of some kind, that enables us, for example, to reach down or up or out for something without falling and without knocking over everything else nearby, or to go down a flight of stairs or move securely along uneven ground without needing to concentrate on where each footstep lands). I had uneven ground in every direction outside the house. The walk from the house down the driveway to the mailbox and back was fifty yards of therapy. I had a physical therapist coming three afternoons a week and a heated swimming pool in which I continued to exercise for one or two hours a day all through the month of September. Outside the house was a road relatively free of pedestrians and automobile traffic. I could walk there in safety for longer and longer distances as I practiced relearning how. I would cross the road to be near a fence whenever I drew near a house that had one; if a knee buckled and I fell, I knew I would have to apply leverage from my arms against something rigid to get back up. I carried a cordless phone in case I had to call for help. I never did fall on my walks there. (It was not until late January, on a beach on Saint Croix, that I was able to rise from the ground to my feet on my own. Thereafter, I practiced that exercise with the others performed each morning on the patio and lawn and in the small pool at the house made available to us by my friends Chet and Blanche Ross and at the beach and in the mild surf each afternoon. Julius Green, down to visit for a weekend, looked perplexed one morning as he studied me occupied with this new exercise. He lay down on the ground to try for himself to understand how it is done, and he did not get back up that much more easily than I could. People lying down can stand up only with considerable exertion. That may explain why many engage in sexual activity instead.)

But back home in East Hampton, as August was drawing to a close, I had a Speed Vogel, who seemed content to stay on a while past Labor Day, especially after his article about me was published in the *Times* and he was encouraged to do a whole book about *his* experiences that summer, which turned out to be this one. And there was Valerie Humphries, who, having signed on until Labor Day, was already getting used to the idea of remaining until at least the eighteenth of September and the small birthday party I had promised her and to continuing the friendships with the many people she'd met and was socializing with amiably. In the end, as I saw my time of privileged residence running out, I could envision no better place for me to be for the rest of that year than the one in which I was.

Jeffrey Cohen concurred, and at the beginning of September we therefore made application to the court to extend the order of exclusive occupancy from September 15, when it was due to expire, until December 31 of that same year.

There was an instant while hearing Ms. Blank's reply in which I was deluded into an expectation of success by that hope that is said to spring eternal in the human breast. Counsel did state that such extension would not be opposed by her client. But then came the rest: There would be no opposition provided I gave up the house for all of the following year and paid $2,500 a month, or "the sum of $8,750 representing the value of comparable accomodations [*sic*] and transportation through December 31, 1982." (In all her arguments in this case, Ms. Blank habitually misspells the word "accommodations.") Not much reason was given as to why money should be provided for comparable accommodations and transportation, and nothing was said at that time disputing my physical disability and needs.

It did not elude my attention that in talking about money for September, October, November, and December we were no longer talking about an allowance for a summer vacation home. The reasoning underlying much of this response was as impenetrable to Jeffrey as to me, and he endorsed my determination to withdraw the application rather than pay anything.

I was not present at the hearing. When the court was disposed to mollify both sides with a figure of $1,000 a month for my three and a half months, Jeffrey reported my objections and instructions. When the court was adamant for compromise, Jeffrey withdrew my motion, and we were back where we'd been before the divorce action was started, with each of the parties again legally free to enter and inhabit the dwelling that the other had grown used to as a home and a sanctuary.

My second encounter with Ms. Blank in court took place soon afterward and centered on requests from her corner that seemed to me at least as extravagant as those made earlier. Now she was writing in support of her client's application for exclusive occupancy of the marital apartment in New York "as well as of the parties' vacation home" in East Hampton. This was a move for both places.

I did not need a lawyer to tell me the motion would ultimately fail. I did need a lawyer, though, to respond to the application.

The papers for this one were voluminous from both sides. Here I was exposed for the first time as an active participant "on the East Hampton party circuit" and there was even a sworn statement that I had been observed "carrying bags of groceries." There were tax returns and financial statements and affidavits, and none of them counted. Had I been the hardiest billionaire on earth it would not have counted. In this country the courts do not summarily deprive people of their property except in instances of compelling need. And here if a need existed, the need was mine.

Jeffrey put the legal issue simply, stating that there was no basis in law or fact for the relief requested and that defendant's counsel had not presented "any statement of law to support her position of defendant's untenable request for exclusive occupancy of one home (much less two)."

He went on with proposals I judged constructive: that the matter be brought forward in an orderly manner to a speedy trial and that a schedule be established to complete the necessary pretrial discovery. He ended as follows:

> I further suggest that until the time of trial, this Court maintain the status quo. Mr. Heller will remain in East Hampton and Mrs. Heller can remain in the seven room marital apartment. . . . I truly believe that a trial preference is the quickest and most appropriate method of resolving this action and eliminating the unnecessary litigation that will otherwise ensue.

This time the court did as he asked, maintaining the status quo by awarding me exclusive use of the house until a final determination was arrived at by trial or settlement agreement. That final determination took two more years. I might seem to be gloating some more if I mentioned that this was better than the extension I had asked for originally, and that I have lived in the same house happily ever after, even unto the present day. (We are now divorced, and my former wife retains the apartment.)

Not long after this, Ms. Blank left her place of employment to establish with her husband the law firm of Blank & Blank. (The names are real, as far as I know, and the partnership is listed that way in the telephone directory.) And not long after that, the Gordon & Shechtman firm was replaced and a new lawyer was involved. This change took place while we were still in Saint Croix. The name of this lawyer was Raoul Lionel Felder, and he entered the scene with an attack on his predecessors for having cooperated in the formulation of a schedule along which matters had been proceeding toward trial.

"Regrettably," Mr. Felder submitted "respectfully," the firm was in a position of being discharged for cause, mainly for "consenting to, rather than vigorously opposing, a groundless and absurd motion for a trial preference" and for participating in the creation of a timetable for pretrial discovery activities. Mr. Felder did not list the flaw in the schedule he was criticizing and, in Jeffrey's words, did not offer "even one fact or example to support their assertion that the consent order was in any way prejudicial." As to me, he seemed scornfully disapproving of my "transparent effort to obtain the sympathy of the Court for a temporary condition which has long since abated. . . ." The way Mr. Felder describes it, his client has been left with a "Sword of Damocles trial date" and is "between a Scylla and Carybdis [*sic*]" on the same page.

One's knowledge of the classics can be refreshed in litigation. While Mr. Norman Sheresky was at the helm, I found out that Hippocrates said more than four hundred years before the birth of Christ: "Healing is a matter of time, but it is sometimes also a matter of opportunity." With Mr. Felder charting the course, I learned that my financial affairs were "labyrinthian." In a letter to me after the whole dispute had been brought to an end through the arbitration judgments of someone else, Mr. Felder informed me, incorrectly, that Shakespeare had said, " 'The fault dear Brutus, lies not within our stars, but within ourselves'. [*sic* punctuation too]" In this same letter misquoting Shakespeare, Mr. Felder regretted that I had not found "contentment and/or quietude of spirit," but wished me, nevertheless, a Happy New Year.

On the legal front, Mr. Felder launched his campaign with a motion to vacate or modify a prior order of the court validating the timetable for pretrial proceedings about which he was complaining. Jeffrey Cohen opposed him, and Mr. Felder lost. Mr. Felder went before a justice of the Appellate Division for a stay of proceedings pending his appeal, and his request was denied. Mr. Felder applied next to a panel of five judges in the Appellate Division with a fourteen-page argument for the same stay of proceedings. Guess what happened. He lost again, and my examination before trial, which was already in progress, was permitted to continue without the interruption for which he was petitioning.

(It cost lots of money—and that's another one of the things that happened.)

In a matrimonial action, the sole purpose of an examination before trial is the disclosure of financial information, and I make mention of mine only for the manner in which Jeffrey brought it to an end after he decided that the purpose for which it was intended had been served.

I remember it was March, and I remember it was cold. The deposition was conducted by an associate of Mr. Felder's in a small conference room in the offices of the firm. His name was William Binderman, and one of the first questions he put to me had to do with where I was staying in the city. Jeffrey broke in immediately to declare that the question was inappropriate to the proceedings and told me not to reply. "If you want to ask if he's paying for accommodations and how much, I'll let him answer." Mr. Binderman said he would reserve that question for a later ruling. Then he asked if I was paying for my accommodations and I said that I was not. By that time I had given up my apartment in Manhattan and I stayed in the dwellings of friends of mine or Speed's or Jeffrey's, to the inconvenience of others as well as myself.

I could get around alone by then, come into the city on the Hampton Jitney unaccompanied, and even carry a small suitcase. To the opposition my illness was "ancient history." To me it was not yet that ancient. I still welcomed help putting on a heavy coat. I could not race anyone for a taxi, I could not even hurry toward one. I would not go down the stairs to the subway, and I did not trust myself on the steps of a public bus. Late one afternoon when the day's questioning was over, a woman I knew from East Hampton, the photographer Susan Wood, spied me floundering in the rush hour trying to find an empty cab and was stunned to see me in the city alone. She parked me under the marquee of a building, where I waited until she came back to the rescue inside a taxi she had commandeered for my use.

At rest, however, I looked like a million. I am only repeating objectively the words of others when I tell you I tan beautifully: my hair turns a luminous silver, my face is of beaten gold. With my color enriched by the Caribbean sun, I looked as good at my examination before trial as when I first lay in the intensive care unit of the hospital.

The deposition dragged through one week and into a second, and toward the end of that second week, Jeffrey suddenly said calmly, as much to my surprise as anyone else's, that he was going to call a halt to it all at the close of business the following day.

At least twice that next day, when the pace seemed to slacken, Jeffrey reminded Mr. Binderman that they were wrapping it up at five o'clock: If Mr. Binderman had more ground to cover we could hurry things, or we could stop right then if he was out of questions. Exactly on the hour, Jeffrey announced the time. He snapped closed his fine leather briefcase, reached for his very fine overcoat and fine snap-brimmed hat, helped me on with the left sleeve of my wool-lined trench coat, and signaled me to follow him out. In the elevator he explained: "Here's what's going to happen. They'll go into court for an order to continue indefinitely. In front of the judge, I'll ask them to state specifically what more information they can get from you that isn't available in the papers they have. There won't be any. They'll get a few more hours and that will be it."

The court allowed them just one more day, not all of which, if I remember correctly, was used. There was one more effort to delay that Jeffrey defeated, and the case eventually came to trial, with Mr. Binderman appearing for the defense.

Mr. William N. Binderman was born in Charleston, West

Virginia, in 1939 and received his law degree from Columbia University in 1964. He was admitted to the bar in 1965, and on July 19, 1983, in the Supreme Court of the State of New York, he accused me of writing the "Mein Kampf of matrimonial warfare."

Naturally, I was surprised.

Among the few others present when Mr. Binderman made this extraordinary charge was Mr. Ira Dickstein, the official court reporter that day, who swears that his transcript is a true one. Also in the courtroom was Justice Martin Evans, presiding, a mild-mannered, soft-spoken man with white hair who talked almost in whispers and whose balanced outlook, inexhaustible patience, and astonishing lucidity and logic kept a restless mastiff like Jeffrey continually on edge.

The book Mr. Binderman had in mind was my novel *Good as Gold,* which had been published in 1979. The unexpected characterization came forth in an exchange between Mr. Binderman and the bench when Mr. Binderman sought to introduce this novel into the proceedings.

"I respectfully offer it . . . ," said Mr. Binderman, after a few preliminary remarks about the work with his client, who was then on the witness stand.

And the dialogue soon went this way:

MR. COHEN: Your Honor, may I ask for what purpose this is being offered, because I don't know.

THE COURT: You may ask it.

MR. COHEN: Mr. Binderman?

THE COURT: It isn't obvious, you say?

MR. COHEN: Not to me, your Honor.

THE COURT: Let me see it.

MR. BINDERMAN: I am offering it for two things, your Honor, the inscription and the contents of the book.

THE COURT: I have to read it.

MR. BINDERMAN: We will give you some abstracts, if your Honor wants.

THE COURT: What is the purpose of the offer?

MR. BINDERMAN: Demonstration as the word, "only" is underlined. Where "only" reflex [reflects?] that there had been someone else. He repeats it twice.

He says, "My wife, my love, my valentine." Then he goes on and says, "My only wife and valentine."

It is an admission not only that Mrs. Heller was supportive, but it is an admission that there had been someone before.

MR. COHEN: May I have that, Mr. Binderman?

THE COURT: I find it hard to sustain that in my mind. Objection sustained.

MR. BINDERMAN: Exception. I offer it as far as the contents of the book, your Honor. If you want me to lay a foundation, I will do that.

THE COURT: If you can tell me the purpose and we will see where we go.

MR. BINDERMAN: Your Honor, "Good as Gold" is a book about an author, middle-aged author, which as Mr. Heller is, from Coney Island, with a loyal wife, who goes through what I would call a middle-age crisis, and plots and schemes throughout the book to juggle women, conceal his philanderings, plot and scheme to find a way to conceal all of that from his wife.

THE COURT: Is this the book in which reference is made to three people being juggled in some hotel?

MR. BINDERMAN: Yes.

THE COURT: Objection sustained.

MR. BINDERMAN: Exception. May I ask your Honor for reasons? This is the first time I have done it.

THE COURT: It probably won't be the last. If we were to say every author is guilty about all the sins of which he writes, Shakespeare would have been hung for murder fifteen times over in his earlier days and for rape and several other things.

MR. BINDERMAN: Well, I would respectfully—

THE COURT: I see no connection. I see no plans of any plot or scheme. Maybe later I will change my mind. But until then there is no adequate relationship between what may be written in a book and the actual action of the author outside of the book.

MR. BINDERMAN: We will show it but there isn't enough time today.

THE COURT: All right.

MR. BINDERMAN: I am saying at a later time I will renew it with a foundation.

THE COURT: You say he has set forth to the world the blueprints of his actions?

MR. BINDERMAN: The Mein Kampf of matrimonial warfare, yes. This is one. It is uncanny and we will show it to your Honor, in fact, with some of his own words.

THE COURT: Next question.

I was on the witness stand, undergoing cross-examination, when Mr. Binderman did renew his efforts, as he had promised, to lay his foundation and show with some of my own words that in my novel *Good as Gold* I had set forth to the world the blueprints of my actions. The transcript reports the following question and answer:

Q: Are these the words of Joseph Heller, "I want a divorce, I need a divorce, I crave a divorce, I pray for divorce, all my life I have wanted a divorce, even before I was married."... You wrote those words in *Good as Gold,* didn't you, Mr. Heller?

A: No.

Mr. Binderman was quoting from my novel *Something Happened.* And that was just about it for his foundation for my *Mein Kampf.*

The firm of Raoul Lionel Felder requested payment of more than $125,000 and settled for $70,000, of which half came from me and half from the first part of the amount awarded my wife as her share of the marital assets after the financial terms had been set by arbitration and we were divorced by the court. Jeffrey and I were told that Mr. Felder already had received $10,000 from his client, but these figures took no account of that.

A family friend named Sidney Elliott Cohn, who had dictated the terms of the settlement in his role of arbitrator, negotiated with the lawyers on their fees. Sidney is an experienced and highly successful attorney in his seventies whom my wife and I had known for close to twenty-five years, and I hope he will not be displeased if I describe him as somewhat owlish and Dickensian in benevolent appearance. More than one person who knew him wondered why he was agreeing to be involved in something contentious he did not need. In explaining him to Jeffrey, who had never met him, I said: "He's got more brains than all of us. And he makes more money than you and Binderman combined, so don't think you're doing him a favor by bringing him work, and please don't waste time with him." I also warned that Sidney was probably the most persuasive person I had ever met.

If he did his work well, as I expected he would, I was sure that all sides would be at least a little disgruntled, and of course I was right. My main discontent was with the fees to the opposing lawyers. I felt they all got more than their services had been worth but concede that I am not the best person to be impartial judge of that.

Mr. Felder, as I've said, received $70,000 at the end and at least $10,000 earlier, of which $35,000 came from me. Mr. Sheresky and the Gordon firm separately asked for $50,000 and settled for $25,000, of which my share was $17,500 for each, and my wife's share was $7,500.

A final payment by me to Jeffrey of $20,000 brought the amount paid him over three years to $100,000; one of us may owe the other a few thousand, but neither of us wishes to find out which.

And Sidney, as I knew in suggesting him as someone acceptable to both sides, does not work for little. His bill was close to $40,000 for the six or seven months spent, of which $25,000 came from me, and the rest was due him from my wife.

The cost of these lawyers, therefore, comes to $270,000 that I know about. (There may have been additional payments on the other side of which I am ignorant.) Throw in the expense of the accountants for both of us, the few thousand to Alan Altman before Jeffrey came in, and the various miscellaneous other charges, and the total easily goes well over $300,000 in professional fees for a divorce I earnestly believe neither my wife nor I wanted.

THE TRIP TO SAINT CROIX was just one more bonus that I had never expected, had not earned, but it was one that I had the good sense not to turn down.

By then summer was long over, though we were reluctant to admit it. Joe planned to remain in East Hampton but was no longer advertising for anyone to stay at the house with him through the winter. Valerie and I were leaving him alone for a few days a week and he was doing all right, working, eating food Valerie and I had prepared for him, even cooking his own meals now and then.

When he asked us to go to Saint Croix, Joe rationalized that being in a warm place might help his physical recovery. It sounded like a fine idea to Valerie and me. He could swim and we could work on our books: he on his, and me on ours. We would go early in January and stay until the middle of February.

The timing was perfect because Craig Claiborne has an annual black-tie New Year's Eve gathering at his home in East Hampton for a small and fortunate group of friends, and Valerie and I did not want to miss it. (Here we thought we were living in the city, but events like this kept Valerie and me coming out to East

Hampton regularly.) Valerie chose the tuxedo Joe rented at a Southampton store. I still had mine, custom-made, from the days when I could afford things like that, and it still fit. We really were all very handsome in our evening clothes. And we had a lot to celebrate.

It had been an extraordinary year for all of us. Joe was happier now than I had ever seen him, and he knew it. Though a divorce was brewing, the whole thing was now in the hands of lawyers and the court.

Through the fall and winter Joe was steadily growing stronger. Now when he emptied the dishwasher, even though his hands still trembled, he seemed to have a firmer grasp and could hold more plates at one time. He could bend lower without holding on and he could extend his arms to stack the dishes higher in the cupboard. He was pleased that the first time he tried, he could drive his car. He was rapidly becoming self-sufficient but seemed to want Valerie and me with him anyway, as a matter of choice rather than necessity.

Every time I leave a freezing New York winter behind and arrive in tropical warmth, I find it thrilling. I love walking across the tarmac from the plane to the baggage area in high humidity and stifling heat. I also like to fly. My companions are different. Heller stopped enjoying air travel after his war experiences and refused to fly for fifteen years afterward. He will now, however, get on planes without persuasion. Valerie, at least at the time we were planning to leave for Saint Croix, didn't like flying one bit.

Valerie was in the city the day before we left for Saint Croix, and I casually asked Heller whether she was coming back to East Hampton or meeting us at the airport. Joe answered bluntly that he did not know. He then sheepishly confessed that Val had called the airline—as she always does—to ask about the equipment. We were booked on a DC-10, she found out. She doesn't like DC-10s and said she might be taking a more roundabout route to the island. (She also doesn't like small planes, and there was no roundabout route that didn't require one of those.) Joe had simply handed her the ticket he'd bought and told her to do as she saw fit. The next day Joe and I left early for the airport, just in case, and hung around to wait for Valerie. It was late and it looked as if she wasn't coming, but at the last minute, she showed up. Joe walked over to the ticket counter to assist her with her luggage and I remained with our carry-ons at a discreet distance. Valerie was smoking a cigarette. (I never saw her smoke before; she looked like a Bette Davis impersonator.) Joe claims he still hasn't any idea what they were talking about, but it lasted for the next six hours. Valerie, under the best conditions, is animated and speaks rapidly, but her state at the airport, on the plane, collecting the luggage in Saint Croix, and for the next two days left little doubt that she could have gotten a scholarship to Mel Brooks's Institute for the Very, Very Nervous.

When we arrived in Saint Croix, we left Valerie watching the luggage while Joe and I went to the car rental place. We were filling out a form when Joe asked, "That girl rushing over there after the porter—is that Valerie?" and took off after her. It turns out Valerie thought half our luggage was being transferred to another plane.

After we picked up our rental car and drove to the house, I observed that once again Heller was having difficulties coping with Valerie. Joe was muttering to himself and intimating (to me only) that he might send her packing. We both knew that was nonsense, but I did hear him say, "If you're not going to relax and enjoy yourself here, you might as well plan to go back. I need a nurse, not a martyr."

Suddenly, to our immense relief, whatever it was that put Valerie in that super-hyper state vanished, and she was once more the laughing and cheerful chronicler of newspaper stories and magazine articles. (Joe says he can still rely on her to keep him well informed by reading stories aloud to him an hour or two after he's finished reading them.) Val also became an enthusiastic chauffeur-guide on our rides to various spots on the island. She never allowed us to miss any cute goats, darling kiddies, or adorable ponies as we drove to the beaches or markets and back to the house. (Even though she might be pointing out the same goats, kiddies, and ponies we'd already seen.)

Almost daily we passed a nursing home that was under construction. A large sign announced when it would be ready for occupancy. Valerie laughed every time we passed. She thought one day Joe and I might wind up there, and she would be our nurse. When she stopped the car and asked us to pose in front of the sign for a picture, we gladly accommodated her. She was laughing so hard she could hardly hold the camera. Joe was grateful for this miraculous transformation and so was I. (Valerie was too.)

The Rosses' house is situated at the highest point of an area known as Mary's Fancy, at the end of a private road. There is a constant breeze from the ocean, the air is clear, and views in every direction are unobstructed. The one house nearby is well hidden by shrubbery. Though we all preferred swimming in the ocean, Joe exercised in the small private pool, which overlooks a wide expanse of lush vegetation. From poolside we had a breathtaking view of the Caribbean and we could see Saint John and Saint Thomas. The kitchen (the heart of any house for me) was well equipped, each of the two large bedrooms had a private bath, and the living room was comfortable with a conversation pit. A brochure prepared by the Rosses contained all the information we could possibly need, including maps and restaurant recommendations. Each morning, at a respectable hour, a sweet-natured woman appeared to take care of the house and our laundry. My life at that time was so tough that I suggested we call this book "Poor Speed: His Friend Joe Is Sick."

After several days of acclimating ourselves to our surroundings, Heller and I "took a meeting" to discuss our book and apportion responsibilities. Joe was in charge of negotiating the contract, supplying the paper, pencils, and carbon sets, and borrowing a typewriter. I had the easy job—to write the book, while he went on with his novel.

Our daily routine suited us all: The first one up in the morning cut the grapefruits and made coffee. (We excluded Valerie, who would not be up before us unless someone set fire to her bed.) After breakfast, Joe and I sat in the sun, worked on our tans, and wrote a few pages of our separate books in silence. At this time I really did find it easy to write. (It was only much later that I found out what was hard. Writing is, I repeat, easy. Reading what you have written is hard. Oh boy, is it hard. When you have to read it again, and again, that's torture. Now I knew what writers are talking about when I hear them complain.)

By the time Valerie awoke and was ready for her breakfast (not as spartan as ours), we usually were through working for the day. While she was fixing and eating her breakfast, we began our session of Valerie's daily "I wonders." Out of the blue, Valerie would ask such questions as, "I wonder how cold it is in Finland right now?" or "I wonder if Cristina DeLorean will write a book?" or "I wonder if Lady Di really likes his mother?" By then it was almost time to eat lunch. At lunch we talked about dinner. We had important matters to decide: What kind of fish should we buy, or should I make blintzes with sour cream? If blintzes, should blintzes be the main course? Which markets should we try or should we eat out for a change? Then we had to decide which beach to choose for the afternoon. We found the restaurants wanting, so we usually preferred to shop the local markets and cook at home. Valerie talked about piña coladas one day, and even though Joe and I prefer martinis, we bought rum and other essential ingredients at the market and I started making piña coladas. They seemed to get better and better and we drank more and more as I kept making them.

When Heller was not causing trouble between us—which he did at times just for the fun of it—Valerie and I got along fine. We share interests that Joe doesn't begin to appreciate, such as skiing, sailing, golf, country and rock music, and even horseback riding. She and I never disagreed about the menus or anything else about food—with the exception of the proper way to store bread. (But this started way back when we were beginning to live as a family in East Hampton.) Valerie prefers to leave it wrapped in plastic. (It gets moldy that way.) I prefer wrapping it in plain paper. (Then it gets stale.) Now, in Saint Croix, we were just like any old married threesome, and none of us cared which way the bread got wrapped and eventually went bad.

We soon discovered that the locally grown white corn and tomatoes were as good as anything we ever had in the Hamptons, and we found real sweet potatoes, the kind Joe remembered from childhood and couldn't swallow that day. The fish markets were good and we ate flounder, salmon, and swordfish steaks.

We all swam and did some snorkeling. Valerie took windsurfing lessons, Sunfish-sailing lessons, tennis lessons, and would have taken horseback-riding lessons but was unable to find a teaching stable, even though she went looking several times. There were many excellent beaches, but the Buccaneer became our favorite. Joe took long walks in the surf back and forth, and at the water's edge he actually managed a few jogging steps in the sand. We all were living a healthy and active outdoor existence. It was an uneventful life, and I did not like the thought of leaving.

Actually, there was, or may have been, a hair-raising event that made me laugh when I found out about it. One morning Valerie asked me if I'd heard the loud noise outside the house the night before. When I told her I had not, she was incredulous. And as she started to tell me what happened, I heard Heller groan. It seems that Valerie was startled in the middle of the night by a loud noise and was sure it was a prowler. She woke Joe, who was prepared to investigate, but she forbade him to leave the room or turn on the lights. Val decided simply to stay awake in the dark until daylight.

The groan from Heller, of course, had broken out when his hopes got dashed: he thought there was a chance I would never find out what a dumbbell he had been!

SHE WOKE ME UP when she thought she heard the noise, then would not let me go outside to investigate: I might be in danger and she did not know if she would be able to save me. She would not let me slip out the door on the other side to peek: he might burst in upon her when I was outside and not there to protect her. She would not let me turn on the lights to frighten him off: that would show him where we were. She would not let me telephone the police for the same reason: the sound of my voice would give us away. When she heard no noise our danger was greater: he was lying in ambush or sneaking up. Another thing she would not let me do was try to go back to sleep: he would come upon me unawares. We had no chance if we remained where we were; we were goners if we tried to save ourselves. So I lay awake all night listening to her whispering to me not to make a sound.

BUT JOE'S INDULGENCE and patient behavior did not surprise me at all. By then I had never seen anyone *a zoi fahliebed* ("so much in love") as my friend Joe.

In Saint Croix there was real sailing too. Peter Reed, Chet Ross's business partner, who lives on the island and loaned Joe the typewriter, invited us for lunch at his small sailing club and we helped him celebrate his boat-racing win at the bar, where we met Gest Hodge, one of his crew that day. Gest, a friendly sailorman, used to breed horses in Kentucky, and was now the skipper of a forty-two-foot Hinckley. (I've since been informed that it's the Rolls-Royce of sailboats.) Gest invited us to sail with him to the federal preserve and well-known snorkeling ground, Buck Island.

The following Saturday, loaded with potables and edibles, we went on this outing and we all enjoyed it, with the possible exception of Heller, who isn't crazy about boats. Sailing homeward, Valerie suddenly pointed and exclaimed, "Look, isn't that terrific?" It was an amphibian taking off. Heller said, "Val, do you mean that seaplane?" "Yes," she said, "I wonder where it takes off from?" Joe and I did not answer. But Gest, removing his hand from the wheel, pointed in the direction of the seaplane and said, "From there! From where you're seeing it taking off! Where else? God! That woman asks the damndest questions." Joe and I were used to hearing things like that and we just laughed at Gest's reaction.

Heller was now the most patient and considerate of men. Nothing like the man he used to be. He strove to gratify Valerie's every wish. "Would you like to drive to the other side of the island, Val? Do you want to ride a horse? Or would you prefer a windsurfing lesson at the Buccaneer? Or maybe you would like lunch at Sprat Hall? Shall I ask Speed to make some more piña coladas before I take you to the Grand Stand disco?" Yes, Joe even went dancing, an activity he loathed even more than sailing. Oh boy, was he ever *fahliebed!*

Several weeks after our voyage to Buck Island with Gest, my friends Ken and Barbara Cooke arrived and I asked Joe to speak to Gest about arranging another day trip, since the Cookes are avid snorkelers. I, of course, expected Joe to avoid another sail, but to my amazement, he chose to join us again. He knew that Gest was taking the boat out only for him. Heller does hate sailing, but perhaps he was learning to find some joy in pleasing others, and the rest of us did want to sail. Joe even tried snorkeling, but his mask didn't fit properly and he had to give up. We had some difficulty getting him back on board, but we had enough manpower to manage it.

The next morning Joe suddenly said, "You people might have had fun on that boat, but I was sitting in back there doing nothing, with that pitiless sun burning my thighs." Just a few moments before Joe made his little speech, I was thinking about how reluctant I was going to be to leave the island in a few days. But much as I hated to go back home, I could now hardly wait to get there to tell the boys in the Gourmet Club, freezing in ten-degree weather, about Joe's harrowing experience with the pitiless sun. Especially Julie Green, who had visited us briefly and witnessed how much Joe was suffering with his pool, the ocean, constant breezes from the Caribbean, and ice-cold piña coladas.

"It's not such a bad life you writers have," Julie had said to Joe and me. "Maybe I should throw in with you."

Green might have second thoughts now about entering our field when I told him about that pitiless sun.

The day before we left, Joe and I were talking, as usual, about death. We spoke of plane crashes, who would finish our books after we died, responsibilities to families, loved ones, and publishers if either one survived, and funny things like that. Valerie (God knows why) took a dim view of our banter and spoke sharply to us. "Don't talk about plane crashes, snowstorms, DC-10s, sickness, or anything like that till we're safely on the ground in New York. You know what that does to me!" I then decided to double the rum in our piña coladas until we left the island.

Fortified with my libations, Valerie was not so nervous as we drove to the airport. Joe looked well and rested. The five weeks in the Virgin Islands had done wonders for all of us.

At the check-in counter, Valerie asked for the weather reports and heard that we were probably going to arrive in New York in the middle of a storm. She became a bit wild-eyed again when she reported the forecast, but when we started to comment about the possibilities of a snowstorm, Val stopped us, saying, "Didn't I tell you not to talk about things like that?" We stopped talking about snowstorms, but nothing stopped her from talking about them.

In fact, Valerie talked nonstop from the time we boarded the plane until we landed at JFK. I was there, but I could not believe it was possible—and that Joe listened! The love bug had given my friend some bite! In the old days he would not have put up with one percent of that much talking from anyone. I stared in awe. He did not stop her, strike her, or even move to another seat. I kept mumbling, just loud enough for him to hear, *"a zoi fahliebed."*

We knew that when we landed after Saint Croix we were to disband. Valerie would go directly to the city to return to work at the hospital, though she thought she might come to East Hampton for the weekend. Joe and I were going to East Hampton together. I understood that with me or without me he could now get along okay, and after that week I was planning to go back to the city too. But when we landed, I felt again that winter would soon be over, and East Hampton was not a bad place for me to be also. There were meals to prepare and a book to coauthor, so I thought I might as well continue my routine of two days in New York and five in East Hampton.

The heavy snowstorm that had been predicted had not hit, and we landed smoothly at JFK. A slightly tipsy Nurse Humphries left for her apartment in the city, and Joe and I arranged for transportation out to Long Island. That snowfall was still in the forecast, though, so we immediately went shopping in anticipation of being snowed in. I'd decided to try a pot roast. Joe liked my pot roast. Provided the butcher had the right cut of brisket, I would give Heller a homecoming meal to remember.

The snows came the next day. A veritable blizzard. We were soon blanketed with drifts as high as three feet. When we awoke the sun was out, the air was clear and cold, and there was no wind. We were in good spirits and completely comfortable indoors.

That day my friend Joe, the picture of health, much of his former strength almost completely restored, volunteered to help as I shoveled a path from the main house to the studio and started to clear the patio for sunbathing—it was going to be Saint Croix in goose-down jackets. I thought Joe would be proud to be of assistance to me, so when he asked to help, I said, "That would be fine, Joe. Why don't you clear enough space so we can both lie down on the beach chairs and catch some rays."

He picked up the other shovel and pursued the task with gusto and vigor. As I was momentarily at rest, my arms atop my shovel, I glanced in Joe's direction. He seemed to falter. Uttering a soft moan, he started to sink to the ground. I rushed to his side, catching him as he fell. His massive head rested upon my shoulder, his body was slack. With a peaceful smile, he turned his face toward mine and softly murmured, "It's been such a wonderful year." He looked up into my misty eyes and said, "I'm going now. Thank you." Slowly his eyes fell closed and he died in my arms.

I DID NO SUCH THING. What the hell's the matter with him? I have no recollection whatsoever of dying in his arms and I don't know why the damned fool keeps insisting that I did. What I did do that evening was enjoy a hearty dinner of the pot roast he cooked, and a few weeks later I flew down to Florida to visit my brother and sister, largely to prove to them and to myself that I was now able to travel alone. Lee had not seen me since the time I was just out of the hospital, when I was emaciated and could not stand up. Sylvia had not seen me at all since the illness. But now my weight was back to normal. My nephew, Paul, was there, with his fiancée, Susan, and I was well enough to dive from the side of a pool and to have swimming races with his young son, Chris, and to allow myself to be beaten each time in just the last few strokes. I flew back alone too, managing a small suitcase and an over-the-shoulder tote bag. Valerie had let me know that she thought she could make room for me in her apartment if I'd like to spend the night in Manhattan instead of making the long trip out to East Hampton.

In the words of Montaigne: *"Mes lèvres sont fermées à clef."**

Today, my right arm and shoulder are just about the only muscle groups in my body that work naturally. If you see me walk on level ground, you might not notice any irregularities, but I do. On an incline or staircase my difficulties are conspicuous. I still cannot move in a hurry, so I try never to let myself be in one. Although the right side of my mouth was the one more seriously affected, the left remains weaker today. (The lips on the left side are used hardly at all when I make an *m* sound.) My *l*'s are still indistinct, especially on the telephone (I usually will have to spell my surname), and I still believe I have trouble with

---

* "My lips are sealed."

sounds that require a pursed mouth, although people say kindly that they are not aware of any difference. A sneeze, a yawn, or even a deep sigh of relief can bring painful cramps for a minute in the muscles of my trunk and around all my chest and in the right side of my neck. My legs and feet are susceptible to cramps when stretched, especially if I've been biking or have walked a lot. Because my ankles tend to turn inward, there is extra pressure on the small toes, and these often become sore.

Apart from defects like these, I'm a great guy. A question remains that is of interest to many and which I can escape answering no longer: the effect of the disease on my sexual powers. I report with some regret that the improvement is barely measurable and that I am no better now at satisfying a romantic woman than I was before. Recommended alternatives to Guillain-Barré in this area are ginseng root, the dried cantharides beetle, and powdered rhinoceros horn. Avoid wishful thinking. It hardly ever does the trick.